European Integration in Times of Crisis

Few events over the past few decades have given rise to an amount of debate and speculation concerning the state of the European Union (EU) and the future of European integration as the economic and financial crisis that began in 2007. In spite of substantial media, policy-making and academic attention, the fundamental questions of why and how the euro area (EA) has remained not only intact but also expanded and integrated further during the crisis require deeper theoretical investigation. One needs to understand not only the economics but also the politics and institutions of the crisis. A lack of such an understanding is the reason why a number of observers, at least initially, had a hard time making sense of policy-makers' decisions (and pace thereof), including why the EA did not implode as some predicted. Economic theories provide a certain perspective for why the crisis occurred and what economic policies were and are needed to resolve it; however, they fail to capture the deeper roots and management of the crisis.

In order to improve our understanding of a discussion that has oscillated between fears of EA disintegration on the one hand and the concrete advancement of integration during the crisis on the other, this special collection brings together leading scholars of European integration who apply key theoretical approaches – from liberal intergovernmentalism and neofunctionalism to other prominent theoretical accounts that have been applied to European integration, such as historical institutionalism, critical political economy, normative theory, and a public opinion approach – to the economic and financial crisis. The contributions seek to analyse, understand and/or explain the events that occurred and the (re)actions to them in order to draw conclusions concerning the applicability and usefulness of their respective theoretical perspectives.

This book was originally published as a special issue of the *Journal of European Public Policy*.

Demosthenes Ioannou is Principal Economist in the Directorate General International and European Relations of the European Central Bank.

Patrick Leblond is Associate Professor of Public and International Affairs at the University of Ottawa, Senior Fellow at the Centre for International Governance Innovation (CIGI) and Research Associate at CIRANO.

Arne Niemann is Professor of International Politics and Jean Monnet Professor of European Integration at the University of Mainz.

Journal of European Public Policy Series
Series Editor: Jeremy Richardson is Emeritus Fellow at Nuffield College, Oxford University, UK, and an Adjunct Professor in the National Centre for Research on Europe, University of Canterbury, New Zealand.

This series seeks to bring together some of the finest edited works on European Public Policy. Reprinting from Special Issues of the *Journal of European Public Policy*, the focus is on using a wide range of social sciences approaches, both qualitative and quantitative, to gain a comprehensive and definitive understanding of Public Policy in Europe.

European Integration in Times of Crisis

Theoretical perspectives

Edited by
Demosthenes Ioannou, Patrick Leblond and Arne Niemann

Routledge
Taylor & Francis Group

LONDON AND NEW YORK

First published 2016 by Routledge

2 Park Square, Milton Park, Abingdon, Oxon OX14 4RN
711 Third Avenue, New York, NY 10017, USA

Routledge is an imprint of the Taylor & Francis Group, an informa business

First issued in paperback 2017

British Library Cataloguing in Publication Data
A catalogue record for this book is available from the British Library

ISBN 13: 978-1-138-93490-0 (hbk)
ISBN 13: 978-1-138-09913-5 (pbk)

Typeset in Garamond
by RefineCatch Limited, Bungay, Suffolk

Publisher's Note
The publisher accepts responsibility for any inconsistencies that may have
arisen during the conversion of this book from journal articles to book chapters,
namely the possible inclusion of journal terminology.

Disclaimer
Every effort has been made to contact copyright holders for their permission to
reprint material in this book. The publishers would be grateful to hear from any
copyright holder who is not here acknowledged and will undertake to rectify
any errors or omissions in future editions of this book.

Contents

Citation Information

The chapters in this book were originally published in the *Journal of European Public Policy*, volume 22, issue 2 (December 2014). When citing this material, please use the original page numbering for each article, as follows:

Chapter 1
European integration and the crisis: practice and theory
Demosthenes Ioannou, Patrick Leblond and Arne Niemann
Journal of European Public Policy, volume 22, issue 2 (December 2014) pp. 155–176

Chapter 2
Liberal intergovernmentalism and the euro area crisis
Frank Schimmelfennig
Journal of European Public Policy, volume 22, issue 2 (December 2014) pp. 177–195

Chapter 3
European economic integration in times of crisis: a case of neofunctionalism?
Arne Niemann and Demosthenes Ioannou
Journal of European Public Policy, volume 22, issue 2 (December 2014) pp. 196–218

Chapter 4
A historical institutionalist explanation of the EU's responses to the euro area financial crisis
Amy Verdun
Journal of European Public Policy, volume 22, issue 2 (December 2014) pp. 219–237

Chapter 5
Public opinion and the crisis: the dynamics of support for the euro
Sara B. Hobolt and Christopher Wratil
Journal of European Public Policy, volume 22, issue 2 (December 2014) pp. 238–256

Chapter 6

Political legitimacy and European monetary union: contracts, constitutionalism and the normative logic of two-level games
Richard Bellamy and Albert Weale
Journal of European Public Policy, volume 22, issue 2 (December 2014) pp. 257–274

Chapter 7

Europe's ordoliberal iron cage: critical political economy, the euro area crisis and its management
Magnus Ryner
Journal of European Public Policy, volume 22, issue 2 (December 2014) pp. 275–294

For any permission-related enquiries please visit:
http://www.tandfonline.com/page/help/permissions

European integration and the crisis: practice and theory

Demosthenes Ioannou, Patrick Leblond and
Arne Niemann

ABSTRACT   This is the introduction to a special collection of contributions that
analyse the financial and economic crisis through various theoretical lenses. Accordingly, it does four things. First, it describes the EU's institutional response to the
crisis in order to provide a reference point for the contributions. Second, it summarizes the contributions. Third, it compares them in order to develop a theoretical dialogue. Finally, it answers the fundamental question at the heart of the crisis and this
special collection: why did Economic and Monetary Union become deeper and more
integrated when many feared for its survival?

INTRODUCTION

Few events over the past few decades have given rise to an amount of debate and
speculation concerning the state of the European Union (EU) and the future of
European integration as the financial and economic crisis that began in 2007. In
spite of substantial media, policy-making and academic attention, the fundamental questions of why and how the euro area (EA) has remained not only
intact but also expanded and integrated further during the crisis require
deeper theoretical investigation. One needs to understand not only the economics but also the politics and institutions of the crisis. A lack of such an understanding is the reason why a number of observers, at least initially, had a hard
time making sense of policy-makers' decisions (and pace thereof), including
why the EA did not implode as some predicted.[1] Economic theories provide
a certain perspective for why the crisis occurred and what economic policies
were and are needed to resolve it (e.g., Pisani-Ferry [2014]); however, they
fail to capture the crisis's deeper roots and management (see Leblond [2012]).

In order to improve our understanding of a discussion that has oscillated
between fears of EA disintegration on the one hand and the concrete advancement of integration during the crisis on the other, this special collection brings
together leading scholars of European integration who apply key theoretical
approaches – from liberal intergovernmentalism and neofunctionalism to

1

other prominent theoretical accounts that have been applied to European integration such as historical institutionalism, critical political economy, normative theory and a public opinion approach – to the financial and economic crisis. The contributions seek to analyse, understand and/or explain the events that occurred and the (re)actions to them in order to draw conclusions concerning the applicability and usefulness of their respective theoretical perspectives.

We view the approaches included in this special collection as complementary rather than competitive and search for a productive coexistence of the various perspectives advanced here (see Diez and Wiener [2009]). In addition, there may be scope to identify the 'home domains' of each approach, thus enabling us to ascertain how a division of labour between them may add up to a larger picture, in the sense of additive theory (Jupille et al. 2003: 21), without being combined or subsumed into a single grand theory through full-fledged synthesis.

In this introductory contribution, we do three things. First, we describe the EU's institutional response to the crisis, which serves as a reference point for the contributions in this special collection in order to avoid unnecessary repetition across them. Second, we present in summary form the contributions to this special collection. Third, we compare the different theories and offer some thoughts concerning the possibility for dialogue among them. Finally, we conclude by answering a key question posed earlier: why did EMU become deeper and more integrated when many feared for its survival during the crisis?

EUROPEAN INTEGRATION DEEPENS WITH THE CRISIS

The contributions to this special collection have either explicitly or implicitly chosen as their dependent variable the events that took place during the crisis, and in particular the decisions taken and integrative steps that were agreed in relation to EMU. This section therefore provides a brief overview of the crisis and the integrative steps taken. We provide as much as possible a factual overview and leave the (theoretical) explanations behind the events to the contributors, which we summarize and discuss in the next sections.

A (very) short history of the crisis

The crisis began as financial turmoil in the United States (US) and Europe in 2007, when some credit institutions found themselves in an increasingly precarious position arising from 'toxic financial assets' on their balance sheets, which had been produced over a prolonged period of credit expansion and public and private over-indebtedness. Within a very short period of time these assets proved to be of much lower value than previously assumed. In the context of the liquidity shortages that ensued worldwide, the European Central Bank (ECB) injected liquidity into the European banking system in August 2007. Illiquidity became acute in the US and elsewhere following the collapse of Lehman Brothers in September 2008. The collapse of a systemic financial intermediary at the heart of the US financial system led to a confidence crisis and a rapid and widespread repricing of risk and retrenchment in international capital markets, which quickly led to sharp drops in economic activity. In such a situation, illiquidity may quickly lead to insolvency and the collapse of the financial system (Rajan 2011). Nevertheless, in the European context, the support of illiquid banks to ensure financial stability became difficult for over-indebted national governments, especially given the absence of a clear crisis management framework that included a lender of last resort and a fiscal backstop (de Grauwe 2011).

A number of EA member states proved too weak, not only in defending their banking systems but also in allowing automatic fiscal stabilizers to fully absorb the impact of the resulting economic recession, let alone considering fiscal and financial policy activism in an environment where imbalances had been building up for a number of years. Against this background, the shortcomings in the EMU's architecture came to the fore, as did the political economy spanning 17 EA members sharing the single currency. The crisis uncovered among other things the lack of appropriate firewalls that could ensure shock absorption and the prevention of contagion, while at the same time avoiding moral hazard in public and private actors and across the borders of member states.

For the sake of brevity, Figure 1 illustrates the key decisions taken since 2007 against the background of one measure of financial tension and of sovereign bond yields, which are used as a simplified barometer of the intensity of the financial and sovereign debt crisis in various EA member states. The details of the institutional reforms that took place in the same period are described below.

Integrative steps taken in response to the crisis

In December 2012, the presidents of the European Council, the European Commission, the Eurogroup and the ECB published a report whose objective was to develop 'a vision for the future of the Economic and Monetary Union [EMU] and how it can best contribute to growth, jobs and stability' (Van Rompuy *et al.* 2012). According to the report, there are four building blocks necessary to create a 'genuine' EMU: an integrated financial framework (i.e., banking union); an integrated budgetary framework (i.e., fiscal union); an integrated economic policy framework; and appropriate mechanisms of democratic legitimacy and accountability commensurate to the increased levels of integration (i.e., political union). As a result of the crisis, the EU and the EA implemented several governance reforms and put together a series of institutional mechanisms to help resolve the crisis and prevent others in the future. Many of these mechanisms came before the 'Four Presidents' Report' was published. As such, they form part of the building blocks identified in the report and on which future steps would be built.[2]

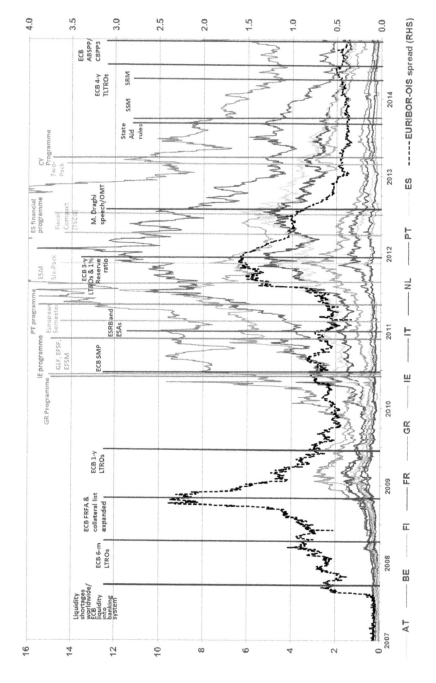

Liquidity shortages worldwide/ECB liquidity into banking system

ECB 6-m LTROs

ECB FRFA & collateral list expanded

ECB 1-y LTROs

GR Programme

IE programme

GLF, EFSF, EFSM

ECB SMP

PT programme

European Semester

ESRB and ESAs

ESM

Six-Pack

ECB 3-y LTROs & 1% Reserve ratio

ES financial programme

Fiscal Compact (TSCG)

M. Draghi speech/OMT

CY Programme

Two-Pack

State Aid rules

SSM

SRM

ECB 4-y TLTROs

ECB ABSPP/CBPP3

AT ——— BE ——— FI ——— FR ——— GR ——— IE ——— IT ——— NL ——— PT ——— ES ----- EURIBOR-OIS spread (RHS)

Figure 1 The European financial and economic crisis at a glance: money market spreads and 10-year government bond spreads against German Bunds (%)

Source: Bloomberg for money market data and *Haver Analytics* for bond yield data (cut-off date: 21 October 2014), and authors' calculations, and, for the signposting of the main events, judgement taking into account EU/EA decision-making procedures and possible differences between i.a. announcement of Commission proposals, political agreements between EU Council and Parliament, adoption of legislation, entry into force of legislation and so on (see more below).

Notes: The measure of tension in government bond spreads is shown as the difference between each country's 10-year government bond yield and that of the German government's 10-year bond yield (in percentages on the left hand scale). The measure of tension in money market spreads is here shown as the difference between the longer-term 12-month Euribor and short-term Overnight Index Swap (in percentages on the Right Hand Scale (RHS)).

- ECB: European Central Bank; LTROs: ECB Long-Term Refinancing Operations (six-month, one-year, three-year); TLTROs: ECB Targeted Long-Term Refinancing Operations; FRFA: ECB refinancing operations conducted with a Fixed (as opposed to minimum-bid) Rate and with Full Allotment; SMP: ECB Securities Markets Programme; OMT: ECB Outright Monetary Transactions; ABSPP: ECB Asset-Backed Securities Purchase Programme; CBPP3: ECB third Covered Bond Purchase Programme. All these events are shown as dark blue vertical lines in the colour (online) version of this Figure.

- GLF: Greek Loan Facility; EFSF: European Financial Stability Facility; EFSM: European Financial Stability Mechanism; ESM: European Stability Mechanism. All these events are shown as green vertical lines in the colour (online) version of this Figure.

- GR/IE/PT/ES/CY Programme: EU Economic Adjustment Programme for EFSF/EFSM/ESM financial support. All these events are shown as red vertical lines in the colour (online) version of this Figure.

- ESRB: European Systemic Risk Board; ESAs: European Supervisory Authorities, i.e., European Banking Authority (EBA), European Securities Markets Authority (ESMA), European Insurance and Occupational Pensions Authority (EIOPA); SSM: Single Supervisory Mechanism (SSM); SRM: Single Resolution Mechanism

- State Aid Rules: the Commission's COM of 1 August 2013 updating the framework of the Single Market's State Aid rules. All these events are shown as magenta vertical lines in the colour (online) version of this Figure.

- Economic and fiscal governance events are shown as light blue vertical lines in the colour (online) version of this Figure, and include: the initiation of European Semester (January 2011), the political agreement on the 'Six-Pack' (November 2011), the signature of Treaty on Stability Co-ordination and Governance (TSCG/'Fiscal Compact') (March 2012), the political agreement between Council and Parliament on the 'Two-Pack' (February 2013).

European Stability Mechanism

When Greece was shut out of capital markets in May 2010, there was no crisis 'firewall' for supporting EA member states that were faced with bond investors' panic. The Greek Loan Facility (GLF) was thus constructed under severe time pressures and as an *ad hoc* solution for Greece. However, the GLF quickly led to the creation of the European Financial Stability Facility (EFSF) as a broader (albeit also temporary) rescue mechanism for EA member states experiencing fiscal problems. Nevertheless, soon after the EFSF had become official, sovereign bond investors began worrying about what would happen when it expired at the end of June 2013. It quickly became obvious that the fiscal and banking problems experienced by Greece and others would not be resolved in the ESFS's three-year time frame. The solution was to set up a permanent firewall/financial assistance mechanism: the European Stability Mechanism (ESM).[3]

The European Council adopted the ESM in principle at its meeting on 16–17 December 2010. On 11 July 2011, finance ministers from EA member states signed the Treaty Establishing the European Stability Mechanism, which is an intergovernmental agreement between the 18 members of the euro area.[4] The treaty came into force on 27 September 2012 when Germany ratified it, thereby surpassing the minimum ratification threshold of 90 per cent of the ESM's original capital requirements. The ESM began its operations on 8 October 2012 with a lending capacity of €700 billion (including the remaining capacity of the EFSF). Unlike the EFSF, which was based on guarantees, the ESM has €80 billion of paid-in capital and €620 billion of callable capital used to issue money market instruments and medium- to long-term debt. It disbursed its first loans to Spain on 11 December 2012. As will be made clearer below, the ESM is an important element of both fiscal and banking unions.

Towards a European fiscal union

In light of the severe fiscal problems experienced by numerous EU member states, Greece being the most notable, it was clear that the existing Stability and Growth Pact (SGP) was insufficient to prevent EU governments' public finances from becoming unsustainable (Ioannou and Stracca 2014), though its weakness was widely acknowledged even before the crisis (see Heipertz and Verdun [2010]). Therefore, fiscal co-operation had to be bolstered, along with stricter rules.

The first step towards tighter fiscal governance at the EU level was the so-called 'Six-Pack', whose process was launched in March 2010 in the midst of the Greek debt crisis to culminate in five regulations and one directive adopted in October 2011, with entry into force on 13 December 2011. The Six-Pack reinforces the SGP's fiscal surveillance, which is now embedded in a pre-determined yearly economic policy co-ordination cycle called the European Semester. One of the Six-Pack's key components is the so-called 'reverse qualified majority', whereby the imposition of financial sanctions on member states that do not bring their fiscal deficits or debts into line quickly enough under the Excessive Deficit Procedure (EDP) is semi-automatic upon a Commission recommendation to the Council unless a qualified-majority of member states votes *against* the sanctions. In contrast, before the Six-Pack a qualified-majority of votes was necessary to *impose* sanctions. In other words, a qualified-minority of member states (including those in excessive deficit) was sufficient to block sanctions from being imposed, which, together with an unclear procedure,[5] was among the causes for the SGP impasse in the Economic and Financial (ECOFIN) Council of 25 November 2003 (see Leblond [2006]). Another important feature of the Six-Pack is that public debt levels are now explicitly incorporated in the EDP, along with deficit levels. This means that a member state whose public debt is above 60 per cent of gross domestic product (GDP) can be put in an EDP even if its deficit is below the 3 per cent of GDP threshold. The Six-Pack also provides the SGP with a stronger 'preventive arm' in the form of country-specific, medium-term budgetary objectives (MTOs) based *inter alia* on expected economic growth rates. Finally, the Six-Pack offers a new surveillance mechanism called the Macroeconomic Imbalances Procedure (MIP) and a related enforcement mechanism known as the Excessive Imbalances Procedure (EIP), which deal with macroeconomic imbalances (such as excessive current account deficits or unit labour cost growth) between EU member state economies.

The second step towards a fiscal union in the EU is the Treaty on Stability, Co-ordination and Governance in the Economic and Monetary Union (TSCG), also known as the 'Fiscal Compact' or the 'Fiscal (Stability) Treaty'.[6] This is an intergovernmental agreement, not part of EU law, signed on 2 March 2012 (it entered into force on 1 January 2013) that builds on the Six-Pack/SGP and Two-Pack (see below).[7] One of the TSCG's main features is the commitment by the signatories to include a permanent and binding balanced budget rule in national legislation, which includes a self-correcting mechanism, preferably of a constitutional nature. Moreover, under this rule annual structural (i.e., taking into account the business cycle) government deficits must not be above 0.5 per cent of GDP. This commitment is subject to review by the European Court of Justice, including the possibility of financial sanctions imposed by the Court. Another important feature is the requirement for the signatories to report to each other their public debt issuance plans, which accompanies a non-binding commitment to have greater economic policy discussion *ex ante* and, where and when necessary, co-ordination. Finally, it is important to note that only countries that follow the TSCG can receive funding from the ESM.

The final legal mechanism that the EU put together to enhance fiscal discipline among its member states is the 'Two-Pack', which consists of two EU regulations applying, on the basis of Article 136 TFEU, only to EA members. The Two-Pack entered into force on 30 May 2013 and consists of two core elements: (1) a common budgetary timeline and rules in which the

Commission examines and gives an opinion on each EA member state's draft budgetary plans, possibly leading to revisions before the budget is tabled in national parliaments;[8] (2) enhanced monitoring requirements for countries subject to an EDP, whereby the latter have to report not only additional but also more timely fiscal information to the Commission than what is already provided by the Six-Pack/SGP.

The above fiscal policy measures put in place by the EU and its member states go some way to achieve the four Presidents' objective of creating an integrated budgetary framework that enhances fiscal discipline. However, it is still a long way from a fully fledged fiscal union with an EU-level fiscal policy with a central budget, supranational taxes, commonly issued debt (e.g., Eurobonds) and fiscal transfers between member states.

The European banking union[9]

The decision to move forward towards an 'integrated financial framework' was taken at the European Council summit of 28–29 June 2012, where a first draft of the Four Presidents' Report was also presented. The first element of what became the European banking union was the Single Supervisory Mechanism (SSM), which was announced in a parallel EA summit with the intention of breaking the so-called bank–sovereign nexus.[10] Eventually, the banking union would also include: an advanced form of the single book of EU prudential regulation; a single resolution mechanism; the possibility of the ESM to directly (as opposed to only indirectly) recapitalize banks; and a common deposit guarantee framework.

The 'single rulebook of prudential regulation' (the term was first coined at the June 2009 European Council) corresponds to a common set of principles and rules governing the adequate regulation and supervision of banks in the EU. Essentially, it consists of transposing the new Basel III standards into the EU's legal framework, which was done with the adoption of the Capital Requirements Directive IV and the Capital Requirements Regulation (CRR) that came into force on 17 July 2013.[11] Because EU regulations have direct effect into member states' national law, the CRR aims to maximize the harmonization of prudential regulation across the EU. For instance, it contains detailed prescriptive provisions on capital and liquidity requirements, including limits on leverage. It also deals with disclosure requirements and counterparty risk. The directive (CRD IV), for its part, is less prescriptive, as it has to be adapted to national law. It focuses particularly on the powers and responsibilities of national authorities (and the ECB following its assumption of supervisory tasks) in terms of authorization, supervision and sanctions. It also includes provisions on banks' internal risk management and corporate governance.

As for banking supervision, on the basis of Article 127(6) TFEU, the SSM was developed after the June 2012 European Council summit and came into full operation in November 2014. As a result, the ECB acquired microprudential supervision[12] of all EA banks, though the SSM also foresees the possibility of non-EA member states joining the mechanism. Through the creation of a Supervisory Board at the ECB, the latter supervises directly the 120 most significant banking groups.[13] After one year of preparations during which a comprehensive assessment of these groups' balance sheets was performed (an Asset Quality Review and a Stress Test), the ECB assumed fully its supervisory tasks under the SSM framework on 4 November 2014.

With the SSM in operation, the ESM is able to provide temporary financial assistance directly to banks experiencing liquidity problems, not just indirectly through governments that take up an EU programme. This ESM Direct Recapitalization Instrument is to act under strict rules that fully respect the new 'bail-in' regime (see below) created by the EU-wide framework of the Bank Recovery and Resolution Directive (BRRD)[14] and against the backdrop of the single market's state aid rules that the European Commission revised in August 2013. In late June 2013, the Eurogroup decided to limit the ESM's ability to intervene directly in banks' recapitalization at €60 billion. This was concomitant to the notion that under the bail-in regime taxpayer funds would be made available only as a very last resort and only after the bail-in of a bank's creditors, including senior creditors from 1 January 2016.

Together with the SSM, another key institutional pillar of an effective banking union emerged in the form of the Single Resolution Mechanism (SRM), which deals with banks that need to be resolved, especially the most significant ones supervised by the SSM. The SRM was agreed to on 30 July 2014 to begin operating on 1 January 2015. It applies to banks supervised by the ECB and is expected to be fully operational by 1 January 2016 (when the BRRD's senior bail-in provision comes into effect). Moreover, a Single Resolution Fund (SRF) was agreed to in May 2014. Bank levies will fund the SRM and be gradually pooled over eight years via national resolution funds.[15]

The banking union's final pillar, a deposit guarantee framework, has started to take shape under the revised Deposit Guarantee Schemes Directive (DGSD), which was adopted on 12 June 2014. The DGSD harmonizes the following elements: deposit coverage to €100,000; arrangements for paying out depositors, in terms of speed and cross-border co-ordination; and the financing of national deposit guarantee schemes (DGSs), including mutual borrowing in the case of large bank failures. Such DGSs are deemed important because they could prevent bank runs by giving depositors confidence that their money is safe. Moreover, to maintain a level playing field in an integrated financial services market like the EU, a minimum harmonization is required because customers could be tempted to deposit their money in the banks of member states where deposit insurance levels are higher. Nonetheless, deposit insurance remains the banking union's weak link, because no progress has been made towards a single EU- or euro-area-level DGS.

In sum, the crisis in Europe has led to a great deal of institutional activity at the EU and EA level (for a timeline and more details on these institutional mechanisms, including the various pieces of legislation underpinning them, see the online Appendix [online supplemental material]). Together with the

ECB's actions, the resulting institutions contributed to overcoming the peak of the crisis (Chang and Leblond 2014) and will provide a better framework for preventing and managing future crises.

In terms of European integration, these achievements are remarkable, not only for their scale and scope but also the speed with which they were adopted and put into place. For instance, writing in 2010 as the sovereign debt portion of the crisis was reaching its apex, Leblond (2011) was critical of what had been achieved in terms of supranational financial (most especially banking) regulation and supervision. Yet, four years later, the EA has a banking union already in operation and the regulation and supervision of financial services more broadly have also been further integrated (Grossman and Leblond 2012). On the fiscal side, the story is the same. When the SGP was weakened following the 2003 crisis, many saw fiscal co-ordination in the EU as toothless, which is why it has been partly blamed for the crisis (Schuknecht et al. 2011). However, a significant strengthening of the fiscal rules and co-ordination has taken place in the EU and the EA over the last few years, though there are still concerns about implementation (Organization for Economic Co-operation and Development [OECD] 2014). Finally, although the Maastricht Treaty made clear that the EU and the ECB could not bail out member states experiencing debt problems, the EA now has a permanent mechanism to do exactly that. So how do we explain these achievements? This is the main question that the contributions to this special collection try to answer, but they do so from different theoretical lenses.

THEORETICAL PERSPECTIVES ON THE CRISIS

As mentioned in the introduction, this special collection brings together leading scholars of the EU to apply various theoretical perspectives to analyse, understand and/or explain the European financial and economic crisis and the integration that took place. In doing so, we try to push beyond the 'stones in a mosaic' metaphor (Diez and Wiener 2009) and identify theories' respective 'domain of application', one of four models of theoretical dialogue identified by Jupille et al. (2003),[16] and thus ascertain their division of labour (see next section).

Although the old rivals – neofunctionalism (NF) and liberal intergovernmentalism (LI) – are no longer at the heart of most scholarly analyses, they remain important reference points in the theoretical understanding of the EU (Mattli and Stone Sweet 2012; Richardson 2012). Therefore, it made sense to have LI and NF as the starting perspectives of this special collection.

Frank Schimmelfennig, in his contribution, analyses the crisis from a liberal intergovernmentalist (LI) perspective, which means that it allows him to take an 'essential first cut' at the crisis by considering LI's basic elements: national interests; national preferences; international bargaining; and institutions to facilitate the bargaining's implementation (Schimmelfennig 2015). He focuses his analysis on the crisis's management and the institutional mechanisms put in place in response to the crisis because he considers LI to be a 'theory of integration', which means that it cannot account for the crisis itself. Schimmelfennig characterizes the crisis's management as a 'game of chicken' where hard intergovernmental bargaining and brinkmanship took place to prevent the EA from imploding, something that all the parties involved wanted to avoid. This 'game' was not so much about whether to co-operate (i.e., integrate) or to save the EA but about how to share the adjustment costs of doing so. He argues that the bargains and institutional choices reflected mostly the preferences of the German-led coalition. This is because Germany (and its allies in the 'game') was less immediately threatened by the crisis than those member states facing default, exit from the euro, and overall economic collapse.

For their part, Arne Niemann and Demosthenes Ioannou (2015) shed a neofunctionalist light on the crisis. The authors deal extensively with the crisis's management by applying NF's three spillover mechanisms: functional; political; and cultivated. Interestingly, however, their analysis of functional spillover's role in the crisis is as much about the origins of crisis as its management. Niemann and Ioannou identify three 'functional dissonances' associated with EMU, which are the result of the incomplete architecture agreed to at Maastricht when EMU was decided. Essentially, these dissonances or pressures are the result of monetary policy being decided independently at the supranational level by the ECB, while fiscal policy, financial supervision (and to some extent regulation) have remained largely determined at the national level. If functional spillover provides the logic or impetus for further integration in the context of the crisis (i.e., completing EMU's Maastricht's architecture), political and cultivated spillovers contributed not only impetus to more integration – through the pressuring roles played by business interests, financial markets and supranational institutions such as the Commission, European Parliament and the ECB – but also content to the resulting institutional reforms and mechanisms. Nevertheless, the authors acknowledge that NF's strength in explaining the dynamics of integration is a weakness when it comes to the limits imposed on integration, like the absence of a fully fledged fiscal union. They nevertheless imply that functional dissonances continue to exist and may in the future re-emerge to push forward integration.

If LI and NF are justifiably the starting points of this special collection, we felt that an institutionalist perspective on the crisis was also warranted. After all, Pollack (2009: 141) concludes that new institutionalisms (rational choice, sociological and historical) 'have arguably become the dominant approaches to the study of European integration'. Herein, Amy Verdun (2015) uses the lens of historical institutionalism (HI) to analyse the institutional choices that were made in response to the crisis. Given that all options were open as a result of the crisis being a 'critical juncture', she wonders why the institutions that were created are similar in design to past and present EU institutional arrangements. She argues that only HI can provide an adequate explanation to this apparent puzzle, whereby new institutions were either 'copied' from or 'layered' onto other EU institutions.

If it is crucial to explain the policy and institutional choices that have been made in response to the crisis, as the above-mentioned contributions do, it is also important, as Sara Hobolt and Christopher Wratil (2015) point out, to analyse the role played by mass politics and public opinion (PO) in European integration (see also Hooghe and Marks [2009]). Like Bellamy and Weale (2015) in this special collection (see below), Hobolt and Wratil argue that further integration depends on some form of public (or, in line with Scharpf [1997], input) legitimacy, which is why they study the dynamics of public support for the euro before and during the crisis. Perhaps surprisingly, they confirm that public opinion of the euro has remained relatively stable and favourable in the euro area during the crisis. What is even more interesting for such studies is the fact that this (stable) support became increasingly driven by utilitarian considerations (i.e., based on cost–benefit analysis), as opposed to identity ones (i.e., based on national attachments), as the crisis progressed. This means that support for the euro is in fact not static but dynamic. Hobolt and Wratil conclude that their results challenge the notion, advocated by *inter alia* Hooghe and Marks (2009), that greater politicization of European policy issues implies more constraints on the integration process.

As mentioned above, Richard Bellamy and Albert Weale (2015) also address the issue of legitimacy but they do so from a normative theory (NT) perspective. They argue that as EMU gets reformed in order to become more effective, especially on the fiscal front, there has to be a two-level contract between EU member states themselves on one level and between the member states and their citizens on the other if the European economic governance structure that emerges from the reform process is to be politically legitimate. According to them, such legitimacy for EMU does not come from a single *demos* but from agreements between the EA's various *demoi* via negotiation by their elected representatives. They call this process republican intergovernmentalism and argue that, as a result, national parliaments should be much more involved in EMU decision-making, notably in the integrated budgetary framework.

If Bellamy and Weale (2015) question the legitimacy of the integration path taken by the institutional response to the crisis and offer a remedy, something that is important for European integration theory to do (Diez and Wiener 2009: 18), Magnus Ryner, in the final contribution to this special collection, offers a broader challenge not only to the institutional and policy choices made in the context of the crisis, but also to European integration scholarship prior to the crisis (Ryner 2015). Using a critical political economy (CPE) perspective, he first argues that the causes of the crisis may be understood as a particularly European manifestation of finance-led (over)accumulation inherent to the capitalist system. Second, he considers the steps taken to manage the crisis as a continuation of the German ordoliberal tradition that is embedded within EMU. He concludes that the resulting one-sided attempt to rebalance competitiveness inside the EA will be catastrophic for member states in the periphery and puts EMU's long-term sustainability at risk.

EUROPEAN INTEGRATION THEORY AND THE CRISIS

The above-mentioned contributions represent major stones, though not all, in the European integration theory 'mosaic' (Diez and Wiener 2009). They help to explain why the crisis happened and how public opinion reacted. They also help to explain why certain integrative steps were taken in response to the crisis and why the resulting institutions were designed the way they were. Finally, they address the normative implications of the crisis and its management, especially in terms of legitimacy and socioeconomic justice/development, which are deemed fundamental for EMU's long-term sustainability. However, it is important to step back and look at the whole mosaic in order to see how the pieces fit together and what picture they give us of European integration in the context of the crisis.

Commonalities and differences between theoretical perspectives

When comparing the various contributions, a number of commonalities and differences can be observed. To begin with, all contributors agree, more or less explicitly, that the crisis has led to a noticeable increase of European integration. Even through the lens of LI – an approach that is not known for exaggerating the progress of European integration – one speaks of 'a major leap in financial and fiscal integration' (Schimmelfennig 2015).

Second, while some contributors indicate that 'their' approaches do not offer any proposition to account for the crisis (Schimmelfennig 2015) or remain (justifiably) silent on this point (Bellamy and Weale 2015; Hobolt and Wratil 2015), other contributions implicitly or partly provide an explanation of why the crisis emerged (Niemann and Ioannou 2015; Ryner 2015; Verdun 2015). Niemann and Ioannou (2015) suggest that if functional pressures are not resolved through further integrative steps, this can promote crisis. They observe this process following the introduction of the single currency. Functional dissonances – e.g., between supranational monetary policy and intergovernmental budgetary, fiscal and structural policy, or between increasing financial market integration but largely national supervisory systems – allowed for the disrespect of the SGP's fiscal rules, the build-up of financial imbalances and the loss of competitiveness in a number of economies failing to pursue sound fiscal, wage and structural policies in line with the single monetary and exchange rate policy (see also Verdun 2015). For his part, Ryner (2015) understands the crisis as the result of a capital accumulation regime generated by financial markets driven by ever riskier investments in the absence of productivity growth. In Europe, surplus capital in the northern core was used to finance debt-driven private and public consumption in the periphery.

Third, LI, NF, HI, NT and CPE all provide key pieces of the explanatory puzzle when it comes to specific integrative steps taken in response to the crisis and the scale and scope of the institutions that were created as a result.

For LI, the institutional arrangements were generally aligned with German preferences. For NF, the various spillovers are the key to understanding the need for further integration in particular. In both accounts, however, interest groups play an important role. LI highlights organized interests through the domestic 'transmission belt', whereas NF stresses the transnational organization of interests. Moreover, both approaches emphasize the assumption of interdependence between economies, though NF emphasizes the interdependence between policy and issue areas more strongly. LI accounts for further crisis-related integration by underlining the substantial interdependence within the EA, which led to strong national preferences for the preservation of the euro (Schimmelfennig 2015). Instead, NF highlights more specifically the various functional interdependences that were (cultivated and) acted upon especially by markets, supranational institutions and transnational business interests (Niemann and Ioannou 2015).

For HI, layering on top or copying from existing or past institutional arrangements has been an effective strategy, especially when there is little time to come up with solutions. This explains the particular shape that new crisis-related institutions have taken (Verdun 2015), which is something that NF has difficulty accounting for because it is focused on the dynamics of integration.[17] However, in contrast to LI and NF, the process of institutional structures affecting possible solutions to current problems lacks agency in the HI approach (*cf.* Verdun 2015). The HI approach presented herein by Verdun (2015) places more emphasis on path dependent institutional structures (previous institutional structures affect possible solutions to current problems) and critical junctures (short periods of time when actors' choices are likely to affect outcomes). By contrast, NF highlights functional dissonances prompting further action and concrete agency (usually in line with its interests) pushing these dissonances (Niemann and Ioannou 2015).

For NT, the logic of legal constitutionalism underpins much of the new fiscal co-ordination framework put into place to respond to the SGP's weakness, at the expense of the framework's legitimacy. Similarly, CPE argues that Germany's ordoliberal view of economic policy pervades the Europe project and, as result, has logically found itself in the institutional response to the crisis. Although this is not something that Verdun (2015) considers, one could reasonably argue that a HI perspective could help shed light on how the ideas of legal constitutionalism and ordoliberalism became institutionalized within the EU. Unlike NT, CPE also offers an explanation for further European integration through the Amsterdam School's argument that in capitalist societies élites associated with big capital enjoy privileged positions of power and are therefore able to exercise leadership over the integration process, which they see favourably as capital becomes more international in nature (Ryner 2015). Arguably, such a logic is not (entirely) dissimilar to that offered by LI and NF in terms of the role played by organized interests in the integration process.

Finally, a number of approaches look into the future. Naturally, NT and CPE do so most explicitly. Following from the previous paragraph, NT and CPE consider EMU's long-term sustainability to be at risk because the new institutions are not sufficiently legitimate in the eyes of citizens who suffer them. Bellamy and Weale (2015) hold that EMU should therefore be placed under a political constitution that, by increasing the power of national parliaments, reconciles the European monetary order with the legitimacy of member state governance. Hobolt and Wratil (2015), however, cast serious doubt on the new institutional order's lack of legitimacy, since EA public opinion in favour of the euro and the EU's effectiveness has remained strong (and actually increased) as the crisis progressed and new institutions came into being. This leads them to question the view that national identities will continue to constrain the process of European integration in the long term, because people seem to have become more utilitarian in their understanding of the euro and its institutional framework. Other contributions also, to some extent, make use of their approaches to project into the future. For instance, NF emphasizes the continued potential for further spillover, given remaining functional dissonances, which suggests that the current (post-crisis) institutional design cannot be taken as the endpoint in the process of European integration (Niemann and Ioannou 2015).

Relationship (and division of labour) between approaches: towards domains of application?

Given their commonalities and differences, how do the different theoretical approaches to this special collection add up if we view the approaches as complementary rather than competitive? If we assume that theoretical approaches can have different purposes and scope, it is possible to see them as contributing to our overall understanding and adding up to a larger picture. There is be scope to go one step further and identify the 'respective turfs and "home domains" of each theory' and thus eventually 'bringing together each home turf in some larger picture' (Jupille et al. 2003: 21). This implies both specifying the scope conditions of theories as well as the division of labour between them.

The domain-of-application model of theoretical dialogue 'works best when multiple theories explain similar phenomena, when variables have little overlap, and when these variables do not interact in their influence on outcomes' (Jupille et al. 2003: 22). Of these conditions for making use of the domain-of-application approach, the first one is largely given: all theories focus on the crisis, although some approaches focus more on the management of the crisis, while others concentrate more on the (normative) implications of it. However, the partial overlap between some of the theories makes a clear-cut specification of domains of application difficult at times. For example, interdependence (between issue/policy areas and economies) is viewed as an underlying cause for integration in NF, LI, and also in HI. Having said that, there are some opportunities for engaging in/with this model of theoretical dialogue (at least in a tentative fashion).

One obvious observation is that LI, NF, HI and to some extent PO contribute mainly to explaining integration, while NT and CPE contribute mainly to the normative implications of integration, especially the institutional choices that have been made. But this can be taken a step further. LI has its comparative advantage or 'home domain' when it comes to analysing the actual (crisis management) negotiations, where the national constellation of preferences and differential bargaining power go a long way towards explaining the institutional design chosen by decision-makers during the crisis. To broaden this further, LI is at its best when single (grand) events are analysed, where issues are substantially politicized, when single governments can block decisions and when the stakes and preferences are clear (Schimmelfennig 2015). Under these circumstances national governments are privileged: they are clearly in the driving seat and tend to enter into a bargaining mode (Moravcsik [1998]; also cf. Niemann [2004]).

However, as noted before in the literature, LI does not give us the whole process (e.g., Pierson 1996). To get the larger picture, HI and NF are more useful because they can explain processes over time and how single events are embedded in broader contexts.[18] They show that national preferences are not exogenously given, but are very much influenced by EU membership, prior EU decision-making and socialization processes among negotiators. The two approaches particularly indicate how earlier decisions – like that of an incomplete/deficient institutional EMU design – create pressures on decision-makers for further (integrative) action, and/or affect possible solutions to current problems (in terms of crisis management). They are also complementary in doing so. According to HI, institutional structures affect solutions to problems at hand; however, it is not clear who accomplishes these structural demands.[19] This is where NF may come in to help, whereby supranational agency, transnational interest groups (and market pressures), along with national policy-makers (whose preferences have been affected by functional rationales) act on structures.

The findings from the PO perspective in this special collection further strengthen our understanding of why decision-makers agreed on substantial further integration during the course of the crisis. High and stable public support for the euro inside the EA is very likely to have influenced policy-makers, especially in times of substantial issue politicization. As the PO perspective does not constitute a properly fleshed-out approach to European integration (yet), it is difficult to specify its home turf. As Hobolt and Wratil (2015) suggest, public opinion may best be viewed as a driver (for or against integration) that could be incorporated into larger theories of European integration. At the very least, it would be useful to have a better understanding of how and when public opinion enters into the integration process. This may have been what Hooghe and Marks (2009) had in mind when they devised their postfunctionalist theory of European integration; however, they ended up seeing public opinion mostly as a structural constraint on the integration process, which is the opposite of what seems to have happened during the crisis.

If public opinion matters for European integration, then why does capital continue to determine the integration process against the interest of labour, as the CPE perspective argues? Even more puzzling is why EA voters continued to support the euro as the crisis progressed and ordoliberal institutional arrangements were put in place. CPE's comparative advantage is certainly its ability to understand the institutional conditions under which the inherent crisis tendencies in capitalism are contained and managed by certain powers, as well as the uneven (power and distributive) effects of particular crisis management strategies. It provides us with a perspective to critically analyse the development of the EU's (capitalist) economic system and its implications in terms of socio-economic justice/development. However, as with HI, it lacks a certain degree of agency: the economic structure is determinant. Socioeconomic agents are forced to wait for the so-called 'inherent contradictions' of the capitalist system to play out and, thereby, bring an end to the system. In the EU's case, the crisis could have been this momentous occasion, as Ryner (2015) implicitly argues in the first part of his contribution. Why voters did not seize this moment, CPE does not say. Again, this demonstrates the importance for European integration theory to have a PO perspective in order to make the picture not only more complete but also clearer.

NT is least ambitious in its explanatory claims. This is because it seeks to explain the legitimacy of binding agreements between democratic states in the EU's political system rather than the emergence of the financial and economic crisis and the subsequent process of economic integration. NT elaborates the normative implications stemming from the crisis, by analysing key concepts and their inter-relationships in a norm-governed order, with political legitimacy depending on the intelligibility of the norms. In that sense NT provides a normative complement to the more explanatory theories, such as LI, NF, HI and CPE. Unlike LI, NF and HI, and more in line with PO, it sees input legitimacy (*cf.* Scharpf 1999) as the key issue of the EU order. LI, NF and HI consider the integrative steps taken as solutions to increase the effectiveness of EMU governance and, thereby, output legitimacy. By contrast, NT sees input legitimacy as a *sine qua non* complement to such output legitimacy. Like CPE, NT also offers a critical–analytical complement to the more established theories, through its critical evaluation of the norms that are at work in the EU's economic constitution and the extent to which those norms are at variance with democratic values. Contrary to CPE, however, it offers a solution to the required legitimization of economic integration that can emerge within the existing system, by moving from the existing legal constitutionalism to political constitutionalism as a basis for further integration. Finally, like CPE, it is able to make concrete policy and institutional proposals that might improve the integration process, like Bellamy and Weale's (2015) suggestion that national parliaments should be more involved into the EU/EA fiscal co-ordination framework in order to increase the latter's legitimacy and, therefore, improve EMU's long-term sustainability.

In order to move beyond fruitless discussion – where approaches of different purpose and scope either talk past one another, try to outcompete or subsume each other, the evolving and emerging division of labour specified above has, in our view, amounted to a richer overall picture. The result of this dialogue may be viewed as 'minimal synthesis' (Jupille et al. 2003: 21) in the sense that the results of additive theorizing are accepted as useful for gaining a deeper and richer understanding, without combining or subsuming approaches into a single grand theory through full-fledged synthesis. The deeper and richer understanding and insight that we have attained of the crisis and its management through this dialogue seem to prove this point.

CONCLUSIONS

This contribution began with a simple yet crucial question with respect to the European financial and economic crisis: why did EMU not implode but instead further integrate? The contributions in this special collection tell us why. The reason is that economic interdependencies between EA member states, stemming from previous institutional arrangements, were such that no one wanted EMU to fail, including the general public. The issue, then, was how to prevent such a scenario from happening, given time constraints and the distribution of costs (burden-sharing). Spillover logics, past and existing EU institutional arrangements and power relations dictated the institutional choices that were made. Even if ultimately those choices proved effective in quelling the crisis, notwithstanding the ECB's key role in managing the crisis, serious questions remain with respect to EMU's long-term legitimacy and sustainability. Nevertheless, the contributions and the insights they provided clearly demonstrate that there is no crisis in European integration theorizing. The existing picture has not only survived the crisis, but it has also become richer: theories' domain of application and their division of labour have manifested themselves more clearly.

Biographical notes: Demosthenes Ioannou is principal economist in the Directorate General International and European Relations of the European Central Bank. Patrick Leblond is associate professor of public and international affairs at the University of Ottawa and Research Associate at CIRANO. Arne Niemann is professor of international politics and Jean Monnet Professor of European Integration at the University of Mainz.

ACKNOWLEDGEMENTS

We would like to express our deep gratitude to Jeremy Richardson and Berthold Rittberger for their valuable support, advice and comments with respect to this special collection. Richard Bellamy, Magnus Ryner, Amy Verdun, and Albert Weale also deserve special thanks for their useful comments on parts of the introduction to this special collection. Patrick Leblond would like to acknowledge the support received from the European University Institute, where he was Visiting Fellow during the final stages of this project. The views expressed are those of the authors and do not necessarily reflect those of their employers or parent organizations.

SUPPLEMENTAL DATA AND RESEARCH MATERIALS

Supplemental data for this article can be accessed on the Taylor & Francis website, http://dx.doi.org/10.1080/13501763.2014.994021

NOTES

1 For dire predictions about the future of the euro area, see, for example, Brittan (2013) and Greenspan (Ahuja 2011). Amongst the best-known critics of the euro and the EU's crisis management are: Blyth (2013); Feldstein (2012); Krugman (2011); Marsh (2013); Roubini (2012); Sinn 2014; and Soros with Schmitz (2014).
2 At the Euro summit on 24 October 2014, EA heads of state or government called for closer co-ordination of economic policy in the EA and invited the four Presidents to make further progress on the basis of their 2012 recommendations (http://www.consilium.europa.eu/uedocs/cms_data/docs/pressdata/en/ec/145444.pdf) (accessed 22 January 2015).
3 Since 1 July 2013, the EFSF no longer extends new loans. It only manages those it has already made (i.e., repayment), alongside the financial instruments that it has used to fund those loans. Once all the loans have been reimbursed by member states and all the funding instruments have also been repaid in full, then the EFSF will cease to exist.
4 A modified version of the ESM treaty, incorporating amendments to make the ESM more effective, was signed on 2 February 2012. Moreover, Article 136 of the Treaty on the Functioning of the European Union (TFEU) was amended to incorporate the possibility under EU law of establishing the ESM.
5 See European Court of Justice Case C–27/04, Commission v. Council, judgment of 13 July 2004.
6 It is important to note that the term 'Fiscal Compact' only refers to the fiscal component of the TSCG, not the parts dealing with economic policy co-operation.
7 The Czech Republic and the United Kingdom are the only two EU member states that have not signed the TSCG.
8 The Two-Pack also obliges member states to base their draft budgets on independent macroeconomic forecasts and put in place independent bodies (e.g., a parliamentary budget officer) to monitor compliance with national fiscal rules.

9 This subsection draws heavily on Leblond (2014).

10 The bank–sovereign nexus is also known as the 'doom-loop' whereby sovereign debt problems lead to bank vulnerabilities, which in turn make the sovereign debt problem worse as bond investors fear that the government might have to come to the banking system's rescue, and so on and so forth.

11 EU politics have created discrepancies between Basel III and the CRD IV package, according to Howarth and Quaglia (2013).

12 Microprudential supervision means the supervision of individual banks while macroprudential supervision means supervisory measures covering more than one bank or wider measures that avoid *inter alia* the creation of market bubbles. The SSM Regulation and the application of CRD IV also to the ECB as supervisor mean that the ECB has also acquired certain macroprudential powers beyond its previous financial stability responsibilities.

13 The ECB supervises the remaining banks in co-operation with national supervisors (National Competent Authorities).

14 The BRRD was a further addition to the single rulebook and aims to harmonize national rules and procedures for restructuring and recapitalizing failing or failed banks. Importantly in such a situation, it provides for 'bailing in' creditors of banks to avoid that taxpayer money is used to rescue banks.

15 The transfer and mutualization of funds collected from national credit institutions is to be done through an intergovernmental agreement that requires ratification by national parliaments.

16 The three other models are: competitive testing; sequencing; and incorporation (subsumption).

17 One may argue that NF is at a certain disadvantage here because early neofunctionalism was taken as a point for departure. A revised neofunctionalist framework that takes countervailing pressures in account may arguably better equip the approach for analysing such issues (*cf.* Niemann 2006).

18 While several studies have shown that spillover processes may also occur in more politicized 'high politics' arenas (Niemann 2008; Niemann and Ioannou 2015), the natural 'home turf' that is most conducive to the NF spillover logic has often been that of technical and depoliticized settings (see Burley and Mattli [1993]).

19 It would be unfair to say that scholars working in the HI tradition have not taken agency into consideration at all (*cf.* Pierson 1998: 43ff). However, on the whole agents are rather reduced to servants of structure, and the latter is arguably assigned a more important ontological status, which also comes out of the HI contribution to this special collection (Verdun 2015).

REFERENCES

Ahuja, M. (2011) 'Greenspan: why the euro zone is doomed to fail', *CNBC.com*, 25 October, available at http://www.cnbc.com/id/45033013 (accessed 26 October 2014).

Bellamy, R. and Weale, A. (2015) 'Political legitimacy and European monetary union: contracts, constitutionalism and the normative logic of two-level games', *Journal of European Public Policy*, doi: 10.1080/13501763.2014.995118.

Blyth, M. (2013) *Austerity: The History of a Dangerous Idea*, New York: Oxford University Press.

Brittan, S. (2013) 'Why the eurozone will come apart sooner or later', *FT.com*, 8 August, available at http://www.ft.com/intl/cms/s/0/c0bbc01a-fec0-11e2-97dc-00144feabdc0.html#axzz3HJG1EwAu (accessed 26 October 2014)

Burley, A.M. and Mattli, W. (1993) 'Europe before the court: a political theory of legal integration' *International Organization* 47(1): 41–76.

Chang, M. and Leblond, P. (2014) 'All in: market expectations of eurozone integrity in the sovereign debt crisis', *Review of International Political Economy*, doi: 10.1080/09692290.2014.941905.

De Grauwe, P. (2011) 'The governance of a fragile eurozone', ceps working document no. 346, May 2011, Brussels: Centre for European Policy Studies.

Diez, T. and Wiener, A. (2009) 'Introducing the mosaic of integration theory', in A. Wiener and T. Diez (eds), *European Integration Theory*, 2nd edn, Oxford: Oxford University Press, pp. 1–22.

Feldstein, M. (2012) 'The failure of the euro: the little currency that couldn't', *Foreign Affairs* 91(1): 105–16.

Grossman, E. and Leblond, P. (2012) 'Financial regulation in Europe: from the battle of the systems to a Jacobinist EU', in J. Richardson (ed.), *Constructing a Policy-making State? Policy Dynamics in the European Union*, Oxford University Press, pp. 189–208.

Heipertz, M. and Verdun, A. (2010) *Ruling Europe: The Politics of the Stability and Growth Pact*, New York: Cambridge University Press.

Hobolt, S.B. and Wratil, C. (2015) 'Public opinion and the crisis: the dynamics of support for the euro', *Journal of European Public Policy*, doi: 10.1080/13501763.2014.994022.

Hooghe, L. and Marks, G. (2009) 'A postfunctionalist theory of European integration: from permissive consensus to constraining dissensus', *British Journal of Political Science* 39(1): 1–23.

Howarth, D. and Quaglia, L. (2013) 'Banking on stability: the political economy of new capital requirements in the European Union', *Journal of European Integration* 35(3): 333–46.

Ioannou, D. and Stracca L. (2014) 'Have euro area and EU economic governance worked? Just the facts', *European Journal of Political Economy* 34: 1–17.

Jupille, J., Caporaso, J.A. and Checkel, J.T. (2003) 'Integrating institutions: rationalism, constructivism, and the study of the European Union', *Comparative Political Studies* 36(7): 7–40.

Krugman, P. (2011) 'Can Europe be saved?', *New York Times Magazine*, 16 January, 26.

Leblond, P. (2006) 'The political stability and growth pact is dead: long live the economic stability and growth pact', *Journal of Common Market Studies* 44(5): 969–90.

Leblond, P. (2011) 'A Canadian perspective on the EU's financial architecture and the crisis', in K. Hübner (ed.), *Europe, Canada and the Comprehensive Economic Partnership*, Abingdon: Routledge, pp. 165–79.

Leblond, P. (2012) 'One for all and all for one: the global financial crisis and the European integration project', in L. Fioramonti (ed.), *Regions and Crises: New Challenges for Contemporary Regionalisms*, New York: Palgrave Macmillan, pp. 50–66.

Leblond, P. (2014) 'The logic of a banking union for Europe', *Journal of Banking Regulation* 15(3/4): 288–98.

Marsh, D. (2013) *Europe's Deadlock: How the Euro Crisis Could Be Solved – and Why it Won't Happen*, New Haven, CT: Yale University Press.

Mattli, W. and Stone Sweet, A. (2012) 'Regional integration and the evolution of the European polity: on the fiftieth anniversary of the *Journal of Common Market Studies*', *Journal of Common Market Studies* 50(S1): 1–17.

Moravcsik, A. (1998) *The Choice for Europe: Social Purpose & State Power from Messina to Maastricht*, Ithaca, NY: Cornell University Press.

Niemann, A. (2004) 'Between communicative action and strategic action: the Article 113 Committee and the negotiations on the WTO Basic Telecommunications Services Agreement', *Journal of European Public Policy* 11(3): 379–407.

Niemann, A. (2006) *Explaining Decisions in the European Union*, Cambridge: Cambridge University Press.

Niemann, A. (2008) 'Dynamics and countervailing pressures of visa, asylum and immigration policy treaty revision: explaining change and stagnation from the Amsterdam IGC to the IGC 2003–2004', *Journal of Common Market Studies* 46(3): 559–91.

Niemann, A. and Ioannou, D. (2015) 'European economic integration in times of crisis: a case of neofunctionalism?', *Journal of European Public Policy*, doi: 10.1080/13501763.2014.994021.

Organisation for Economic Co-operation and Development (OECD) (2014) *OECD Economic Surveys: Euro Area 2014*, Paris: Organisation for Economic Co-operation and Development.

Pierson, P. (1996) 'The path to European integration: a historical institutionalist analysis', *Comparative Political Studies* 29: 123–63.

Pierson, P. (1998) 'The path to European integration: a historical institutionalist analysis', in W. Sandholtz and A. Stone Sweet (eds), *European Integration and Supranational Governance*, Oxford: Oxford University Press, pp. 27–58.

Pisani-Ferry, J. (2014) *The Euro Crisis and its Aftermath*, Oxford: Oxford University Press.

Pollack, M.A. (2009) 'The new institutionalisms and European integration', in A. Wiener and T. Diez (eds), *European Integration Theory*, 2nd edn, Oxford: Oxford University Press: 125–43.

Rajan, R. (2011) *Fault Lines: How Hidden Fractures Still Threaten the World Economy*, Princeton, NJ: Princeton University Press.

Richardson, J. (2012) 'The onward march of Europeanization: tectonic movement and seismic events', in J. Richardson (ed.), *Constructing a Policy-making State? Policy dynamics in the European Union*, Oxford: Oxford University Press, pp. 334–59.

Roubini, N. (2012) 'Early retirement for the eurozone?', *Project Syndicate*, 15 August, available at https://www.project-syndicate.org/commentary/early-retirement-for-the-eurozone-by-nouriel-roubini (accessed 26 October 2014).

Ryner, M. (2015) 'Europe's ordoliberal iron cage: critical political economy, the euro area crisis and its management', *Journal of European Public Policy*, doi: 10.1080/13501763.2014.995119.

Scharpf, F. (1997) 'Economic integration, democracy and the welfare state'. *Journal of European Public Policy* 4(1): 18–36.

Scharpf, F. (1999) *Governing in Europe: Effective and Democratic?* Oxford: Oxford University Press.

Schimmelfennig, F. (2015) 'Liberal intergovernmentalism and the euro area crisis', *Journal of European Public Policy*, doi: 10.1080/13501763.2014.994020.

Schuknecht, L., Moutot, P., Rotter, P. and Stark, J. (2011) 'The Stability and Growth Pact: crisis and reform', *Occasional Paper Series #129*, Frankfurt: European Central Bank.

Sinn, H.W. (2014) *The Euro Trap: On Bursting Bubbles, Budgets, and Beliefs*, Oxford: Oxford University Press.

Soros, G., with Schmitz, G. (2014) *The Tragedy of the European Union: Disintegration or Revival?* New York: PublicAffairs.

Van Rompuy, H., Barroso, J.M., Juncker, J.C. and Draghi, M. (2012) 'Towards a genuine economic and monetary union', 5 December, available at http://www.consilium.europa.eu/uedocs/cms_data/docs/pressdata/en/ec/134069.pdf (accessed 16 October 2014).

Verdun, A. (2015) 'A historical institutionalist explanation of the EU's responses to the euro area financial crisis', *Journal of European Public Policy*, doi: 10.1080/13501763.2014.994023.

Liberal intergovernmentalism and the euro area crisis

Frank Schimmelfennig

ABSTRACT   Liberal intergovernmentalism explains the politics to cope with the euro area crisis by the constellation of national preferences and bargaining power and by institutional choices designed to commit euro area countries credibly to the currency union. National preferences resulted from high negative interdependence in the euro area and the fiscal position of its member states: a common preference for the preservation of the euro was accompanied by divergent preferences regarding the distribution of adjustment costs. These mixed motives constituted a 'chicken game' situation characterized by hard intergovernmental bargaining and brinkmanship. Whereas negotiations produced a co-operative solution averting the breakdown of the euro area and strengthening the credibility of member state commitments, asymmetrical interdependence resulted in a burden-sharing and institutional design that reflected German preferences predominantly.

INTRODUCTION

The eurozone crisis has been the deepest in European integration. In many member states, it featured a major economic downturn and fiscal squeeze, a sharp decrease in citizen support for European integration, and mass protest against European Union (EU)-imposed austerity policies. It also put in question the euro area (EA) membership of some countries – and potentially the survival of the common currency, the EU's flagship integration project. At the same time, the crisis produced a major leap in financial and fiscal integration designed to stabilize the euro and the EA. The EU strengthened its regime of fiscal and economic surveillance; it created a permanent bailout mechanism for insolvent countries (the European Stability Mechanism [ESM]) and a banking union (Ioannou *et al.* 2015).

Both deep crises and major progress in European integration have regularly triggered and reshaped debate between theories of integration. From the mid-1960s, the 'empty chair crisis' and the subsequent period of stagnation in supranational integration did much to boost 'intergovernmentalism' as an alternative to the dominant neofunctionalist paradigm (e.g., Hoffmann [1966]). The new dynamism in European integration from the Internal Market Programme to Monetary Union was accompanied by a revival of neofunctionalism (e.g., Stone Sweet and Sandholtz [1997]) and a reformulation of intergovernmentalism (Moravcsik 1993). In turn, the politicization of European integration spurred by this dynamism was reflected in a 'postfunctionalist' approach (Hooghe and Marks 2009) focusing on the mass-level politics of European integration.

Liberal intergovernmentalism (LI) is a major contender in this debate. Developed by Andrew Moravcsik in the 1990s by fitting a liberal theory of state preferences and a neoliberal theory of international interdependence and institutions to earlier – predominantly 'realist' – approaches, LI has quickly established itself as the most elaborate version of intergovernmentalism (Moravcsik 1993, 1998). In a one-sentence summary of his theory, Moravcsik (1998: 4) argues 'that a tripartite explanation of integration – economic interests, relative power, credible commitments – accounts for the form, substance, and timing of major steps toward European integration'. LI conceives of 'European integration ... as a series of rational choices made by national leaders' in response to international interdependence (Moravcsik 1998: 18). Integration results from three steps that translate the incentives created by international interdependence into collective institutional outcomes: the domestic formation of national preferences, intergovernmental bargaining to substantive agreements and the creation of institutions to secure these agreements. In a nutshell, LI argues that national preferences are shaped by the economic interests of powerful domestic groups in a situation of international interdependence; substantive agreements reflect the constellation of national preferences and bargaining power; and the design of international institutions is a function of the kind and size of co-operation problems they are supposed to manage.

LI has arguably acquired the status of a reference or baseline theory: 'an essential first cut against which other theories are often compared' (Moravcsik and Schimmelfennig 2009: 67). On the other hand, LI has been criticized for providing mere 'snapshot' views of individual intergovernmental bargaining episodes and for failing to account for the endogeneity of the integration process, i.e., for how integration decisions at one point in time are shaped and constrained by the effects of earlier integration decisions (e.g., Pierson [1996: 127]; Wallace *et al.* [1999]). I argue in this contribution that LI does, indeed, provide an 'essential first cut' in explaining the 'major steps toward European integration' taken in EA crisis.[1] Because LI is a theory of integration, it offers no specific propositions to account for the crisis as such. The EA's responses to the crisis, however, can be explained plausibly as a result of intergovernmental bargaining based on partly converging and partly diverging member state interests and designed to strengthen the credibility of member state commitments to the common currency. National preferences resulted from strong interdependence in the EA and the fiscal position of its member states: a common preference for the preservation of the euro was accompanied by divergent preferences regarding the distribution of adjustment costs. These mixed motives constituted a 'chicken game' situation characterized by dynamics of hard bargaining and brinkmanship. Whereas negotiations produced a co-operative solution averting the breakdown of the EA and strengthening the credibility of member state commitments, asymmetrical interdependence resulted in a burden-sharing and institutional design that reflected the preferences of Germany and its allies predominantly. In a broader historical perspective, however, crisis bargaining was very much constrained by the unintended spillovers and path-dependencies of the original decision for and design of monetary union. These spillovers resulted both in the endogenous interdependence of the EA and in the converging preferences for the preservation of the EA, which shaped the bargaining dynamics and outcomes.

The main sections of this contribution follow LI's tripartite analysis of preferences, bargaining and institution-building. In each section, I develop case-specific expectations on the eurozone crisis and put them to a series of simple congruence tests with the empirical record. I do not provide a chronological narrative of negotiations and integration in the EA crisis but need to limit myself to a few crucial episodes at the height of the crisis between 2010 and 2012. In addition to the scholarly literature, I rely mainly on newspaper reports and official documents on the integration outcomes. Moreover, I cannot systematically test alternative explanations to check whether LI offers the only or best explanation of integration in the crisis. I hope to show, however, that the LI expectations fit the broad pattern of preferences, negotiating behaviour, and outcomes reasonably well. The concluding section summarizes the results and discusses the merits and limitations of LI.

NATIONAL PREFERENCES IN THE EA CRISIS

According to LI, the preferences of governments on European integration are national and issue-specific. They result from a domestic process of preference formation and are oriented towards increasing (and possibly maximizing) national welfare in the issue-area at hand. This assumption distinguishes LI from other integration theories. In contrast with both supranationalist and constructivist assumptions, preferences are conceived as exogenous to integration. They are neither the result of institutionally induced international learning or socialization processes nor primarily shaped by domestic ideas. Finally, states do not pursue strategic geopolitical interests as assumed by realist intergovernmentalism.

Most fundamentally, preferences for integration result from critical positive or negative interdependence. Actors seek policy integration if they are convinced to reap higher net benefits than from unilateral, autonomous or only loosely co-ordinated national policies. LI thus expects steps of integration taken in the EA crisis to be driven by common perceptions of interdependence and the desire to avoid losses and reap benefits. Among the various forms of integration and substantive rules that produce such net benefits, actors strive to realize those that maximize their gains.

The nature of the preferences and the relevant domestic actors and interests vary by issue area. Domestic economic interests most clearly shape state preferences on issues of commercial or economic policy, the 'more intense, certain, and institutionally represented and organized' they are (Moravcsik 1998: 36) and the less 'uncertainty there is about cause-effect relations' between EU rules and individual welfare. Conversely, 'the weaker and more diffuse the domestic constituency behind a policy' (Wallace et al. 1999: 171) and the more uncertain and modest 'the substantive implications of a choice', the less predictable are national interests and the more likely ideological prefer-ences will prevail (Moravcsik and Nicolaïdis [1999: 61]; see also Moravcsik [1998: 486–9]). In Moravcsik's original formulation, macroeconomic policies such as monetary policy and fiscal policy are generally less likely to have strong or clear substantive implications for specific interest groups than market-making or market-regulating rules. Therefore, he expects integration preferences in this area to reflect 'the macro-economic preferences of ruling governmental coalitions' (Moravcsik 1998: 3). Because the EA crisis started out as a financial and banking sector crisis before it turned into a sovereign debt crisis, and because the reforms included supranational regulations of the financial market, however, business interests need to be taken into account as well. In the sovereign–bank nexus that developed during the crisis, financial market and state interests became strongly intertwined. Finally, the short-term welfare implications of many crisis policy alternatives, especially the austerity policies, were clear and strong. For this reason, LI would assume material inter-ests to prevail over ideological preferences.

Monetary union brought together countries pursuing different growth strat-egies: a supply-side or export-led growth strategy based on wage restraint, pro-ductivity and competitiveness in Germany and the 'north' of the EA, and a demand-led growth strategy based on fiscal expansion and wage inflation in the 'south' (Hall 2012: 358–9).[2] Monetary union increased the divergence of these strategies, forcing Germany into even stronger supply-side reform in the early 2000s and allowing the southern countries to borrow at low cost (Scharpf 2011: 13–16). As a result, the financial market shifted large balance-of-payment surpluses generated in the north to the south, fuelling real-estate bubbles (mainly in Ireland and Spain) and public sector debt (above all in Greece, Italy and Portugal) and leaving southern countries highly vulnerable to the financial market turbulence and credit squeeze that followed the US subprime mortgage crisis of 2008 (Hall 2012: 360; Scharpf 2011: 17–22). Because Economic and Monetary Union (EMU) left the responsibility for rescuing national banks and banking systems with the member states, a dynamic sovereign–bank nexus developed: governments undertook financial sector bailouts that increased sovereign credit risk, which in turn increased the vulnerability of banks invested in sovereign bonds (Acharya et al. 2011). In Ireland and Spain, the bursting of the real-estate bubble forced states with balanced budgets to go into debt and risk their creditworthiness; in Greece, a government facing sovereign default was about to drag down its national financial system; and both banking and sover-eign debt crises in the south left French, German and other northern banks heavily exposed, threatening northern governments with the prospect of having to bail them out.

This negative financial and fiscal interdependence provides the background for the development of state preferences at the outset of the EA crisis. LI expects that such interdependence creates a strong incentive for more integration under the condition that EA governments perceive that integration would produce lower losses than stagnation or even disintegration. According to the mainstream scenarios, this was the case.[3] For the highly indebted countries, abandoning the euro would have meant sovereign default, a likely breakdown of the monetary and financial system, hyperinflation and being cut off from external capital. Moreover, contagion effects were widely expected. Whereas the other euro countries may probably have been able to cope with a default and exit of Greece alone, there was reason to fear that financial markets would lose trust in the euro more generally, withdraw from further debt countries and force the EA to back countries (such as Spain and Italy) that were too big to rescue. For Germany and the north, a breakdown of the euro would have resulted in a steep appreciation of its currency, a concurrent slump in exports, and deep and long-lasting recession.

Any common interest in avoiding the costs of non-integration, however, would be accompanied by distributional conflict about the terms of integration. Simply put, the costs of adjustment in the crisis could either be mutualized, e.g., in the form of Eurobonds or fiscal equalization schemes, in which case the solvent member states of the north would pay for the heavily indebted member states and their banking systems; or adjustment could be nationalized in the form of fiscal austerity, wage and price depression, thus putting the burden of adjustment on the debt-ridden southern countries, forcing them to create the means to service their credits, and sparing the northern countries from bailing out their banks. These considerations lead to two propositions on national preferences in the EA crisis:

(1) States prefer (more) integration to disintegration or the *status quo* in order to avoid welfare losses in a situation of negative international interdependence.
(2) National preferences on the terms of integration depend on the fiscal position of the state:
    (a) solvent northern countries prefer national adjustment;
    (b) heavily indebted southern countries prefer mutualized adjustment.

LI thus expects mixed state motives in the EA crisis: a common interest in the survival of the euro (area) based on perceptions of interdependence and potential net losses *and* conflicting preferences on the distribution of the burdens of adjustment depending on their fiscal position.

From the beginning of the acute crisis, governments have, indeed, been united in their commitment to the survival and defence of the euro (area), and this position was underpinned by a strong sense of negative interdependence and prohibitive costs. No government of a highly indebted country intended to give up the euro. Greek Prime Minister Papandreou asserted there was 'no chance' this was going to happen.[4] The same is true for the solvent countries. Early on in the crisis, the German government vowed to 'act decisively' if the 'stability of the euro' was in danger.[5] Accordingly, German Chancellor Merkel and Finance Minister Schäuble publicly defended the rescue of Greece as necessary to ensure the 'stability of the euro' and the 'entire euro area'.[6] Schäuble considered the damage of a default of a euro country to be incalculable and more costly than the rescue.[7] In fact, he likened a potential default of Greece to the bankruptcy of Lehman Brothers that accelerated the global financial crisis in 2008.[8] In this vein, Merkel and Schäuble repeatedly declared the rescue to be '*alternativlos*' (without any alternative). Merkel, furthermore, strictly refused to push for the exit of Greece from the EA.[9] Similarly, French President Sarkozy stated: 'If we created the euro, we cannot let a country fall that is in the euro zone.'[10] He declared France to be 'fully determined to support the euro and to support Greece'.[11] Later in the crisis, EU heads of state and government have continued to stress their public commitment. Merkel vowed to do everything to defend the euro;[12] French President Hollande and Italian Prime Minister Monti expressed 'their will to do everything ... to defend, preserve, and consolidate the euro zone'.[13]

According to a *Financial Times* background series on the crisis, there was indeed no questioning of defending and consolidating the euro, but support for Greek membership did not remain rock solid behind the scenes (Spiegel 2014). Reportedly, at the height of the crisis, Schäuble headed the 'infected leg camp' of policy-makers and advisers arguing that the exit of Greece from the EA was necessary to save and strengthen the euro. By contrast, the 'domino camp' feared that 'Grexit' would result in market panic and contagion including Spain and Italy and lead to the unravelling of the EA. In a situation rife with uncertainty, Merkel ultimately decided against taking the risk of Grexit. This debate shows that the preferences of Germany, a core actor, on Grexit, a core policy question during the crisis, were not unitary, fixed or internalized but resulted from calculations of negative interdependence and risk in a situation of high uncertainty.

Whereas the EA countries (ultimately) agreed on the supreme goal of preserving the euro and the EA, they held strongly conflicting reviews on the means to achieve this goal. Germany, together with Austria, Finland and the Netherlands, sought to minimize their liabilities and financial assistance. What unites these countries is their high solvency and credit rating, which made them independent of external assistance. In early 2010, Germany was the most reluctant EA country to commit itself to the Greek bailout. The governments of Austria, Finland and the Netherlands sympathized with the German position, however.[14] The German government favoured bringing in assistance from the International Monetary Fund (IMF),[15] rejected Eurobonds and capital-raising by the European Commission, called for a strengthening of the Stability and Growth Pact (SGP), including automatic sanctions, the withdrawal of voting rights, an orderly sovereign default procedure and a procedure to exclude countries in breach of the rules.[16] Later in the crisis, Germany opposed the expansion of the European Financial Stability Facility (EFSF), the direct recapitalization of banks through the rescue funds, and a supranational resolution fund for European banks.

By contrast, France urged the EU early on to take active measures against the Greek credit crunch and to rein in financial markets. Together with Belgium, Greece, Italy, Portugal and Spain, it pushed for the 'Europeanization' of sovereign debt and for soft adjustment policies but opposed harsh sanctions for high deficit countries. These countries were in a worse economic and fiscal position than the first group: less wealthy, more highly indebted, and under pressure from the financial market. It was therefore in their self-interest to get access to additional liquidity with minor strings attached. For this reason, the southern EA countries led by France demanded, among others, the establishment and expansion of rescue funds, unlimited bond purchases by the European Central Bank (ECB), a bank licence for the EFSF and ESM, the direct European recapitalization of banks, a European bank resolution fund and the introduction of Eurobonds – but opposed rigid austerity conditions and automatic sanctions (Schild 2013).

In general, LI offers a plausible explanation of state preferences in the EA crisis. All EA countries were in favour of deepening economic integration to manage the high actual and potential negative interdependence created by the debt crisis. They differed starkly regarding the preferred terms of integration, however, and this difference was in line with their fiscal positions. France, however, fits the pattern only partly.[17] At the outset of the crisis, France was certainly the most fiscally and economically stable country of the 'southern coalition'. It enjoyed triple-A credit ratings and bond yields that were only marginally higher than Germany. Yet, French bonds already suffered from relative weak fiscal fundamentals and contagion effects of the Greek crisis in the spring of 2010 (De Santis 2012); French preferences might therefore have resulted from incipient and anticipated vulnerability. The stark difference to German preferences, however, is difficult to explain by material conditions only, but points to the relevance of ordoliberal vs Keynesian economic ideas (Hall 2012: 367; Olender 2012; Schild 2013).

The intergovernmental preference constellation developed early in the crisis and has remained stable across changes in government and issues. In France, the shift from Sarkozy to Hollande was characterized by a general continuity of crisis policy – in spite of Hollande's support for Eurobonds and criticism of the Fiscal Compact (Schild 2013). Moreover, all issues, from the first bailouts via the establishment of the rescue funds and the reforms of budget monitoring policies to the development of banking union, were structured by the same coalitions and the same basic conflict between fiscally healthy countries advocating limited financial commitment together with strict fiscal and financial supervision on the one hand, and fiscally pressurized countries advocating strong European financial commitment in combination with looser fiscal and financial regulation, on the other.

INTERGOVERNMENTAL BARGAINING IN THE EA CRISIS

Starting from their preference constellation, governments enter into negotiations on integration. New treaties or treaty revisions require unanimous agreement and domestic ratification by each participating state. For this reason, integration needs to be Pareto-efficient, i.e., each state must expect to increase its welfare as a result. At least, states must not incur net costs from integration lest they veto the agreement. Potential Pareto-efficient outcomes vary with regard to the distribution of costs and benefits across the participating states. In negotiations on integration, states therefore bargain to attain the agreement that maximizes their gains. Negotiations consist in hard bargaining, including 'credible threats to veto proposals, to withhold financial side-payments, and to form alternative alliances excluding recalcitrant governments' (Moravcsik 1998: 3). The outcomes of negotiations reflect the intergovernmental constellation of bargaining power. Bargaining power results from asymmetrical interdependence: states that are less vulnerable to interdependence gain less from integration. In turn, they can successfully bargain for side payments or terms of integration that work in their favour.

As in the case of preferences, the hypothesis of hard intergovernmental bargaining is most likely to hold if stakes are high and the distribution of costs and benefits is clear. The hypothesis of hard intergovernmental bargaining distinguishes LI from other integration theories in two ways. First, in contrast to supranationalism, LI does not attribute a relevant role to supranational organizations and supranational entrepreneurship in facilitating integration or in shaping the substantive outcomes of negotiations. Second, in contrast to constructivism, LI does not attribute a relevant role to normative constraints on bargaining or to argumentative behaviour and persuasion (Moravcsik 1998: 54–8).

In the EA crisis, the mixed-motive preference constellation of the member states corresponds to a 'chicken game' situation.[18] Chicken game situations have several characteristic features. First, the actors have a strong joint preference for avoiding an extremely costly common bad – such as the breakdown of the euro – but also seek to avoid the costs of backing down and making the first move to avert catastrophe. In other words, although non-co-operation is everybody's least preferred outcome, the players receive the highest payoff from not co-operating while the other player does. Whereas all governments perceived a breakdown of the euro to be the worst case, the solvent countries would have benefited most from shifting the burden of adaptation to the highly indebted countries, and the indebted countries would have benefited most from being bailed out without having to impose austerity on their economies.

Second, chicken games tend to produce 'brinkmanship' in bargaining behaviour. The players send each other signals of resolve as they move closer to the brink and make co-operative moves at the latest opportunity to avert disaster. Assuming that the other player is rational and will do everything to avoid the crash in the end, hard bargaining pays off. Because both players count on the other's rational co-operation, it is useful to send signals of irrationality or incapacity. If actors demonstrate credibly that their hands are tied or that they have lost control over events, they can force the other side to back down. In the EA crisis, solvent countries had an incentive to refer to legal, political and financial constraints and push the highly indebted countries to make fiscal cuts and sell state assets up to the point at which sovereign default was imminent. The indebted countries, in turn, had an incentive to postpone painful adjustment measures and demonstrate their incapacity to counter financial market pressure until the solvent countries came to the conclusion that rescue was inevitable.

If a chicken game is symmetrical, i.e., the costs of disaster and backing down are the same for both players, it is hard to predict who will back down – unless one player is better at demonstrating irrationality or incapacity. In the EA crisis, however, interdependence was asymmetrical. Whereas the stakes were prohibitively high for all EA countries, the *immediate* consequences of the crisis were significantly more severe for the highly indebted countries than for the solvent countries. The highly indebted countries were faced with increasingly unsustainable bond rates and, in the case of Greece, imminent bankruptcy. In addition, as the largest economy of the EA and the country enjoying the strongest confidence of the markets, Germany was pivotal for the survival of the euro and any rescue scheme. Because they were less immediately and heavily threatened by the crisis and held the key to remedying the situation, the solvent countries, and Germany in particular, were in principle in a better position to realize their preferences on the terms of integration than the southern countries.

However, Germany could not fully exploit its relatively secure and pivotal situation. First, it had to cope with the fact that the highly indebted countries were objectively unable to 'swerve' without damaging the EA. Unilateral adaptation measures by Greece and other debtor countries alone were unlikely to avoid default, contagion and potential exit from the euro. Some form of rescue therefore seemed inevitable to avoid disaster. Second, exactly because Germany's contribution to the rescue was indispensable, and because it did not have a credible option to abandon the euro, the German government was forced to commit itself financially at some point. The observable implications of LI for the EA crisis negotiations are:

(1) Intergovernmental negotiations are characterized by hard bargaining and brinkmanship.
(2) Solvent countries (and Germany in particular) ultimately come to the rescue of the highly indebted countries, but shape the terms of the rescue in return.

There is ample evidence for hard, brinkmanship bargaining behaviour on the part of the participants. The characteristic pattern for the highly indebted countries was to evoke imminent disaster and stress their incapacity in order to force reluctant creditor countries to come to their rescue. They further sought to delay or block the stringent conditions attached to the rescue measures in order to limit or deflect adverse domestic political reactions. The characteristic pattern for Germany was to reject or delay financial commitments at first and point towards the domestic political impediments (the Bundesbank and public opinion) for making such commitments – before finally agreeing to do (just) what was necessary to keep the indebted countries afloat under the impression of imminent breakdown. Peter Spiegel's summary assessment of interviews with numerous participants of EA decision-making at the height of the crisis from late 2011 through 2012 is reminiscent of the chicken game metaphor: 'From mid-level bureaucrats to prime ministers, they tell an unsettling tale of accidents, near misses and seemingly foolhardy brinkmanship. But in the end, these same leaders appear to have prevailed. The euro has been saved' (Spiegel 2014).

In the run-up to the Greek bailout in mid-March 2010, the German government tried to deny any need for concrete commitments to aid Greece, insisted on unilateral austerity measures and threatened to exclude deficit countries as the *ultima ratio*. Only one week later, Germany redefined the 'last resort' in a co-operative way: as granting credit to countries that did not have access to capital on the market.[19] When this situation occurred and Greece asked for assistance in April 2010, Germany tried to delay again. When financial markets were targeting further countries (whose credit rating was downgraded), the EA countries finally granted Greece a 110 billion euro bailout and established the EFSF. According to unconfirmed Spanish leaks from the negotiations, Sarkozy threatened to walk away from the talks and abandon the euro if Merkel did not agree.[20] In turn, Merkel allegedly hinted at the possibility to quit the euro when her demand to strip non-compliant EA countries of their voting rights was criticized as undemocratic at a summit dinner in October 2010. The next day, however, her spokesman dismissed such a threat as 'not plausible'.[21] Whereas such exit threats were indeed not ultimately credible, they are indicative of the hard bargaining style.

In their part of brinkmanship, highly indebted governments delayed seeking money from the EFSF or the ESM in order to avoid the strict conditionality and the loss of reputation attached. Irish Prime Minister Cowen denied the Irish government's intent to seek financial help in November 2010 under pressure from its partners to accept a loan from the EFSF.[22] Spain similarly hesitated for weeks, during which financial pressure on the country increased, before it accepted a bailout and then sought to limit international control to the banking sector.[23] Negotiations between Cyprus and the EU dragged on for months; a first agreement was rejected in the Cypriot parliament, and it took a threat by the ECB to cut off liquidity for the Cypriot government to accept a second agreement – not without threats by Prime Minister Anastasiades to resign and even to abandon the euro.[24]

The most dramatic case occurred in October 2011 when Greek Prime Minister Papandreou announced a national referendum on the bailout plan and the euro in order to close ranks within his own party, force opposition leader Samaras to back the plan, and thereby strengthen his government domestically (Spiegel 2014). This announcement made Greek and Italian bond yields soar and sent the EA closer to the brink. At the Cannes G20 meeting shortly after-wards, Sarkozy and Merkel forced Papandreou to choose between the referendum, on the one hand, and staying in the euro and receiving further financial support, on the other.[25] In the end, Papandreou's government was replaced by a national unity government, which called off the referendum and supported the bailout package. Otherwise, however, the G20 meeting failed to bring a solution to the mounting crisis. Italy resisted being put in an IMF programme; in turn, Merkel, pointing to the opposition of the Bundesbank, refused to replete the EFSF with freshly created IMF special drawing rights (Spiegel 2014).

In the final crisis episode during the spring and summer of 2012, Merkel came around to tacitly accepting a new role for the ECB as a lender of last resort, which she had vehemently opposed before. At the G20 summit in June 2012, she still refused the plan of Italian Prime Minister Monti envisaging ECB bond-buying for rule-abiding EA countries under attack from financial markets (Spiegel 2014). At the European Council meeting in the same month, when Monti and Spanish Prime Minister Rajoy warned that they could not sustain funding their states for very long at current interest rates, this was still dismissed as 'exaggerated panic-mongering' by a German official.[26] As Italian and Spanish bond yields continued to rise and the Bankia crisis in Spain continued to unfold, a long-term 'shift of thinking in Berlin' appears to have come to a close: 'Germany's original vision of the eurozone – no bail-outs, no shared debts and, in some quarters, no Greece – was becoming unachievable'. In return for her support to the ECB's Outright Monetary Transactions (OMT) bailout programme, however, 'Berlin was going to ensure that shared burdens came with centralised control' (Spiegel 2014).

At each step of crisis decision-making, Germany was able to shape the terms of integration in return for giving up its opposition to bailing out insolvent EA members. Germany prevented the introduction of Eurobonds or any other formally mutualized sovereign debt. Debt would remain national, and financial assistance would come in the form of credits and with the involvement of the IMF. For the same reason, Germany successfully rejected bank licenses for the EFSF and the ESM. In addition, Germany was able to link financial assistance to strict austerity conditionality, the strengthening of the EU's monitoring and sanctioning of national budgets, and the adoption of the Fiscal Compact, including a balanced budget rule to be enshrined 'preferably' in domestic constitutional law. Only some of the harsher measures proposed by Germany – fully automatic sanctions and the suspension of voting rights for countries in excessive deficit – did not find support. According to an unnamed observer, however, the suspension of voting rights was generally understood as 'essentially just a bargaining chip on Germany's part to get what they really want'.[27]

In sum, the evidence from the negotiations is broadly in line with LI expectations. First, the major crisis management and reform deals have been reached in intergovernmental negotiations. This is especially true for the bailout packages, the rescue funds EFSF and ESM and the Fiscal Compact, all based on intergovernmental agreements. The guidelines for the reforms of the procedures to monitor EU budgets and banking union were also hammered out in intergovernmental negotiations before they entered the legislative process. Whereas the Commission launched numerous initiatives and proposals in favour of supranational reform solutions, they were only successful if and when they chimed with the preferences of Germany and its allies: for instance, the proposal for Eurobonds did not fly; the proposal for banking union was adopted in 2012 with modifications reflecting German concerns (see below). Finally, the ECB has, of course, made a major contribution to mitigating the crisis and buying governments time to find agreement – but it does not seem to have had a noteworthy agenda-setting role in institutional reform.

Second, there is strong evidence of hard bargaining and brinkmanship. Hard bargaining included threats to abandon the euro, exclude countries from the euro or suspend their rights, and let countries go bankrupt. Brinkmanship is evident in persistent German efforts to avoid or delay coming to the rescue of the debtor countries and persistent efforts by the debtor countries to escape rescue conditionality. Finally, EA reform generally bears the hallmark of Germany, the country with superior bargaining power. In return for Germany's (reluctant) agreement to the rescue of the highly indebted countries, the rest of the EA largely accepted the terms that Germany preferred.

INSTITUTIONAL CHOICE AND CREDIBLE COMMITMENT

Governments not only negotiate on the substantive terms of integration but also on its institutional design. In line with functional, neoliberal theory, states establish international institutions to monitor and sanction state compliance and to lock in the substantive negotiation outcomes. To what extent governments are in favour of ceding competences to supranational organizations depends on the value they place on the issues and substantive outcomes in question and on their uncertainty about the future behaviour of other governments (Moravcsik 1998: 9, 486–7). For instance, states are more willing to centralize decision-making and delegate powers of monitoring and sanctioning to supranational organizations in the case of enforcement problems, which produce incentives to defect unilaterally, than in the case of co-ordination problems, which do not. Because the institutional preferences of states are likely to differ as much as their preferences on the substantive terms of integration, intergovernmental bargaining affects institutional choice as well: institutional design tends to follow the institutional preferences of the states with superior bargaining power.

By focusing on the functional exigencies of credible commitment, LI assumptions about institutional choice differ again from those of other theories. In contrast to constructivism, institutional choice is not thought to be shaped by federalist ideology, democratic norms or other standards of legitimacy. In contrast to supranationalism, LI disputes a general tendency towards technocratic governance based on 'need for centralized expertise and information' (Moravcsik 1998: 71). Finally, LI does not share the realist assumption that states are primarily motivated by maximizing autonomy (Grieco 1996).

The EA crisis revealed several enforcement problems in EMU. First, the SGP, established to commit countries to fiscal discipline, had already proven malleable and, ultimately, toothless ahead of the financial crisis. Second, the EA crisis demonstrated that even countries without excessive budget deficits (such as Ireland or Spain) could be hit by exogenous shocks, sudden stops and balance of payment difficulties. In this case, the enforcement problem was how to commit other member states to coming to their rescue. Finally, EMU was accompanied by financial market integration based on mutual recognition of national banking regulation. The EA crisis highlighted the inadequacies of national banking supervision and resolution: lax supervision owing to cosy relations between bankers and politicians and the sovereign–bank nexus, regulatory arbitrage across member states, and burden- as well as blame-shifting among national regulators when transnationally operating banks ran into trouble.

Thus, institutional choice during the EA crisis was mainly confronted by enforcement problems calling for more supranational delegation and stricter surveillance. However, because the asymmetry of interdependence in the EA crisis accords the solvent countries superior bargaining powersupranational delegation and enforcement are mainly to be expected in the area of fiscal discipline, which commits the indebted countries, whereas financial assistance and transfers that would commit the solvent countries should remain under intergovernmental control. LI thus predicts the following pattern of institutional choice in the euro crisis.

(1) New and reformed institutions increase the credibility of the member states' commitment to eurozone stability.
(2) Institutions of financial assistance are more intergovernmental than institutions of supervision.

Institution-building and institutional reforms during the EA crisis were, indeed, to a large extent motivated by strengthening – or avoiding – credible commitments. Institutional preferences were strongly linked to material preferences. Germany and the solvent countries sought to limit their own financial commitment but to strengthen the credibility of the highly indebted countries' commitment to fiscal discipline. That explains Germany's preferences for intergovernmental rescue funds based on fixed limits of lending capacity. Whereas supranational funds or Eurobonds would certainly have strengthened the credibility of the EA's commitment to rescuing insolvent countries, they would also have meant higher costs and less control for the solvent countries. On the other hand, Germany's proposals for harsh and automatic sanctions of countries violating the excessive deficit rules and for embedding balanced budget rules in constitutional law were intended to invest the earlier rules of the Excessive Deficit Procedure and the SGP with the credibility they had lacked or lost in the first decade of the euro. In these cases, Germany was also willing to invest non-majoritarian supranational institutions, the European Commission and European Court of Justice, with new monitoring and enforcement competencies. In the case of banking union, the mix of commitment-enhancing and commitment-avoiding preferences and proposals is apparent, too. Whereas the German government strongly favoured supranational banking supervision (even though it tried to exclude many German banks), it opposed a supranational resolution and recovery mechanism underpinned by a Europe-wide fund, fearing massive transfers to countries with ramshackle banks.

Conversely, the highly indebted countries sought to limit their commitment to fiscal discipline and to strengthen the credibility of the solvent countries' commitment to put their financial clout behind the eurozone. Accordingly, they favoured supranational bailout solutions that could not be undermined by the veto of Germany and other solvent countries and did not require a new intergovernmental agreement every time a crisis flared up in one of the member states. At the same time, they opposed the automaticity and harshness of the sanctions proposed by Germany for countries not complying with the EU's budget deficit rules, and favoured more flexibility. Their institutional preferences on banking union also reversed those of Germany: their priority was a supranational resolution and recovery mechanism and fund, not supranational banking supervision.

In spite of these divergent institutional preferences, there was a common interest in creating institutions that would enhance the member states' credible commitment to the common currency. This corresponds to their common interest in stabilizing the EA. The three major blocks of institutional reform are clearly linked to the three major problems that together made the EA crisis possible: the financial crisis; the sovereign debt crisis; and the lack of instruments to counter loss of financial market confidence and sudden stops. The Fiscal Compact and the legislation on the surveillance of member states' fiscal and economic policies are designed to overcome the enforcement problems of the SGP; the legislation on banking union is designed to tackle the sovereign–bank nexus and the enforcement problems of national regulation in an integrated financial market; and the ESM is designed to overcome the problem of committing solvent countries to the rescue of insolvent ones.

Whereas these institutions reflect a common interest of the EA governments in strengthening the credibility of their commitment to the euro, their design generally matches the preferences of Germany, the country with the strongest bargaining power: intergovernmental financial assistance, supranational fiscal and economic surveillance, and a banking union that combines supranational supervision with more intergovernmental resolution. First, the ESM is an intergovernmental organization whose Board of Governors generally decides by unanimity. Even under the emergency voting procedure, which is used when the Commission and the ECB conclude that a failure to grant financial assistance would threaten the stability of the EA, a majority of 85 per cent of the voting shares is required: this means, in effect, that the big member states retain a veto. Second, the surveillance of fiscal and economic policies now includes an earlier and stronger involvement of the Commission in the budget planning process of member states, stronger balanced budget rules, and earlier and more credible sanctions. Most notably, enforcement is based on 'reverse qualified majority voting', i.e., a qualified majority of member states is required to reject (rather than to adopt) a Commission proposal. Finally, whereas the ECB is vested with the power to supervise system-relevant banks directly and may also look into smaller banks, the resolution mechanism retains more national and intergovernmental elements. Decisions on bank resolution will be taken by an independent board of national authorities; finance ministers can overturn resolution decisions; and the build-up and mutualization of the fund is phased in over an eight-year period.

Institutional choice thus broadly fits LI expectations again. Institutional reform generally conveys a concern for a more credible commitment to the stability of the EA. In addition, however, the design of the common institutions has largely followed the preferences of the solvent countries and Germany in particular. That supranational institutions have seen their competences strengthened during the crisis is not an argument against LI – if it can be shown that competence growth was a response to important enforcement problems and followed the preferences of the most powerful governments.

CONCLUSIONS: PUTTING LIBERAL INTERGOVERNMENTALISM IN PERSPECTIVE

The main process characteristics and outcomes of European integration decision-making in the EA crisis match LI assumptions and expectations well. National preferences reflected international interdependence as well as the fiscal position of the state (with France being a partial outlier). Governments agreed on more integration in order to manage a common condition of negative interdependence and in order to avoid the prohibitive costs perceived to result from a breakdown of the euro (area). In doing so, however, they sought to shift the costs of adaptation and reform as much as possible to other states. This preference constellation resulted in a chicken game situation characterized by a strong joint preference to avert a breakdown of the euro (area) – while flirting with disaster at the same time. Negotiations included hard bargaining and brinkmanship. The new institutions and policies are designed to stabilize the EA by vesting policies of financial assistance, fiscal surveillance and banking regulation with a more credible commitment of member states to stick to and enforce the rules. Both the terms of stabilization in the EA and the design of integrated institutions largely follow the preferences of Germany, the country with superior bargaining power. By explaining the basic features and outcomes of European negotiations in a decisive phase of EU development, LI buttresses its claim to explain the major steps toward European integration.

Yet, critics of LI have rightly pointed out that LI is best at accounting for isolated, individual intergovernmental negotiation processes and treaty outcomes, but fails to account for the endogeneity of the integration process, i.e., how current integration decisions are shaped by the effects of earlier integration decisions. In the words of Paul Pierson (1996: 127), 'Attempts to cut into ongoing social processes at a single point in time produce a "snapshot" view that is distorted in crucial respects.' According to his historical-institutionalist analysis, any integration decision produces unanticipated consequences, adaptations of preferences and endogenous interdependencies, which shape and constrain the next integration decision and create a path-dependent process over time. Most importantly, the common interest of EA countries in preserving and stabilizing the euro and their preparedness to engage in institutional reforms strengthening the credibility of their commitment to the euro is best explained as endogenous to the previous decision to create a common currency (Verdun 2015). Faced with unanticipated negative consequences of integration and realizing that the earlier decision to join EMU had increased international interdependence and put them in a situation without credible exit options, the member states reluctantly agreed on new rules and institutions that they had rejected in the original negotiations on EMU and would not have agreed to had the financial crisis occurred in a pre-EMU institutional setting (see also Niemann and Ioannou [2015]). This counterfactual argument is supported by the factual observation that EU member states outside the EA have in general not committed themselves to the rescue or banking resolution funds, the stricter sanctioning of excessive deficits or supranational banking supervision. The decision for more integration in the EA crisis is thus dependent on the path that states embarked on 20 years before. Moreover, the intergovernmental bargaining highlighted by LI is likely to recede together with the acuteness of the crisis and as institutional reform moves back from intergovernmental settings to the ordinary legislative procedure, Commission initiative and parliamentary co-decision. This could already be seen in the concessions Germany had to make during the legislative process on banking union.

The EA crisis suggests that LI is best embedded as a theory of intergovernmental negotiations and decisions in a supranationalist theory of long-term, path-dependent development of integration. Whereas supranationalism explains how earlier integration decisions create endogenous interdependence and preference updates, LI captures how governments negotiate and decide on the basis of the changed constellation of interdependence and preferences. It also shows that divergent national preferences, hard intergovernmental bargaining, asymmetrical interdependence, and differential bargaining power remain consequential, even in a path-dependent integration process.

Biographical note: Frank Schimmelfennig is professor of European politics at ETH Zurich, Center for Comparative and International Studies.

ACKNOWLEDGEMENTS

For comments on earlier versions of this contribution, I thank members of the European Politics research group at ETH Zurich, the editors of the special issue and two anonymous reviewers.

NOTES

1 Moravcsik has not provided a published LI interpretation or explanation of the crisis and its outcomes so far. Moravcsik (2012) is a current affairs commentary mainly analysing the roots of the crisis and discussing the adequacy of the reform steps taken to solve it.

2 I use north and south as convenient shortcuts even though Ireland is not geographically in the south.

3 Compare the scenarios in Straubhaar (2011: 30–1) and *The Economist*, 26 May 2012, 26–7.

4 http://www.theguardian.com/business/2010/feb/15/will-greece-leave-euro, 15 February 2010.

5 http://www.faz.net/aktuell/wirtschaft/eurokrise/im-gespraech-wolfgang-schaeuble-erst-die-strafe-dann-der-fonds-1954060-p2.html, 24 March 2010.

6 http://www.tagesschau.de/inland/griechenland678.html, 3 May 2010; http://www.stern.de/politik/ausland/schaeuble-verteidigt-griechenland-hilfe-es-geht-um-die-sta bilitaet-des-euro-raums-1562349.html, 29 April 2010.

7 http://www.wolfgang-schaeuble.de/index.php?id=37&textid=1380&page=1, 27 March 2010.

8 http://www.faz.net/aktuell/wirtschaft/eurokrise/im-gespraech-wolfgang-schaeuble-erst-die-strafe-dann-der-fonds-1954060-p2.html, 24 March 2010.

9 http://www.stern.de/politik/deutschland/griechenland-krise-schaeuble-will-tempo-merkel-bremst-1561613.html, 26 April 2010.

10 http://www.ft.com/intl/cms/s/0/db2dd602-2914-11df-972b-00144feabdc0.html#a xzz2r26Tgv00, 6 March 2010.

11 http://www.20minutes.fr/economie/401218-comment-france-peut-preter-milliards-a-grece, 29 April 2010.

12 http://www.angela-merkel.de/page/103_686.htm.

13 http://www.lemonde.fr/economie/article/2012/07/31/hollande-et-monti-determin es-a-tout-faire-pour-consolider-la-zone-euro_1740722_3234.html, 31 July 2012.

14 http://www.zeit.de/politik/ausland/2010-03/eu-gipfel-hilfe-griechenland, 22 March 2010.

15 http://www.faz.net/aktuell/wirtschaft/eurokrise/schuldenkrise-deutschland-hilft-den-griechen-wenn-der-iwf-hilft-1950816.html, 25 March 2010.

16 http://www.faz.net/aktuell/wirtschaft/eurokrise/bundesregierung-taeglich-eine-neue-haltung-zu-griechenland-1956003.html, 21 March 2010; http://www.faz.net/ aktuell/wirtschaft/eurokrise/im-gespraech-wolfgang-schaeuble-erst-die-strafe-dann-der-fonds-1954060-p2.html, 24 March 2010.

17 I thank one of the reviewers for alerting me to this point.

18 LI does not follow any formal game-theoretic assumptions, but its rationalist underpinnings are compatible with such an analysis. I do not present a formal game-theoretic analysis of the crisis, but use the basic intuition of the chicken game heuristically to point to the dynamics of the bargaining situation.

19 See http://www.euractiv.de/finanzen-und-wachstum/artikel/merkels-ultima-ratio-rauswurf-aus-euro-zone-002866, 18 March 2010; http://www.euractiv.de/euro pa-2020-und-reformen/artikel/merkels-neues-ultima-ratio-milliarden-fr-griechenland-002895, 25 March 2010.

20 http://www.theguardian.com/world/2010/may/14/nicolas-sarkozy-threat-greece-row-angela-merkel; http://www.theguardian.com/business/2010/may/14/nicolas-sarkozy-angela-merkel-euro-crisis-summit, 14 May 2010.
21 http://www.theguardian.com/world/2010/dec/03/angela-merkel-germany-abandon-euro, 3 December 2010.
22 http://www.telegraph.co.uk/finance/financialcrisis/8139167/Eurozone-debt-crisis-EU-officials-sent-to-Ireland.html, 17 November 2010.
23 http://www.nytimes.com/2012/06/10/business/global/spain-moves-closer-to-bailout-of-banks.html?pagewanted=all, 9 June 2012.
24 http://www.economist.com/blogs/charlemagne/2013/03/cyprus-bail-out, 25 March 2013.
25 Spiegel 2014; http://www.reuters.com/article/2011/11/03/us-g-idUSTRE7A20E9 20111103.
26 http://www.theguardian.com/business/2012/jun/28/eurozone-crisis-live-summit-brussels, 28 June 2012.
27 'EU leaders give green light to tweak treaty', http://euobserver.com/institutional/31154, 28 October 2010.

REFERENCES

Acharya, V., Schnabl, P. and Drechsler, I. (2011) 'A Pyrrhic victory? Bank bailouts and sovereign credit risk', *NBER Working Paper* 17136, Cambridge, MA: National Bureau of Economic Research.

De Santis, R. (2012) 'The euro area sovereign debt crisis. Safe haven, credit rating agencies and the spread of the fever From Greece, Ireland, and Portugal', *ECB Working Paper Series* 1419, Frankfurt: European Central Bank.

Grieco, J. (1996) 'State interests and international rule trajectories: a neorealist interpretation of the Maastricht Treaty and European Economic and Monetary Union', *Security Studies* 5(3): 261–306.

Hall, P. (2012) 'The economics and politics of the Euro crisis', *German Politics* 21(4): 355–71.

Hooghe, L. and Marks, G. (2009) 'A postfunctionalist theory of European integration: from permissive consensus to constraining dissensus', *British Journal of Political Science* 39(1): 1–23.

Hoffmann, S. (1966) 'Obstinate or obsolete? The fate of the nation state and the future of Western Europe', *Daedalus* 95(4): 861–98.

Ioannou, D., Leblond, P. and Niemann, A. (2015) 'European integration and the crisis: practice and theory', *Journal of European Public Policy*, doi: 10.1080/13501763. 2014.994979.

Moravcsik, A. (1993) 'Preferences and power in the European Community: a liberal intergovernmentalist approach', *Journal of Common Market Studies* 31(4): 473–524.

Moravcsik, A. (1998) *The Choice for Europe. Social Purpose and State Power from Messina to Maastricht*, Ithaca, NY: Cornell University Press.

Moravcsik, A. (2012) 'Europe after the crisis. How to sustain a common currency', *Foreign Affairs*, May/June, available at http://www.foreignaffairs.com/articles/137421/andrew-moravcsik/europe-after-the-crisis, accessed 21 December 2014.

Moravcsik, A. and Nicolaïdis, K. (1999) 'Explaining the Treaty of Amsterdam: inter-ests, influence, institutions', *Journal of Common Market Studies* 37(1): 59–85.

Moravcsik, A. and Schimmelfennig, F. (2009) 'Liberal intergovernmentalism', in A. Wiener and T. Diez (eds), *European Integration Theory*, 2nd edn, Oxford: Oxford University Press, pp. 67–87.

Niemann, A. and Ioannou, D. (2015) 'European economic integration in times of crisis: a case of neofunctionalism?', *Journal of European Public Policy*, doi: 10.1080/13501763.2014.994021.

Olender, M. (2012) 'Germany's euro crisis. Preferences, management, and contingencies', *Review of European and Russian Affairs* 7(2): 1–17.

Pierson, P. (1996) 'The path to European integration: a historical institutionalist perspective', *Comparative Political Studies* 29(2): 123–63.

Scharpf, F. (2011) 'Monetary union, fiscal crisis and the preemption of democracy', *LEQS Paper* 36, available at http://ssrn.com/abstract=1852316, accessed 21 December 2014.

Schild, J. (2013) 'Leadership in hard times: Germany, France, and the management of the eurozone crisis', *German Politics & Society* 3(1): 24–47.

Spiegel, P. (2014) 'How the euro was saved', *Financial Times*, available at http://www.ft.com/intl/indepth/euro-in-crisis, accessed 21 December 2014.

Stone Sweet, A. and Sandholtz, W. (1997) 'European integration and supranational governance', *Journal of European Public Policy* 4(3): 297–317.

Straubhaar, T. (2011) 'Drei Euro-Zukunftsszenarien', *Die Volkswirtschaft* 11: 30–3.

Verdun, A. (2015) 'A historical-institutionalist explanation of the EU's responses to the euro area financial crisis', *Journal of European Public Policy*, doi: 10.1080/13501763. 2014.994023.

Wallace, H., Caporaso, J., Scharpf, F. and Moravcsik, A. (1999) 'Review section symposium: The Choice for Europe: Social Purpose and State Power from Messina to Maastricht', *Journal of European Public Policy* 6(1): 155–79.

European economic integration in times of crisis: a case of neofunctionalism?

Arne Niemann and Demosthenes Ioannou

ABSTRACT   This contribution analyses the relevance of neofunctionalist theory and the various spillover mechanisms for explaining the management of the crisis and the drive towards a more complete Economic and Monetary Union (EMU). The management of the crisis resulted in integrative outcomes owing to significant functional dissonances that arose from the incomplete EMU architecture created at Maastricht. These functional rationales were reinforced by integrative pressures exercised by supranational institutions, transnational organized interests and markets. The contribution concludes that, despite shortcomings, neofunctionalism provides important insights for understanding the integrative steps taken during the crisis.

1. INTRODUCTION

In a special collection that investigates the development of European (economic) integration (in times of crisis) from different theoretical perspectives, neofunctionalism is arguably one of the more obvious choices for analysis. First, as pointed out in the introduction to this collection (Ioannou *et al.* 2015), we have witnessed quite a number of integrative steps in the area of Economic and Monetary Union (EMU) over the past few years relating to crisis management mechanisms such as the European Financial Stability Facility (EFSF) and European Stability Mechanism (ESM), the streamlining and tightening of fiscal and economic policy co-ordination such as the Two-Pack, or the creation of the banking union with single supervision and resolution. Neofunctionalism, with its particular focus on *explaining* policy-making outcomes (Wiener and Diez 2009) and its core competence with regard to the *dynamics* of European integration, should be apt to account for these changes. Second, and closely related, many observers agree that one of the insights gained from the crisis is that the introduction of the euro cannot be taken as the endpoint in the process of economic integration. Although EMU solved some of the economic dilemmas of an integrated single market with liberalized capital movements, variable exchange rates and national monetary policies, it also laid the ground for new ones, for example

42

stemming from the mismatch between centralized monetary and decentralized fiscal and financial policies. This seems to be a fertile breeding ground for neo-functionalist spillover pressures. Third, although neofunctionalism is one of the most widely criticized theories of European integration, it has remained relevant in the academic discourse over the years (Niemann and Schmitter 2009).

In view of these aspects, it appears rather astonishing that there is relatively little research on the crisis that (explicitly) draws on neofunctionalism. Interest-ingly, economic integration during the crisis arguably constitutes a crucial (hard) case for neofunctionalism, mainly because it is an area of 'high politics' – i.e., close to the heart of national sovereignty and substantially politicized (Hobolt and Wratil 2015) – while it has often been assumed that the neofunc-tionalist logic only works in a depoliticized environment (Hoffmann 1966). This contribution tries to address this gap by posing the following research ques-tion: to what extent is neofunctionalism (still) relevant for explaining the man-agement of the crisis and the drive towards a more complete EMU; i.e., to what degree are neofunctionalist propositions supported by empirical findings?

We proceed as follows: Section 2 specifies the neofunctionalist tenets and the concept of spillover. In Section 3, we briefly elaborate our dependent variable (the degree of European economic integration in response to the crisis). Sections 4, 5 and 6 analyse the extent to which the concepts of functional, political and cultivated spillover contribute to explaining the integrative steps taken to resolve the crisis. Finally, we draw some conclusions from our analysis.

2. NEOFUNCTIONALISM AND THE CONCEPT OF SPILLVOVER

The basic neofunctionalist assumptions can be summarized as follows:

(1) Integration is understood as a process. Implicit in the notion of process is the assumption that integration processes evolve over time and take on their own dynamic.
(2) Regional integration is assumed to be characterized by multiple, diverse and changing actors who also build transnational coalitions (Haas 1964: 68ff).
(3) Decisions are taken by rational actors, who nevertheless have the capacity to learn from their experiences in co-operative decision-making (Haas 1958: 291).
(4) Incremental decision-making is given primacy over grand designs, where seemingly marginal adjustments are often driven by the unintended conse-quences of previous decisions, as most political actors tend to be incapable of long-range purposive behaviour, since decisions on integration are nor-mally taken with very imperfect knowledge of their consequences and fre-quently under the pressure of deadlines (Haas 2004: xxiv).
(5) Neofunctionalists pointed out that interaction in the Community setting is often characterized by positive-sum games and a supranational style of decision-making where participants seek to attain agreement by means of compromises upgrading common interests (Haas 1964: 66).

The neofunctionalist conception of change is succinctly encapsulated in the notion of 'spillover'. Three types of spillover have generally been identified: functional; political; and cultivated spillover (Tranholm-Mikkelsen (1991).

2.1 Functional spillover

Functional spillover pressures come about when an original objective can be assured only by taking further integrative actions (Lindberg 1963: 10). The basis for the development of these pressures is the interdependence of policy sectors and issue areas. Individual sectors and issues tend to be so interdependent in modern polities and economies that it is difficult to isolate them from the rest (Haas 1958: 297). Functional pressures thus encompass the various endogenous interdependencies, i.e., the tensions and contradictions arising from within, or which are closely related to, the European integration project, which induce policy-makers to take additional integrative steps in order to achieve their original goals. Owing to such 'inherent linkages of tasks' (Nye 1970: 804), 'actors discover that they cannot [satisfactorily] do A ... without also doing B and perhaps C (Lindberg and Scheingold 1970: 117).

In the subsequent academic debate it has been suggested that the strength of functional spillover logics does not only depend on the degree of interdependence between policy areas. Two aspects influence when, and the extent to which, functional tensions impact on actors. First, when functional dissonances are not balanced or offset through further integrative steps, this may foster shocks or crises that may in the process of their management/mastery generate amplified functional pressures, which are likely to prompt the 'necessary' integrational steps. Second, functional structures do not determine actors' behaviour in a mechanical or predictable manner. Actors must regard functional logics as plausible or compelling in order for them to unfold their potential (cf. Niemann 2006: 31). In other words, functional logics are only as strong as they are perceived by (relevant/important) actors. The development of the political discourse can be suggested as an indicator for the persuasiveness of functional logics on decision-makers. When arguments along the lines of functional spillover rationales are substantially taken up by decision-makers, and especially when they become part of the dominant discourse, they also tend to find expression in political decisions (Niemann 2006: ch. 4). Through such modifications and extensions of the concept we should be able to better specify when and how functional pressures impact on the policy process.

2.2. Political spillover

Political spillover encapsulates the process whereby (national) élites come to perceive that problems of substantial interest cannot be effectively addressed at the domestic level. This should lead to a gradual learning process whereby élites shift their expectations, political activities and – according to Haas – even loyalties to a new European centre.[1] Consequently, national élites would come to promote further integration, thus adding a political stimulus to the process. Haas (1958: ch. 9–10) in particular focused on the pressures exerted by non-governmental élites, especially trade associations and trade unions, while second-generation neofunctionalists tended to refer to a broader range of interest groups (e.g., Schmitter [1971: 257]). Interest groups were thought to expose functional interdependencies between policy areas and organize increasingly at the European level (Haas: 1958: ch. 9; Nye 1970: 806ff).[2] Lindberg (1963: ch. I, IV) attributed greater significance to the role of governmental élites and socialization processes, which tended to foster consensus formation among member governments and would eventually lead to more integrative outcomes.

2.3. Cultivated spillover

This pressure concerns the role of supranational institutions[3] that, concerned with increasing their own powers, become agents of integration because they are likely to benefit from the progression of this process. Once established, they tend to take on a life of their own and are difficult to control by those who created them. Supranational institutions may foster the integration process; for example, by acting as policy entrepreneurs, through promotional brokerage, lifting agreements beyond the lowest common denominator (e.g., Haas 1964: 75ff; Lindberg 1963: ch. 3), or through positions of centrality and authority in the Community's political system capable of directing the dynamics of relations with various types of actors (Lindberg and Scheingold 1970: ch. 3; Nye 1970: 809).

3. EUROPEAN ECONOMIC INTEGRATION IN RESPONSE TO THE CRISIS

With regard to the dependent variable – i.e., the degree of European economic integration – the pre-crisis institutional framework considerably advanced under all main policy areas of EMU. The integrative steps followed a chronological order that reflected the nature of the crisis (and thereby the rise in pressures owing to functional dissonances), as well as the fact that in some cases more than one iteration was necessary to reach a point where functional pressures had adequately subsided.

Thus, the first integrative steps in the area of crisis-related firewalls were of an emergency nature, and included in May 2010 first bilateral loans to Greece and the agreement to establish the European Financial Stability Mechanism (EFSM) and European Financial Stability Facility (EFSF) in combination with macroeconomic conditionality in the form of European Union (EU) Economic Adjustment Programmes for the worst hit crisis countries. The EFSF developed into the more permanent ESM in March 2011, which took over new financing of programmes from the EFSF in July 2013 and, despite its intergovernmental nature, was also linked to the Treaty through an addition to Article 136.

In parallel, and in terms of fiscal and macroeconomic surveillance, the so-called 'Six-Pack' of legislative measures was adopted, with the intention of strengthening the fiscal rules of the Stability and Growth Pact (SGP) and the national fiscal frameworks, and setting up a framework to tackle macroeconomic imbalances. The Six-Pack was then further supplemented by the so-called 'Two-Pack' and the Fiscal Compact, increasing the co-ordination of fiscal and budgetary policy (Begg 2013).

In the financial sphere, the original reaction to the crisis in 2009 was in the form of elevating the committees responsible for co-ordinating micro-prudential supervision and regulation to authorities with greater autonomy and powers. These were also complemented by the new European Systemic Risk Board (ESRB) for macro-prudential policy. However, when functional dissonances escalated further through the coupling of public and private over indebtedness into the bank-sovereign nexus, the response in the financial sphere went a step further with the creation of the Banking Union; i.e., the creation of centralized banking supervision at the European Central Bank (ECB) and its resolution counterpart, the Single Resolution Mechanism (SRM) with a Single Resolution Fund (SRF) at the Commission. All these steps deepened to a remarkable degree European economic integration within a relatively very short period of time (also *cf.* Ioannou *et al.* [2015]). Some observers have suggested that banking union in particular represents the most important integrative step since the inception of the euro at Maastricht (Merler 2014).

4. FUNCTIONAL SPILLOVER

The concept of functional spillover will be operationalized by probing several indicators and mechanisms including:

(1) The salience of the original goal, which determines the strength of the functional pressure for further action.
(2) The existence of functional interdependence between issue A (original objective) and issue B (requiring further action). To what extent do changes/tensions in issue area A (EMU) have significant consequences for issue area B, thus requiring more collective action?
(3) The availability of functional solutions: is further action in a particular issue area necessary to achieve the initial objective, or are there alternative solutions? If the original goal cannot be reached by other means, the functional connection is likely to be a strong one.
(4) Functional dynamics are only as strong as they are perceived by (key) actors. If important policy-makers have used the functional argument(s) in political discourse repeatedly, this strengthens the functional rationale.

4.1. The salience of the original goal(s)

A significant and/or urgent original policy objective is required to let functional pressures develop. With regard to the integrative measures taken since the crisis, there has been one prime original objective: (financial) stability of EMU/safeguarding the euro. This fundamental objective was endorsed by a vast majority of, if not all, member governments and the EU institutions (Schimmelfennig 2012: 403). This objective is inextricably linked to an even more elementary one, that of protecting the Single European Market (SEM), as cited by several key policy-makers (Schäuble [*Der Spiegel* 2012a]; Rajoy [2012]). In addition, it has been argued that EMU and the SEM constitute policy goals crucial for the entire EU project, epitomized by Chancellor Merkel's statement 'Europe fails if the euro fails' (Merkel 2012). In sum, the original goals have been (considered) very salient indeed.

4.2 Functional interdependencies

Functional interdependencies between policy areas explain why the desire to achieve an original integrative objective may lead to further integration in a related area. In this case the developments towards deeper economic integration can be explained as steps taken in order to alleviate functional pressures arising from an incomplete architecture created at Maastricht.

Such functional interdependencies are based on the multitude of policy areas that are conducted in parallel and interconnected over different time horizons. Key in this interaction is that policy, which would normally take place at the same level of governance, has been allocated at different levels of government under the EMU design of the Maastricht Treaty. While monetary and exchange rate policy is an exclusive EU competence, fiscal policies are largely determined at national level. Financial sector regulation is determined at European and national level, while financial sector supervision and structural policies (beyond the single market) were loosely co-ordinated at EU level but legislated at national level.

Three functional dissonances can be identified, which brought about substantial integrative pressures during the crisis. First, a functional dissonance manifested itself between supranational monetary policy and intergovernmental budgetary, fiscal and structural policy, resulting in negative externalities. While these externalities were meant to be contained by the SGP and the non-bailout clause of the Treaty as well as loosely co-ordinated structural policies, this framework proved inadequate and provided incentives for free riding behaviour. At the same time, member states with severe imbalances found their policy options restricted when their sovereign debt came under pressure in financial markets, as they no longer had the possibility to counter such pressures through, for example, nominal exchange rate adjustment (Leuffen *et al.* 2013: 173; Schimmelfennig 2012). The creation of crisis management tools such as the ESM and concomitant conditionality, and a tighter fiscal and economic framework, sought to alleviate the functional dissonances between a stable single currency and the 'no-bailout' clause and decentralized national policies leading to public over-indebtedness.

Second, monetary union relied on the adequate supervision by national authorities of nationally based credit institutions within the single financial market, even though a number of them were exposing their balance sheets across national borders and/or were systemically important. More broadly, the degree of financial market integration increased substantially with the introduction of the euro (European Central Bank [ECB] 2005). Yet, while cross-border activity in the EU banking sector and financial markets prospered, supervision remained largely inward-looking at the national level and without (sufficient) institutional adaptations. In other words, the limited institutional framework and financial public policy at European level did not match the extensive Europeanization of the banking system and single financial market. A financial trilemma emerged between financial integration, national financial policies and financial stability, which became untenable (Schoenmaker 2011). The establishment of the banking union reflects steps taken to reduce the functional dissonances emanating from European financial stability and integration on the one hand, and a banking system that was functioning under essentially national policy allowing private over indebtedness on the other hand.

The third dissonance manifested itself through the interaction of the first two in what became known as the bank–sovereign nexus (European Council 2012a). Fragile public and private debt developments became intertwined at the national level, either because domestic banks were overexposed to failing domestic sovereign debt or because the sovereign had to rescue the systemically important credit institutions. A close correlation thus arose between sovereign and bank debt with European-wide financial instability implications, simultaneously interrupting the smooth transmission of monetary policy by the banking system. The nexus thus endangered EU- and euro-area-wide public goods such as financial stability and the single currency, and required emergency measures involving both the national and European level. A combination of fiscal backstops like the ESM (and the possibility of bank recapitalization), together with a centralized supervisory and resolution framework, sought to alleviate the additional functional pressures emerging as the crisis mutated into the bank–sovereign nexus.

4.3. The crisis: the result of existing, and amplifier of subsequent, functional pressures

If functional pressures are not resolved through further integrative steps, this can promote crises which in turn cause further functional pressures during the process of crisis management, thereby eventually triggering the necessary steps of integration. We can observe this process following the introduction of the single currency in 1999. During the time of broadly positive economic developments in the early years of monetary union, existing functional logics went largely unnoticed and did not give rise to sufficient integrative pressures. However, the functional dissonances described above allowed for the disrespect of the SGP's fiscal rules (already in 2003), the build-up of financial imbalances, and the loss of competitiveness in a number of economies failing to pursue sound fiscal, wage and structural policies in line with the single monetary and exchange rate policy. Thus, at least some of the elements of the crisis can be attributed to the first two functional dissonances described above (Schmidt 2012: 76).

Functional pressures were amplified during the crisis because the institutional framework did not include crisis management tools. This lead to the third dissonance described above whereby the support of illiquid banks to ensure financial stability became difficult for over-indebted national governments (Dyson 2013: 216). In the European context, the crisis uncovered, among other things 'that European authorities had no means to stop the spiral of the European sovereign debt crisis. In particular, no pan-European fiscal mechanism to face the global crisis [was] available' (Bordo *et al.* 2011: 1). Eventually, both crisis management and broader institutional integrational steps took place to alleviate these functional pressures, including the pooling of resources to manage the crisis and ensure economic and financial stability, the adjustment of the fiscal and economic co-ordination rules especially in the euro area, together with rules governing the regulation, supervision and resolution of banking institutions.

4.4. Alternative solutions?

If the original goal – here the stability of EMU and safeguarding the euro – cannot be (adequately) reached by means other than further integration, the functional spillover logic is likely to be strong. Several other scenarios could be imagined, such as retaining the *status quo*, a break-up of the euro area and a return to national currencies, or several intermediate scenarios, such as dividing EMU into a north and south euro, the establishment of a core EMU, etc. (Schmidt 2012: 165–92). We argue that these alternative solutions were considered politically and economically far too costly and/or risky by euro area policy-makers and that path dependencies point in a different direction.

First, the crisis convincingly demonstrated that the *status quo* was untenable. Second, spillback scenarios were (considered) highly undesirable. The change to the euro and a supranational monetary policy came to imply very significant 'sunk costs' for states and firms. In addition, as pointed out above, EMU reinforced the integration of capital markets and thus interdependencies between the euro area member states. Consequently, a break-up of EMU and/or the exit of a member state would have posed very considerable costs and risks. Therefore, euro area governments across the board strongly supported the maintenance of the entire euro area (Schimmelfennig 2012: 404). Where dissenting views were expressed in national politics – such as sporadically by representatives of the Christian Social Union and the Free Democratic Party in Germany – these were met by heavy criticism (Handelsblatt 2011). Overall, top eurozone policy-makers clearly dismissed such alternatives.

4.5. Increased shaping of the political discourse through functional logic

As described in Section 2, actors also have to consider functional logics as plausible or urgent in order for them to substantially unfold. The crisis, as a result and amplifier of functional pressures, has apparently fostered learning effects and thus decisively reinforced the functional spillover logic. Although the functional spillover dynamic emanating from EMU had been (sporadically) articulated since the late 1980s (Delors Committee 1989), it found little traction in political discourse until the crisis.

Through the crisis, functional spillover argumentation became the dominant political discourse relatively quickly. This discourse is evident throughout nearly all national governments and EU institutions. The functional link between the Single European Market and the single currency was referred to repeatedly during the crisis. According to German Finance Minister Schäuble:

> There is certainly the risk that, in the event of a collapse of the euro – which, by the way, I don't believe is going to happen – much of what we have achieved and become fond of would be called into question, from the common market to freedom of travel in Europe. (*Der Spiegel* 2012a)

Spanish Prime Minister Rajoy argued similarly: 'The euro is on a path of no return, and its connection with the entire European project, starting with the common market, is undissolvable' (Rajoy 2012).

As for the functional consequences emanating from the common currency, politicians in Europe also increasingly make use of functional spillover logic. Chancellor Merkel, for example, suggested that 'a renewed EMU requires a common fiscal and economic policy' (*Der Spiegel* 2012b, authors' translation). Commission President Barroso likewise argued: 'It was an illusion to think that we could have a common currency and a single market with national approaches to economic and budgetary policy' (Barroso 2011: 4). Similar arguments were expounded, for instance, in the four Presidents report (Van Rompuy *et al.* 2012: 3).

Subsequently, the functional link between EMU and an often ill-defined but much broader political union was cited by a multitude of decision-makers at national and European level.[4] Apart from Chancellor Merkel and the four Presidents,[5] French President Hollande also followed this logic: 'This Eurozone must take a political dimension … [but] political union comes afterwards. It is the step that follows the fiscal union, the banking union, the social union' (*Le Monde* 2012). Political union as a necessary result of the single currency was also seen as uncontroversial, less surprisingly, of course, in wide sections of the European Parliament and the European Commission. For example, Commissioner Almunia declared:

> It's legitimate to pursue national interests. But, at the end of the day, individual nations need to do what is necessary in order to save Europe as a whole. This also means that Germans are right to push for a political union after having achieved the economic and monetary union. (Spiegel Online 2012)

Steps towards a European financial market union are mostly constructed as a logical result of functional constraints in the political discourse. Even politicians of governments follow this logic, whom one would expect rather to advocate the importance of national sovereignty. As suggested by British Chancellor of the Exchequer Osborne: 'We've always said a banking union was a necessary part of a more stable single currency for the Eurozone' (*The Guardian* 2012).

The above indicates that functional logic found increased acceptance in the political discourse of senior policy-makers in the EU and its member states during the crisis. This seems to imply that functional pressures were, during the crisis's development, increasingly perceived to be convincing by political élites in the EU. Since discourses tend to restrict decision-makers' freedom of action in the political process (Jachtenfuchs 1997: 47), one can tentatively deduce that this discourse should also be evident in consequent political decisions.

5. POLITICAL SPILLOVER

Owing to the limited scope of this contribution, our analysis of political spillover – i.e., the integrative role that élites play owing to their awareness of the benefits of supranational solutions – focuses only on non-governmental élites. First, we discuss the role of interest groups before we turn to that of financial markets.[6]

5.1. The role of interest groups

In this section the concept of political spillover will be probed by (1) examining the extent to which supranational solutions have been regarded beneficial by interest groups,[7] (2) analysing the degree to which interest group representation and articulation has taken place through Brussels-based umbrella organizations and/or in a co-ordinated fashion transnationally, rather than nationally, and (3) approximating the impact of organized interests on decision-makers.

First, we look at the degree to which supranational solutions are/have been regarded beneficial for solving the crisis. Generally speaking, business leaders have strongly favoured European solutions in this regard. Grant Thornton survey data suggest that 78 per cent of eurozone business leaders are positive about the overall impact of joining the euro, 94 per cent support the survival of the euro, and 89 per cent favour further economic integration (Grant Thornton International Business Report 2013). The position papers, reports and statements of business interest groups further corroborate their interest in supranational solutions (e.g., BusinessEurope [2011]; European Roundtable of Industrialists [2011, 2012]). In particular, those economic interest groups representing businesses substantially involved in intra-currency union trade tend to favour the euro owing to reduced transaction costs resulting from the eradication of exchange rate risks (Jäger 2013: 120).

Second, as neofunctionalism suggests, much of the corporate interest representation and articulation has taken place through Brussels-based umbrella organizations and/or in a co-ordinated fashion transnationally during the crisis. For example, in the run-up to the European Council summit of June 2011, a coalition of 51 German and French top representatives from major corporations, such as Air France, BASF, Deutsche Bank, Michelin and Siemens, launched a newspaper campaign entitled 'The euro is necessary', calling for further financial aid for the highly indebted countries (Büschemann 2011; Jäger 2013). In addition, the euro area's three largest national business interest groups, the Bundesverband der Deutschen Industrie (BDI), Le Mouvement des entreprises de France (MEDEF) and Confederazione Generale dell'Industria Italia (Confindustra), issued a joint statement in 2011. They demanded safeguarding the euro and deeper European economic integration (BDI, Confindustria and MEDEF 2011). Furthermore, the European Roundtable of Industrialists (ERT) – which brings together some 50 chief executive officers (CEOs) of major European corporations – got significantly involved in the business campaign for stabilizing the euro by advocating measures reinforcing and deepening the entire eurozone architecture (ERT 2011, 2012). In addition, BusinessEurope (2010a, 2010b, 2010c), the largest European umbrella business association, has continuously and unequivocally pushed for such objectives, and also did so jointly with other European industrial and financial umbrella organizations (BusinessEurope *et al.* 2010).

Third, the precise impact of organized interests on decision-makers is difficult to ascertain, as can be seen from other works on the role of EU corporate groups (Green Cowles 1995). Nonetheless, it seems that the above-mentioned interest groups have had direct access to key decision-makers. Cromme of Thyssen-Krupp, the initiator of the Franco-German newspaper campaign described above, together with Diekmann of Allianz and Todenhöfer of Bosch, went to meet Chancellor Merkel on 10 May 2011 to report their concerns with regard to 'the ailing euro' (Büschemann 2011). Furthermore, in the autumn of 2011 ERT representatives met with Chancellor Merkel in Berlin, with Council President Thorning-Schmidt in Copenhagen and with French President Sarkozy in Paris to draw their attention to the ERT crisis management proposals for deepening the euro area architecture (Corporate Europe Observatory 2012a; Embassy of France in London 2011).

In more tangible terms, the influence of organized interests can be discerned on the various legislative dossiers leading to further integration such as the so-called Six-Pack that aims at strengthening the procedures to reduce public deficits and address macroeconomic imbalances. Evidence suggests that BusinessEurope acted as a policy entrepreneur during the Six-Pack (pre-)negotiations. On important issues that ended up in the legislation, BusinessEurope was the first group/entity to argue for their inclusion. For example, BusinessEurope argued for stricter binding sanctions – both in terms of greater automatism and a transfer of fines to a crisis resolution fund – before this was taken up by the Commission or Task force.[8] There is no evidence that the Commission and Task Force included certain provisions in the legislation because of the efforts undertaken by BusinessEurope; however, the similarity of content, the timing of the proposals and the intensive contacts cultivated by BusinessEurope with representatives from the Commission and Parliament, along with four letters directly addressed to Van Rompuy (e.g., BusinessEurope [2011]), suggest that BusinessEurope's lobbying efforts have at least been conducive (Knedelhans 2014).

In addition, BusinessEurope contently concluded that it was 'glad to see a large number of [their] recommendations reflected in the legislative package', for example in terms of the exceptions for meeting the envisaged budgetary targets (BusinessEurope 2010c: 2; cf. Official Journal 23/11/2011: 17), which is a telling statement, because interest groups tend to understate their influence (Dür 2008).

BusinessEurope also appears to have played an active role in advocating economic governance reform eventually codified in the fiscal compact. Already, in its 2010 'European Action Plan', it proposed, binding fiscal rules and stronger institutions to ensure long-run budgetary discipline (BusinessEurope 2010a). The crisis provided a good opportunity for business interests to promote the strengthening of EU economic governance (Mandate 2012). Before the EU summit of December 2011, three major changes were advocated: strengthened voting rules to make it tougher for the Council to overrule the Commission's recommendations regarding deficits; greater ambition and commitment from member states in their national reform programmes; making ESM lending conditional on member states accepting the fiscal compact (BusinessEurope 2011a: 2–3). The final version of the fiscal compact, signed in March 2012, appears to be modelled rather closely on BusinessEurope's demands (Corporate Europe Observatory [2012b]; cf. Council of the European Union [2012: 15–16]).

5.2. The role of the financial markets

While the previous sub-section analysed the role of actors in the 'real' economy, this one examines the role of financial markets.[9] Although financial markets may be treated simply as arenas in which actors play out their individual strategies and respond to each other (Overbeek 2012: 40), a majority of authors have viewed them (mostly implicitly) as actors during the crisis (e.g., Schimmelfennig [2012: 396]; Yiangou et al. [2013: 16ff]).

Overall, we argue that financial markets acted both directly and indirectly during the crisis to promote integration, and with a particularly high level of autonomy (Schmidt 2012: 24). They may not have been organized as a unitary actor but, owing to the high uncertainty and herd-like behaviour observed during the crisis (Dyson 2013:220), their actions appeared unitary vis-à-vis EU policy makers and influenced substantially the EU's crisis management towards the adoption of integrative measures (Schimmelfennig 2012:396). In particular, they bluntly revealed the functional dissonances of the original EMU design and became a serious threat to the euro area through the radical reassessment of a variety of economic and credit risks. Arghyrou and Kontonikas (2012: 672) have argued that, on several occasions, financial markets understood policy-makers' hesitation as a withdrawal of previously perceived fiscal guarantees, which furthered the notion of a significant default risk. Substantial funding pressures emerged in several euro area sovereign debt markets, translating into augmented borrowing rates. The sharp increase in interest rates for new issues of sovereign debt securities, especially for the highly indebted countries, created additional costs for governments and put further pressure on budget deficits (van Scherpenberg 2012: 369). This, together with an ongoing downgrading of several euro area members' creditworthiness, triggered a vicious circle of increasing debt and interest rates, pushing some euro area states to the edge of insolvency (De Grauwe 2011: 1).

At that time, European decision-makers had to act given the magnitude of the negative consequences of a eurozone member's bankruptcy. When EU heads of state and government met for an emergency summit on 7 May 2010, they started to realize the immense risks and necessity for swift action. The amount of market pressure was reportedly dramatic and all-pervading during negotiations (Ludlow 2013). When President of Cyprus Christofias asked for some days of reconsideration regarding the decision on a new European bailout facility, Merkel refused, urging that a decision before the reopening of markets after the weekend (Ehrlich 2010). Late in the night before 10 May, a decision to establish a European stabilization mechanism was taken by the Economic and Financial Affairs Council. This decision represented the first of several integrative measures taken in response to very substantial market pressures during the crisis. Nevertheless, while the measures taken in May 2010 were certainly important for reducing the risk of a deep pan-European financial crisis in the short run, they quickly proved inadequate to prevent speculative attacks on sovereign bonds of some euro area members (Panico and Purificato 2012: 13). Pressure thus continued and even sharpened after the adoption of early crisis management mechanisms, which eventually compelled policy-makers to consider deeper institutional reforms to address the flaws in the EMU design. During numerous 'historic' summits, where decision-makers attempted to persuade the markets of their ability to solve the problems, original positions gradually subsided to the pressure of financial markets, which led to more sustainable measures such as the Six-Pack, Fiscal Compact and Banking Union (Vilpišauskas 2013: 372).

Characteristic in this regard was the case of the Fiscal Compact: by late autumn 2011 it was clear the adopted measures were insufficient to arrest deteriorating market conditions. When Greek government yields reached a new peak and overnight borrowing from the ECB hit its highest level in December 2011, the tone between the participants at the European Council summit became sharper. Head of the EFSF, Regling, talked to investors on the eve of the summit and reported that they aimed to decrease their exposure in the euro area. This raised the pressure on the summiteers to persuade investors that the agreed measures were indeed appropriate to shield the euro area (Spiegel Online 2011).

> The market needs to see a road map of the process by which the Europeans will get to a fiscal-integration situation, not just a statement of intentions. Without it, you get the Euroquake scenario: runs on European banks, forced nationalization of European banks. ... With a healing plan for fiscal union, the markets will feel much more relaxed. If they don't have one, the markets will freak out again. (Wood quoted in Norton 2011)

Such processes revealed functional dissonances, which encouraged institutional reforms to replace 'governance through markets' with 'governance through governments', and hence establish mechanisms to guarantee stable outcomes for the monetary union (Yiangou *et al.* 2013: 239). From a neofunctionalist perspective, financial markets became a 'revealer' of, and barometer for, the degree to which functional dissonances were addressed: when significant crisis management and integrative measures were taken, markets generally reacted positively, reducing pressure on sovereign bonds. By contrast, investors withdrew rapidly from these markets when they saw policy-making inactivity and hesitation in terms of finding durable institutional solutions.

6. CULTIVATED SPILLOVER

As for the potentially integrative role of supranational institutions, the most directly relevant supranational institutions, the Commission, the European Parliament and the European Central Bank, shared a clear preference for substantial action towards further integration. The overall process towards further integration during the crisis would not have taken place to the same extent without their involvement.

6.1. The European Commission

The Commission seems to have played a relatively limited role in cultivating spillover pressures during the crisis. According to Hodson (2013), it appeared little determined to mobilize ideas in support of, and push for, further integration, especially in the initial years of the crisis. This may have been because crisis management solutions such as the EFSF and the ESM were strongly intergovernmental, limiting the Commission's right of initiative. In the talks on the Fiscal Compact, the Commission managed to position itself on the 'winning side', but whenever its interests diverged from that of the 'coalition' headed by Germany, it failed to (fully) realize its preferences. However, the Commission did add impetus towards integrative solutions by emphasizing functional spillover rationales (e.g., Barroso [2011: 4]). It also played a more proactive role once the heads of state broadly agreed to move ahead with further integration, for example by putting forward ambitious legislative proposals in particular for the two main pillars of the banking union, the Single Supervisory Mechanism (SSM) and Single Resolution Mechanism (SRM), despite strong scepticism for its proposals by some member states (European Commission [2009]; cf. Hasselbach [2012]). In the end the Commission gained new competencies with the implementation, in particular of virtually all new surveillance procedures under the Six-Pack, Two-Pack and the Fiscal Compact, together with its role in the SRM, which increased its potential for autonomous action.

6.2. The European Parliament

The European Parliament contributed substantially to the integrative impetus, sometimes playing a notable role even in those areas where it lacked significant powers. As with the Commission, on the negotiations of the EFSF, the ESM and the Fiscal Compact, Parliament was side-lined because heads of state or government decided to conclude intergovernmental contracts. Nevertheless, of every such step taken outside the Community framework, the Parliament was very critical (cf. European Parliament [EP] 2012). Consequently, and under the pressure from Parliament in particular, it was agreed that the ESM was linked to the Treaty through a simplified revision procedure and that the Fiscal Compact would eventually be brought into the Treaties (Ludlow 2013). Moreover, on the negotiations of the Six-Pack, the EP managed to assert itself and forced the Council into tough negotiations and largely prevented the supranational dimension of the legislation from being watered down (e.g., with regard to the role of the Commission; a higher degree of automaticity in the procedures and thus more restricted role of member states). Although the EP had codecision rights for only four out of the six legislative proposals, members of the European Parliament (MEPs) were able to 'sell this to the Council as a package' obliging the Council to negotiate with the EP on the package as a whole (Chang 2013: 263). Parliament ensured the same approach was taken with the SSM by gaining *de facto* codecision with the Council on the SSM Regulation assigning supervisory tasks to the ECB by treating it as a package with the parallel European Banking Authority (EBA) Regulation. Finally, Parliament did not only seek to strengthen the supranational institutions' competencies (e.g., the Commission in the economic and fiscal area; the ECB for supervision) but it also sought to gain a commensurate role in the accountability of the new institutional solutions.

6.3. The European Central Bank

The EU institution that attracted most attention during the crisis was the European Central Bank. A key challenge for the ECB during the crisis was to maintain price stability for the euro area while the transmission of its monetary policy was becoming impaired. In this context, its actions also had to eliminate fears about the reversibility of the euro and the preservation of financial stability. The ECB's standard and non-standard monetary policy measures included the rapid reduction of its key interest rates; changes to its collateral policy and Long Term Refinancing Operations (LTROs); the adoption of three Covered Bond Purchases Programmes (2009, 2011,2014), the Securities Markets Programme (SMP) in 2010 and the announcement of Outright Monetary Transactions (OMT) in 2012, both with the aim of enhancing the transmission of monetary policy through purchases, under different conditions, of securities in secondary markets.[10] With regard to the non-standard measures, while Sinn and Wollmershäuser (2012) claimed that the use of the ECB's balance sheet exceeded its competences, others, such as de Grauwe (2011), criticized it for doing too little, claiming, for example, that it had failed to act as lender of last resort.

Beyond these monetary policy measures, the ECB was an early advocate of integrative deepening to buttress EMU. It did so in the Van Rompuy Task Force of 2010, in its legal opinions on EMU-relevant legislation, and through its interaction with the fiscal authorities in fora such as the Eurogroup and the European Council. It also provided input to the four Presidents report (Van Rompuy *et al.* 2012). Moreover, given the strong interconnection between the different policy domains under EMU, it also played an advisory role in assisting the authorities in shaping the EU-financed economic adjustment programmes and monitoring them.

The ECB's role in advancing integration was perhaps most evident in the development of the banking union. This was in line with its proactive stance towards fostering financial integration (ECB 2005: 3) and closely linked to the efficient transmission of monetary policy through the banking system. The ECB thus strongly supported the establishment of the SSM and took on the role of single supervisor, even if this may not have been the only solution in principle (Angeloni and Ioannou 2013). Furthermore, the ECB also strongly supported the establishment of the Single Resolution Mechanism, seeing the possibility of further functional dissonances emerging if supervision were not to be coupled with an effective European-wide resolution.

According to Traynor (2012), the ECB's calls to strengthen and integrate the institutional architecture of EMU were justified within its remit to secure the single currency. Some observers have also argued that this stance was partly owing to the policy paralysis caused by the prohibition of monetary financing and the no-bail-out clauses of the Treaty (Menz and Smith 2013: 197), as well as poor political leadership (Dyson 2013; Torres 2013). In 2012, *The Economist* also claimed that 'the slow moving response of European leaders to the crisis created a vacuum that has forced the ECB, the only institution in the euro area capable of intervening promptly and decisively, into territory far outside its custom and practice' (quoted in Alessi 2012). Menz and Smith even go as far as to suggest that the ECB was:

[a] decisive, at times even shrewd actor in pursuing its favoured strategy. In fact, much of the empirical story reads like one of quiet, yet powerful, mission creep.' They further claim that ECB 'officials [were] dedicated to

not only salvaging the euro at any cost, but also pushing for fiscal union'. Menz and Smith (2013: 203)

Ultimately, the Central Bank's advocacy to adjust and deepen the EMU framework need to be understood, in neofunctionalist terminology, as resolving functional dissonances between the different policy domains under EMU that jeopardized the ECB's independence and its ability to shield the euro and deliver price stability. Pressures on its independence came as soon as the sovereign debt crisis erupted in May 2010. When French President Sarkozy demanded from ECB President Trichet what essentially amounted to a bailout, Trichet reportedly reacted very strongly, warning that the ECB Governing Council would react very negatively to such pressure with potentially 'catastrophic consequences' (Ehrlich 2010; Ludlow 2010).

Some observers saw the ECB's attitude as 'business as usual' (Schmieding 2012: 182), or even 'inaction'' (Dyson 2013: 217), which may itself have induced further integrative steps (Yiangou *et al.* 2013: 224). Schmieding (2012: 183) has suggested that the ECB was willing to 'tolerate significant economic and financial stress, as such stress gives politicians a strong reason to fortify their economies through fiscal repair and structural reforms'. Referring to the creation of the EFSF and ESM, de Grauwe (2011: 4) has suggested that this approach 'has forced the euro zone members to create [these] surrogate institutions'. That the ECB's proportional monetary policy actions (ECB 2012: 7) and 'encouragement' to deepen EMU were key in this process therefore appears plausible.

7. CONCLUSION

Neofunctionalism – as a framework for analysing EU economic integration during the crisis – has substantially contributed to our understanding of that process. In particular, it identified crucial driving forces and mechanisms of change. From a neofunctionalist perspective, the management of the crisis resulted in integrative outcomes owing to three significant functional dissonances that arose from the incomplete EMU architecture created at Maastricht, based on salient original policy objectives (mainly related to the stability of EMU and safeguarding the euro). The functional dissonances (at least partly) triggered the crisis, which in turn amplified these dissonances. In the absence of credible and sensible alternative solutions, the functional spillover dynamic was reinforced considerably and increasingly shaped the political discourse. In addition to functional pressures, supranational institutions exerted important additional integrative pressure – for example owing to skilful policy entrepreneurship by the EP during the Six-Pack negotiations, as well as the ECB's insistence on integrative solutions for managing the crisis and dealing with the fiscal and economic governance shortcomings of EMU. Interest groups, which largely advocated further economic integration as a means of solving the crisis, provided further significant integrative impetus by lobbying mainly through

Brussels-based umbrella organizations and/or in a co-ordinated fashion transnationally. Still more important was the role of markets, in their own search for economic advantage, uncovered functional dissonances and sanctioned policy-making inactivity and hesitation in terms of finding durable institutional solutions.

The above analysis also makes an important limitation of neofunctionalist theory apparent. Neofunctionalism – in its conventional version that predominantly focuses on the *dynamics* of integration – struggles to account for the limits of European (economic) integration. For example, that decision-makers have not yet agreed on a fully fledged fiscal union by now cannot be adequately explained by (mainstream) neofunctionalist theory because it lacks an account of countervailing or disintegrative pressures.[11]

The seeming continued utility of neofunctionalist theory, the existing potential for further spillover in view of remaining functional dissonances,[12] the tentativeness of parts of the preceding analysis, and the limitations of neofunctionalism to explain certain aspects of economic integration during the crisis suggest that there is considerable scope for further research emanating from this article.

Biographical notes: Arne Niemann is professor of international politics and Jean Monnet Professor of European Integration at the University of Mainz. Demosthenes Ioannou is principal economist in the Directorate General International and European Relations of the European Central Bank.

ACKNOWLEDGEMENTS

We would like to thank Markus Knedelhans, Linda Koch and Tobias Tesche for their research assistance. The views expressed in the article are those of the authors and do not necessarily reflect those of the European Central Bank.

NOTES

1 In his second edition of *The Uniting of Europe*, Haas (1968) pointed out that élites are more likely to follow economic advantages pragmatically rather than developing a deeper concern for European integration, thus no longer banking on their *longer-term* integrative support.
2 This indicated that the various types of spillover are closely interlinked and cannot be clearly separated from each other (Niemann 2006: 50–1).

3 While Haas emphasized the role of the High Authority/ Commission, later on neo-functionalism was often interpreted as viewing the role of supranational institutions, more generally, as an integrative dynamic.
4 Functional spillover logic within EMU is also evident in legal EU texts, such as the 'fiscal compact' (European Council 2012b: 7).
5 That is, European Council President van Rompuy, Commission President Barroso, Eurogroup President Juncker and ECB President Draghi.
6 The section on political spillover as well as those on the Commission and the European Parliament partly draws on Koch (2013), whose masters thesis one of the authors supervized.
7 In this contribution we have focused on business interest groups as the largest and best documented segment of organized interests in this sector.
8 Compare BusinessEurope (2010a, 2010b) with European Commission (2010a, 2010b) and European Council (2010). Also *cf.* Knedelhans (2014).
9 To include financial markets within the notion of political spillover may be contested, as it is doubtful whether they undergo (deeper) learning processes, an assumption that was dropped, however, during the first revisions of the theory in the late 1960s (*cf.* note 3). In that spirit, the inclusion of financial markets as actors seems justified. In addition, their very high degree of autonomous acting fits core neofunctionalist maxims.
10 For a timeline of the measures taken by euro area, EU and global authorities during the crisis, see: https://www.ecb.europa.eu/ecb/html/crisis.en.html (accessed 1 April 2014).
11 But see Niemann (2006) for such a revised neofunctionalist framework.
12 For example, a number of elements identified in the Four Presidents' Report (Van Rompuy 2012) have yet to be dealt with, suggesting that the updated EMU architecture still entails potentially significant functional dissonances.

REFERENCES

Alessi, C. (2012) 'The role of the European Central Bank', *Council on Foreign Relations*, available at http://www.cfr.org/world/role-european-central-bank/p28989
Angeloni, I. and Ioannou, D. (2013) 'The European Banking Union is moving ahead', *Boao Review* 4.
Arghyrou, M. and Kontonikas, A. (2012) 'The EMU sovereign-debt crisis', *Journal of International Financial Markets, Institutions and Money* 22(4): 658–677.
Barroso, J.M. (2011) 'European renewal', available at http://europa.eu/rapid/press-release_SPEECH-11-607_en.htm (accessed 1 April 2014).
BDI, Confindustria and MEDEF (2011) 'Aufruf zu einer tieferen europäischen Integration', 8 October, available at http://www.bdi.eu/download_content/ Gemeinsamer_Aufruf_von_BDI_Confindustria_MEDEF.pdf (accessed 19 December 2014).
Begg, I. (2013) 'Are better defined rules enough? An assessment of the post-crisis reforms of the governance of EMU', *Transfer: European Review of Labour and Research* 19(1): 49–62.
Bordo, M., Markiewicz, A. and Jonung, L. (2011) 'A fiscal union for the euro', *National Bureau of Economic Research, Working Paper 17380*, available at https://www.cesifo-group.de/portal/pls/portal/!PORTAL.wwpob_page.show?_docname=1210229. PDF (accessed 1 April 2014).
Büschemann, K. (2011) 'Bitte, bitte, rettet doch den Euro', available at http://www. sueddeutsche.de/wirtschaft/deutsche-wirtschaft-anzeigenkampagne-bitte-bitte-rettet-doch-den-euro-1.1110669 (accessed 1 April 2014).

BusinessEurope (2010a) 'Combining fiscal sustainability and growth: a European action plan', available at http://www.businesseurope.eu/content/default.asp? PageID=568&DocID=25979 (accessed 1 April 2014).

BusinessEurope (2010b) 'Combining fiscal sustainability and growth: a European action plan', available at http://www.businesseurope.eu/content/default.asp? PageID=568&DocID=25979 (accessed 1 April 2014).

BusinessEurope (2010c) 'Declaration on economic governance', available at http:// www.businesseurope.eu/content/default.asp?PageID=568&DocID=27393 (accessed 1 April 2014).

BusinessEurope (2011) Letter to Council President Van Rompuy, available at http://www.businesseurope.eu/Content/Default.asp?PageID=568&DocID=28181 (accessed 1 April 2014).

BusinessEurope, EBF, EFRP and FEE (2010) 'Financial reforms and the recovery', http://www.evca.eu/uploadedFiles/News1/News_Items/2010-06-25_Financial_ reforms_and_the_recovery-June_2010.pdf (accessed 1 April 2014).

Chang, M. (2013) 'Fiscal policy coordination and the future of the community method', *Journal of European Integration* 35(3): 255–69.

Corporate Europe Observatory (2012a) 'Austerity treaty', available at http:// corporateeurope.org/nl/node/855 (accessed 1 April 2014).

Corporate Europe Observatory (2012b) 'Inspired by big business', available at http:// corporateeurope.org/printpdf/885 (accessed 1 April 2014).

Council of the European Union (2012) *Treaty on Stability, Coordination and Governance in the Economic and Monetary Union*, Brussels, 2 March, available at http:// www.european-council.europa.eu/media/639235/st00tscg26_en12.pdf (accessed 19 December 2014).

De Grauwe, P. (2011) 'Only a more active ECB can solve the euro crisis', *Policy Brief, No. 250*, Brussels: CEPS.

Delors Committee (1989) *Report on Economic and Monetary Union in the European Community*, Luxemburg: EC Publications Office.

Der Spiegel (2012a) 'Finanzminister Schäuble über die Geburtsfehler der Gemeinschaftswährung', available at http://www.spiegel.de/spiegel/finanzminister-schaeuble-ueber-die-geburtsfehler-des-euro-a-840867.html (accessed 1 April 2014).

Der Spiegel (2012b) 'Europa – Die Kuhhändler', available at http://www.spiegel.de/ spiegel/print/d-90254946.html (accessed 1 April 2014).

Dür, A. (2008) 'Measuring interest group influence in the EU', *European Union Politics* 9(4): 585–602.

Dyson, K. (2013) 'Sworn to grim necessity?', *Journal of European Integration* 35(2): 207–22.

Ehrlich, P. (2010) 'Europas heimlicher Chronist', *The Financial Times*, 25 December.

Embassy of France in London (2011) 'European industrialists back euro area stability', http:// www.ambafrance-uk.org/European-industrialists-back-Euro (accessed 1 April 2014).

European Central Bank (2005) 'Indicators of financial integration in the euro area', available at https://www.ecb.europa.eu/pub/pdf/other/indicatorsfinancialin tegration200509en.pdf (accessed 1 April 2014).

European Central Bank (2012) 'Monthly bulletin, October', available at http://www. ecb.europa.eu/pub/pdf/mobu/mb201210en.pdf (accessed 1 April 2014).

European Commission (2009) 'Beschluss der Kommission vom 23. Januar 2009 zur Einsetzung des Ausschusses der europäischen Bankaufsichtsbehörden ... ', http://eur-lex. europa.eu/LexUriServ/LexUriServ.do?uri=OJ:L:2009:025:0023:01:DE:HTML (accessed 1 April 2014).

European Commission (2010a) 'Reinforcing economic policy coordination', *COM (2010) 250 final*, May 2010, avauilable at http://eurlex.europa.eu/LexUriServ/ LexUriServ.do?uri=COM:2010:0250:FIN:EN:PDF (accessed 1 April 2014).

European Commission (2010b) 'Enhancing economic policy coordination for stability, growth and jobs', *30/62010*, available at http://ec.europa.eu/economy_finance/articles/euro/documents/com_2010_367_en.pdf (accessed 1 April 2014).

European Council (2010) 'Strengthening economic governance in the EU; report of the task force to the European Council', Brussels, 21 October, available at http://www.consilium.europa.eu/uedocs/cms_data/docs/pressdata/en/ec/117236.pdf (accessed 1 April 2014).

European Council (2012a) 'Euro area summit statement of 29 June 2012', available at http://www.consilium.europa.eu/uedocs/cms_data/docs/pressdata/en/ec/131359.pdf (accessed 1 April 2014).

European Council (2012b) 'Vertrag über Stabilität, Koordinierung und Steuerung in der Wirtschafts- und Währungsunion', available at http://www.european-council.europa.eu/media/639244/04_-_tscg.de.12.pdf (accessed 1 April 2014).

European Parliament (2012) 'Report with recommendations . . . 'Towards a genuine Economic and Monetary Union', Committee on Economic and Monetary Affairs, 24 October 2012, available at http://www.europarl.europa.eu/sides/getDoc.do?pubRef=-%2f%2fEP%2f%2fNONSGML%2bREPORT%2bA7-2012-0339%2b0%2bDOC%2bPDF%2bV0%2f%2fEN (accessed 1 April 2014).

European Roundtable of Industrialists (2011) 'Euro crisis: European industry leaders call for coordinated actions to reinforce EMU', 12 October, available at http://www.ert.eu/sites/default/files/Euro%20-%20ERT%20Press%20Release%20FINAL%2020121011.pdf (accessed 1 April 2014).

European Roundtable of Industrialists (2012) 'Creating growth in Europe', 16 January 2012, http://www.ert.eu/sites/default/files/2012%20January%20-%20ERT%20Statement%20on%20Creating%20Growth%20in%20Europe.pdf (accessed 1 April 2014).

The Guardian (2012) 'Eurozone moves a decisive step closer to banking union', 3 October, available at http://www.guardian.co.uk/business/2012/dec/13/eurozone-banking-union-step-closer (accessed 1 April 2014).

Grant Thornton International Business Report (2013) 'The future of Europe', available at http://www.internationalbusinessreport.com/files/IBR2013_Future_Europe_FINAL.pdf (accessed 1 April 2014).

Green Cowles, M. (1995) 'Setting the agenda for a new Europe', *Journal of Common Market Studies* 33: 501–26.

Haas, E. (1958) *The Uniting of Europe. Political, Social and Economic Forces, 1950–1957*, London: Stevens.

Haas, E. (1964) 'Technocracy, pluralism and the new Europe', in S. Graubard (ed.), *A New Europe?*, Boston, MA: Beacon Press, pp. 62–88.

Haas, E. (1968) *The Uniting of Europe: Politics, Social and Economic Forces, 1950–1957*, 2nd edn, Stanford, CA: Stanford University Press.

Haas, E. (2004) 'Introduction: institutionalism or constructivism?', in E. Haas, *The Uniting of Europe*, 3rd edn, Notre Dame, IN: University of Notre Dame Press, pp. xiii–lvi.

Handelsblatt (2011) 'Griechenland-Pleite wäre "Brandbeschleuniger"', 12 September, available at http://www.handelsblatt.com/politik/deutschland/kritik-an-roesler-griechenland-pleite-waere-brandbeschleuniger/4602498.html (accessed 1 April 2014).

Hasselbach, C. (2012) 'Kommission stellt Pläne für Bankenunion vor', *Deutsche Welle 11* Se[tember 2012, available at http://www.dw.de/kommission-stellt-pl%C3%A4ne-f%C3%BCr-bankenunion-vor/a-16232356 (accessed 1 April 2014).

Hobolt, S.B. and Wratil, C. (2015) 'Public opinion and the crisis: the dynamics of support for the euro', *Journal of European Public Policy*, doi: 10.1080/13501763.2014.994022.

Hodson, D. (2013) 'The little engine that wouldn't: supranational entrepreneurship and the Barroso Commission', *Journal of European Integration* 35(3): 301–14.

Hoffmann, S. (1966) 'Obstinate or obsolete: the fate of the nation state and the core of Western Europe', *Daedalus* 95(3): 862–915.

Ioannou, D., Leblond, P. and Niemann, A. (2015) 'European integration and the crisis: practice and theory', *Journal of European Public Policy*, doi: 10.1080/13501763. 2014.994979.

Jachtenfuchs, M. (1997) 'Conceptualizing European governance', in K.E. Jorgensen (ed.), *Reflective Approaches to European Governance*, Basingstoke: Macmillan, pp. 39–50.

Jäger, K. (2013) 'Sources of Franco–German corporate support for the euro', *European Union Politics* 14(1): 115–39.

Knedelhans, M. (2014) 'The influence of non-governmental interest groups on the European sovereign debt crisis management', masters thesis, University of Mainz.

Koch, L. (2013) 'Revenge of neo-functionalism?', masters thesis, University of Mainz.

Le Monde (2012) 'François Hollande: »L'Europe ne peut plus être en retard«', 17 October.

Leuffen, D., Rittberger, B. and Schimmelfennig, F. (2013) *Differentiated Integration*, Houndmills : Palgrave Macmillan.

Lindberg, L. (1963) *The Political Dynamics of European Integration*, Stanford, CA: Stanford University Press.

Lindberg, L. and Scheingold, S. (1970) *Europe's would-be Polity*, Englewood Cliffs. NJ: Prentice Hall.

Ludlow, P. (2010) 'In the last resort. the European Council and the euro crisis', *Briefing Note 7/8*, Eurocomment.

Ludlow, P. (2013) 'Eurocomment: economic policy, EMU and enlargement', The European Council of 27–8 June 2013, *Preliminary Evaluation 2013/4*.

Mandate (2012) 'EU unions' No to EU stability treaty', 1 February, available at http://www.mandate.ie/news/Global/470/eu-unions-no-to-eu-stability-treaty.aspx (accessed 1 April 2014).

Menz, G. and Smith, M. (2013) 'Kicking the can down the road to more Europe?', *Journal of European Integration* 35(3): 195–206.

Merkel, A. (2012) 'Regierungserklärung von Bundeskanzlerin Merkel zu Finanzhilfen für Griechenland', 27 February, available at http://www.bundesregierung.de/Content/DE/Regierungserklaerung/2012/2012-02-27-merkel.html (accessed 1 April 2014).

Merler, S. (2014) 'Banking union and beyond', Brussels Think Tank Dialogue, available at http://www.bruegel.org/publications/publication-detail/publication/808-banking-union-and-beyond-discussion-papers-for-brussels-think-tank-dialogue/ (accessed 1 April 2014).

Niemann, A. (2006) *Explaining Decisions in the European Union*, Cambridge: Cambridge University Press.

Niemann, A. and Schmitter, P. (2009) 'Neofunctionalism', in A. Wiener and T. Diez (eds), *European Integration Theory*, Oxford: Oxford University Press, pp. 45–66.

Norton, L. (2011) 'China and the euro: connected concerns', Barron's 10 December, available at http://online.barrons.com/article/SB50001424052748704221204577080512017378308.html#articleTabs_article%3D1 (accessed 1 April 2014).

Nye, J. (1970) 'Comparing common markets: a revised neo-functionalist model', *International Organization* 24: 796–835.

Overbeek, H. (2012) 'Sovereign debt crisis in euroland', *The International Spectator* 47(1): 30–48.

Panico, C. and Purificato, F. (2012) 'The role of institutional and political factors in the European debt crisis', *Working Paper Series No.280*, Amherst: Political Economy Research Institute.

Rajoy, M. (2012) 'Brief an Kommissionspräsident Barroso und Ratspräsident Van Rompuy', available at http://www.cnbc.com/id/47794623/Europe039s_039Worst_Crisis039_Requires_Fiscal_Union_Spain (accessed 1 April 2014).

Schimmelfennig, F. (2012) 'Zwischen Neo- und Postfunktionalismus: Die Integrationstheorien und die Eurokrise', *Politische Vierteljahresschrift* 53(4): 394–413.

Schmidt, S. (2012) *Das Gesetz der Krise*, Munich: Droemer Verlag.

Schmieding, H. (2012) 'Tough love: the true nature of the eurozone crisis', *Business Economics* 47(3): 177–89.

Schmitter, P. (1971) 'A revised theory of regional integration', in L. Lindberg and S. Scheingold (eds), Regional Integration: Theory and Research, Cambridge, MA: Harvard University Press, pp. 232–64.

Schoenmaker, D. (2011) "The financial trilemma", *Economics Letters* 111: 57–9.

Sinn, H. and Wollmershäuser, T. (2012) 'Target loans, current account balances and capital flows: the ECB's rescue facility', *International Tax and Public Finance* 19: 468–508.

Spiegel Online (2011) 'The end of old Europe', 12 December, available at http://www.spiegel.de/international/europe/the-end-of-old-europe-why-merkel-s-triumph-will-come-at-a-high-price-a-803097.html (accessed 1 April 2014).

Spiegel Online (2012) 'Krise in Spanien (Interview mit Joaquín Almunia)', 3 October, available at http://www.spiegel.de/wirtschaft/soziales/eu-kommissar-almunia-zur-spanien-krise-machen-was-europa-rettet-a-859042.html (accessed 1 April 2014).

Torres, F. (2013) 'The EMU's legitimacy and the ECB as a strategic political player in the crisis context', *Journal of European Integration* 35(3): 287–300.

Tranholm-Mikkelsen, J. (1991) 'Neo-functionalism: obstinate or obsolete?', *Millenium* 20(1): 1–22.

Traynor, I. (2012) 'ECB introduces unlimited bond-buying in boldest attempt yet to end euro crisis', *The Guardian*, 06 September 2012.

Van Rompuy, H., Barroso, J.M., Juncker, C. and Draghi, M. (2012) 'Auf dem Weg zu einer echten Wirtschafts- und Währungsunion', available at http://www.consilium.europa.eu/uedocs/cms_data/docs/pressdata/de/ec/134206.pdf (accessed 1 April 2014).

Van Scherpenberg, J. (2012) 'Währungsfragen sind Machtfragen', *Zeitschrift für Außen- und Sicherheitspolitik* 5(3): 367–77.

Vilpišauskas, R. (2013) 'Eurozone crisis and European integration?', *Journal of European Integration* 35(3): 361–73.

Wiener, A. and Diez, T. (2009) 'Taking stock of integration theory', in A. Wiener and T. Diez (eds), *European Integration Theory*, Oxford: Oxford University Press, pp. 241–52.

Yiangou, J. O'Keeffe, M. and Glöckler, G. (2013) 'Tough love': how the ECB's monetary financing prohibition pushes deeper euro area integration', *Journal of European Integration* 35(3): 223–37.

A historical institutionalist explanation of the EU's responses to the euro area financial crisis

Amy Verdun

ABSTRACT How can we understand the European Union's responses to the euro area financial crisis? This contribution examines this question through a historical institutionalist (HI) lens. First it reviews the design of existing institutions. With the help of HI it examines what challenges the institutional design posed on the European Union (EU) when the crisis hit. Next, the responses to the crisis by member state leaders and by EU-level actors are reviewed. An analysis is made of selected new EU institutions created to address the crisis: the European Financial Stability Facility; the European Stability Mechanism; the Six-Pack and Two-Pack; the European Semester; and the Fiscal Compact. Four ideal types – 'displacement', 'layering', 'drift' and 'conversion' – are examined and found not to fit well. In some cases institutions were 'layered' on top of existing institutions. Perhaps an amendment could be made by offering the ideal type 'copying' in those cases where new institutions that borrow from earlier institutions. Although no complex problem can be truly understood by looking at it through one single theoretical lens, this contribution argues that a large of part of the problems that emerged, and the solutions adopted, can be understood by examining it through an HI lens.

INTRODUCTION

The economic and financial crisis hit the European Union (EU) in 2007–8, with banks collapsing, the money markets drying up and severe drops in the stock exchanges throughout Europe and other advanced economies (Sorkin 2009). At this time the EU as a whole collaborated with others in the context of the G20. At the level of the EU it was difficult initially to deal with the immediate crises of the day, as individual member states were uncertain what steps had to be taken at that level, given the speed of the unfolding crisis, the limited budget of the EU and the lack of response mechanisms catering to this kind of crisis (Buti and Carnot 2012).

As the sovereign debt crisis worsened during 2010–12 the question was once again how to deal with it. The EU was heavily criticized during this time;

support for the EU observed a downward trend throughout the entire period since the start of financial crisis and through 2012 (Eurobarometer 2011: 34; Eurobarometer 2012: 85). Also, at the level of member states, support was waning (Armingeon and Ceka [2014]; Roth *et al.* [2011]; although Hobolt and Wratil [2015] show that support for the euro inside the euro area remained stable). Sitting national governments were not spared: in eight countries governments fell or incumbents were not re-elected in national elections (Verdun 2013a).

With such economic and political pressures, the EU member states could have chosen to support, or not, EU member states in need. If so, they could have opted to create institutions within or outside the EU framework to assist these member states in need. Furthermore, they could have decided to create new institutions or alter existing ones to deal with the crisis. Economists from the United States (US) and elsewhere uttered serious criticisms of the design of Europe's Economic and Monetary Union (EMU) and the EU as a whole (De Grauwe 2011, 2012; De Grauwe and Ji 2012; Eichengreen 2012a, 2012b; Feldstein 2012; Krugman 2011; 2012; Sargent 2011). Eventually, in response to the crises, the EU created some remarkable new institutions such as the European Financial Stability Facility (EFSF) – later the European Stability Mechanism (ESM) – the Six-Pack, the Two-Pack, the European Semester and the Fiscal Compact (see Ioannou *et al.* [2015]).

With all options open, and the EU criticized, the question asked in this contribution is how can we explain that the EU responses to the euro area (EA) financial crisis were to create institutions that were so similar to the typical EU institutional structures? This study adopts a historical institutionalist (HI) approach to answer this question. It shows how the existence of earlier institutional structures is used to come up with new institutional structures.

The structure of this contribution is the following. The next section reviews the literature on HI and the origins of the EA financial crisis. The third section reviews the EU institutional design, and the fourth offers an overview of the crises and the responses by the member states and the EU, including an overview of four newly created institutions set up to respond to the crisis. The final section concludes.

HISTORICAL INSTITUTIONALISM AND THE ORIGINS OF THE EURO AREA FINANCIAL CRISIS

EMU has long been discussed in the literature as an example of a policy area that at once has features of far-reaching integration yet with various flaws (e.g., Buiter [1999]; De Grauwe [2006a, 2006b]), sometimes referred to as an 'Asymmetrical EMU' (Verdun 1996). There is a vast literature that examines the path to EMU and the success and failure of the EU to design a system that would be sturdy in the face of difficulty.[1]

An earlier HI analysis of the history of EMU (Verdun 2007) discussed seven important crossroads from the Treaty of Rome to the post-EMU difficulties of implementing the Stability and Growth Pact (SGP). That analysis demonstrated that by looking at a few key points, one is better able to examine the concept of EMU, the actors pushing for it, the institutional context, the role of exogenous shocks and how they affected monetary integration. One of its main findings was that there was a remarkable continuity in the concept of EMU throughout the decades: a transfer of sovereignty over monetary policy to the EU level, but regarding fiscal policy a reliance on rules (EU treaty and regulations) and leaving responsibility with the member states – even though initially, in the 1960s and 1970s, it was thought that EMU would be accompanied by deeper economic (or fiscal) integration (Verdun 2007: 208). In terms of the actors that have been influential, the findings suggest that although the European Commission has been a key player, support had been needed from heads of states or governments. The institutional context, but also the occurrence of any exogenous shocks, played an important role in the pre-crisis period. The analysis concluded that member states' governments were unwilling to transfer sovereignty over fiscal policies to the EU level without there being a felt need (e.g., owing to a major shock). Yet it was assumed there would be some kind of crossroads, some kind of upset, that would force the matter back onto the agenda so that member state governments would have to commit there and then, under major pressure, to consider deeper integration (Verdun 2007: 209).

An HI analysis of the EU responses to the EA financial crisis is attractive because of the nature of the *problématique* that is being studied. Many saw the crisis as an existential crisis: one or more countries could find themselves having to leave the EA, with a potential domino effect in its wake, implying that the EA was at risk of falling apart (Eichengreen 2012b). The question that lay before member state governments and EU institutions was what to do next. What kind of institutional response would be given? Would there be a leap in integration or more gradual institutional change? If the latter, what kind of gradual change? Could we see more 'displacement', 'layering', 'drift' or 'conversion' of institutional structures (Mahoney and Thelen 2010: 15–16; Streeck and Thelen 2005; Thelen 2009)?[2] Could this period be judged as a 'critical juncture' as other HI scholars might do (Capoccia and Kelemen 2007)? Would we be able to understand the chosen institutional structure better by using that analytical tool?

HI is an approach that seeks to understand how political struggles are mediated by the setting in which they take place (Hall and Taylor 1998; Hay and Wincott 1998; Meunier and McNamara 2007: 4; *cf.* Steinmo *et al.* 1992; Thelen 1999; Thelen and Steinmo 1992). Institutions in this context could be either formal (EU institutional structures such as the Council of the EU or formal rules such as the SGP) or informal (norms, practices and unwritten rules), although HI scholars typically focus on formal institutions. Scholars in this tradition study through 'empirical investigation' whether 'institutional structures affect political strategies, outcomes and preferences' (Steinmo 2008: 125). Also, the EU responses to the crisis lend themselves to be examined through a lens that takes into consideration 'the context of rule structures that are themselves human creations ... and ... [examine them] sequentially' (Sanders 2009: 39). In the HI tradition various scholars also draw on the concept of critical junctures (Capoccia and Kelemen 2007; Collier and Collier 1991; Lipset and Rokkan 1967): periods in which major transitions take place. These can be gradual or more rapid. A critical juncture is a period in which there is a transition and there are various alternative options from which to choose. The institutional structure chosen affects the future for considerable time to come. Capoccia and Kelemen (2007: 348) define critical junctures as 'relatively short periods of time during which there is a substantially heightened probability that agents' choices will affect the outcome of interest'. It seems reasonable to think that the EA financial crisis is a good candidate to be considered a critical juncture as is discussed in more detail below.

Finally, this analysis finds that the notion of path dependence (Peters *et al.* 2005; Pierson 1996, 2000) is instrumental for an understanding of the EU response to the EA financial crisis. The only other HI analyses of the crisis that I am aware of is by Gocaj and Meunier (2013), who argue that one can understand the creation of the EFSF and ESM through this lens, and Gabriel Glöckler, Marion Salines and Zbigniew Truchlewski who argue that change in the governance of EMU happened through layering and redirection.

EU INSTITUTIONAL DESIGN

The earlier literature on the EU's institutional structure, going into the financial crisis, suggested that EMU was incomplete and was lacking an adequate supranational structure to complement the role of the European Central Bank (ECB). The latter was an institution at the EU level that was to deal with monetary policy. In nation states, including in federal states, such a body is flanked by an authority that taxes and spends. In federal states such taxing and spending bodies indeed exist at different levels (federal and the provincial or state level). In the EU, however, there is only a set of rules and regulations (rather than another supranational institution) that aim at keeping budgetary deficits and public debts of member states below agreed ceilings (Verdun 2013c). Yet many observers have repeatedly warned that such a loose institutional structure could well prove too weak for the EMU architecture to be successful (Buiter 1999; Eichengreen 2012a). Thus, various authors thought that there would come a day when the EU would be put to the test and that this structure would prove too weak. In the minds of many at that point it would mean that EMU might either disintegrate or lead to a need to integrate further to deal with the incomplete design (De Grauwe 2006a; 2006b; *Der Spiegel* 2011b; Verdun 1996; 2000).

When the financial crisis first took Europe in its grip, it took the form of the collapse of various banks and money markets drying up. The most remarkable action taken in this early period was by the ECB, which made funds available to European banks in August 2007, when it was among the first of the central banks of the advanced economies to take such a bold step (Drudi *et al.*

2012). Following the collapse of Lehman Brothers (*The Economist* 2008), numerous European countries with large financial sectors were first impacted. The fear was that depositors would withdraw funds from banks, with runs on the banks in the worst-case scenario. Rather than having the EU come up with a joint response to this immediate crisis, various EU member states ended up unilaterally (nationally) securing deposits up to an amount of €100,000. It would take until 2009 before the EU had actually revised its own deposit insurance to this same minimum amount (Engineer *et al.* 2013).

The crisis took the EU by surprise and it spent most of the initial period, in autumn 2008, reflecting on whether the crisis was going to be a short-term one that would have only modest impact, or whether the it was foreshadowing something bigger. The EU responded with haphazard decisions that were often announced and then followed soon by other announcements to deal with the immediate aftermath (Buti and Carnot 2012). National governments' officials were surprised that the crisis got hold of the EU so fast and that there was so little that individual member state governments could do offset its impact. It made clear that there was a need for EU level response (Verdun 2013a) and that small and large member states as well as core and periphery countries within and outside the EA were affected differently by the crisis (Verdun 2013b).

The crisis further affected the EU through the onset of an economic recession (*The Economist*, 2011). Production went down and increasingly the effect of the financial crisis became an economic crunch. Given that the EU does not have a large budget (about 1 per cent of EU gross domestic product [GDP]), any decision to stimulate the economy by spending money would have to use member state funds (rather than the small EU budget). Again, in the first instance, member states responded individually rather than orchestrating a major co-ordinated EU response. At this point, however, the EU was not yet feeling the pressure on the EA as such. Rather, turbulence was observed in financial markets (stock exchange, money markets), which soon led to a contraction of GDP in most EU member states.

Although the EU had difficulties responding in a speedy fashion to acute crises in the banking sector, the EU did push ahead with a number of other initiatives. For instance, the Commission President Barroso mandated a group to look into the future of European financial regulation and supervision which resulted in the De Larosière Report (of 25 February 2009) that was a direct response to the crisis and suggested various steps of how to improve the institutional structure of the EU in the area of financial regulation and supervision, including a regulatory framework for crisis management in the EU. Also, in September 2009 the Commission put forward proposals to replace the EU's supervisory institutional structure with a so-called European system of financial supervisors (European Commission 2009a).

By autumn 2009, the next problem that hit the EU was the Greek government announcement that its budgetary deficit was much higher than previously declared. Remarkably, the immediate response was very limited (nothing happened for the first week or so). But soon after, various observers started to reflect on what the implications might be. Seeing that the Greek government had very clearly and massively overshot the SGP limits, the European Commission soon expressed its concern (European Commission 2009b). In various steps, credit agencies incorporated this information into their thinking, which led to a reduction in the value of Greek government bonds. By April 2010 rating agencies had downgraded Greek debt to 'junk' status (Eijffinger 2012). All through the autumn of 2009 and spring 2010 the EU and its member states were trying to find the best response to this situation. It was a difficult time to come to a joint collective EU decision, as financial markets were wreaking havoc with the Greek financial situation.

Throughout the first four months of 2010, there was major speculation as to whether the EU should let Greece default on its own and thereby risk a messy exist from the EA (and a chance of contagion) or offer support so that the problems could be contained (see Gros and Mayer [2010]). The concern that many member state leaders had was that Greece had violated EU rules on budgetary deficits and thus whether, and if so how, EU level support was warranted. In the end it became clear that the main critical juncture had been the creation of EMU. Letting Greece go bankrupt would pose a risk of contagion and thus could possibly put the entire EMU edifice under pressure. Therefore the option became to create some kind of support system.

By May 2010 the EU offered its first major co-ordinated response to the crisis, by providing Greece access to bailout funds: the so-called 'Troika' of the European Commission, the ECB and the International Monetary Fund (IMF), made €110 billion available to assist Greece (through an *ad hoc* arrangement referred to as the Greek Loan Facility). Yet, the crisis was bad: after Greece was provided with the bailout package the situation would still get worse before it would get better. In fact, a second Greek bailout was necessary in spring 2012 (see Ardagna and Caselli [2012]) provided by the EFSF, operational since August 2010. This was only just the beginning of the support that the EU needed to give member states in need; the EU faced many more moments of intense crisis and a need to offer a response (see Ioannou *et al.* [2015]).

How can we understand this response from an HI perspective? From the toolkit of HI we can learn how previous institutional structures affect the possible solutions that can be found to current problems. In this case, one noteworthy starting point is that it was well known that the institutional design of the EU was deficient. First, its actual co-ordination role was limited, as it had no budget and no real mechanism to offer quick or substantial response to a crisis. Second, the EU relies on the Council of the EU and on the European Council for action. Third, in terms of EMU the EU is deficient because it has a centralized monetary body, but no such body on the fiscal and budgetary side. What is remarkable is that the earlier HI analysis of economic and monetary integration in the EU completed just before the crisis (Verdun 2007) pointed to the likelihood that EMU institutional design was deficient and that if a crisis occurred the EU would likely have to address this incomplete institutional structure. When institutions were created or amended they looked to previous

EU institutions and structures for follow up, which is what HI would suggest. These institutions did not, however, end up being the major ones that had been foretold; that is, the EU did not opt for transferring sovereignty to a new supranational fiscal authority, even if there was 'some' more sovereignty transferred. Also it did not adopt the idea to issue Eurobonds. Mahoney and Thelen (2010: 16–18) and others identify circumstances under which one might expect to observe some of these ideal types of institutional change. If the political context is characterized by more veto points (as was the case here), one could possibly expect either 'layering' (institutional rules be placed on top of earlier institutional structures) or rather end up being more of a 'drift' away from the original institutional structure. The former can be expected when the targeted institution can be characterized as having not so much discretion; with more discretion one could expect the latter.

INSTITUTIONAL RESPONSES

In this section we examine how the EU responses to the euro debt crisis are path dependently connected to earlier arrangements and look at whether, and if so which, of the four ideal types – 'displacement', 'layering', 'drift' and 'conversion' – best describe the process of institutional change. Let us now turn to four institutional decisions made by the EU and examine what was going on in each of those cases: the EFSF; the ESM; the European Semester; and the Fiscal Compact. These four cases were chosen because those were the ones that were created as an immediate response to the sovereign debt crisis. Others were considered and either dismissed or their final agreement delayed. For instance, there was a strong call for the issuing of Eurobonds and a banking union. The former did not receive the support from all member states – in particular Germany and the Netherlands did not support (*Der Spiegel* 2011a). The latter was agreed to, in principle, in June 2012, but the details would take time to sort out and were only finalized very recently (European Commission 2014; Ioannou *et al.* 2015; Schure 2013).[3] My purpose here is to identify how we can understand the creation of the institutional structures that came into being at the height of the crisis, rather than the ones that took longer to materialize and only really became accepted after the worst of the crisis was over. (See the online appendix [online supplemental material] for an overview of the institutional structures that were created, how they relate to earlier decisions and who were the main stakeholders.)

European Financial Stability Facility

The EFSF is an institutional structure that came into being following the Council of the EU of Economic and Financial Affairs, on 9 May 2010.[4] The goal of the EFSF was to assist the member states that are unable to refinance their public debt. The Greek Loan Facility (GLF), set up on 2 May 2010, served as a model for the EFSF. An total of €80 million in bilateral loans was pledged from 14 member states of the EA and an additional €30 million from the IMF.[5] The Commission acted as co-ordinator and worked together with the IMF and the ECB. Because of concerns for moral hazard (i.e., if support was too easily forthcoming, it might encourage other member states to flout the rules), various restructuring plans were agreed to in return for the loans to Greece. The GLF offered *ad hoc* support and was set up outside of regular EU treaty. The member states had modelled it on how the IMF offers loans to members in times of crisis. Seeing that it was a crisis at the heart of the euro, the EA member states that participated offered more loans than the IMF. These EA loans were co-ordinated by the Commission. This arrangement resembles the Schengen agreement and the Bologna Process in Higher Education, in that the European Commission took on a co-ordination role but the arrangement was still outside the EU Treaty.

In a nutshell, the EFSF is a special purpose vehicle that serves as a temporary rescue mechanism. The main stakeholders of the EFSF are the member states of the EA countries. Its mandate is to safeguard financial stability in the EU by providing financial assistance to EA member states. Its lending capacity is €440 billion. Support from the EFSF does not come without strings attached. Rather, it is offered within the framework of a macroeconomic adjustment programme. Although it is a vehicle of the EA member states, an EU institution – the European Investment Bank (EIB) – first managed the EFSF's loans, but it is now the ESM (see below) that manages its activities. In fact, the EFSF would only provide temporary support (three years); since 1 July 2013 it no longer offers new financing programmes, but it still continues the ongoing programmes for Greece, Portugal and Ireland.

How is the EFSF related to earlier EU institutions? To some extent, the EFSF is a totally new institutional structure, as it is a body that provides loans in case of crisis. There is no other body that resembles it other than perhaps the EIB, which offers financing for projects in EU member states, not loans to EA member states.[6] Drawing a parallel between the EFSF and the European Monetary Institute (EMI) – the predecessor of the ECB – might be more fruitful. The EMI was an institution whose role was to prepare the ECB's creation. Just as with the EMI, the EFSF was a temporary body (replaced by the ESM) that was created with EMU in mind. There are two important differences, however, between the EMI and the EFSF. First, the EFSF was set up in a hasty fashion, and when it was created it was not yet known that there would be a permanent structure to follow. Second, the EMI was part of the Maastricht Treaty, whereas the EFSF was created as an intergovernmental treaty – not unlike another agreement: the Schengen Agreement. The latter was an arrangement among a select number of EU member states and eventually it got incorporated into the EU Treaty, but is still not applicable to all member states. Thus, one reason why this structure was chosen for the EFSF was expediency – something had to happen fast. To change the existing EU treaties would take more time and was deemed politically unfeasible at that precise time. Another reason was that it was only geared to EU member states in the EA.

As such, it would not even have to address the non-euro countries, in the short run. Thus, we could see some kind of path dependence in this way. The existing ways to create new institutions shaped the options on the table.

In terms of the four ideal types, the EFSF does not fully fit the four ideal types of Streeck and Thelen (2005) and Mahoney and Thelen (2010). The reason seems to be that this particular institution is new in its content but similar to other institutions in how it is set up, thereby having copied from other institutions without having displaced, layered or drifted from an existing institution or converted one. Perhaps the best way to use the logic of these earlier HI scholars is to add a new category, that of 'copying'. Just as there is a fifth category 'exhaustion' (Streeck and Thelen 2005: 29) for institutions in decline, there may be the need for a category for institutions that are emerging. Here we see the EFSF's institutional structure copied somewhat from the EIB, including choosing to headquarter the EFSF in Luxembourg. And just as the EMI/ECB were institutions geared towards EMU, here too one could create an institution to deal with EA financial problems. Finally, the EFSF copied from the Schengen agreement the idea to have a legal structure (intergovernmental treaty) outside the EU treaty rather than wait until all member states accepted this institution as part of the EU treaty (which would have been impossible to amend at the time).

European Stability Mechanism

The ESM is the permanent institutional structure that replaced the EFSF (for details on the ESM's creation, see Ioannou *et al.* [2015]). In a nutshell, the ESM is also a special purpose vehicle whose main shareholders are the member states of the EA countries and whose mandate is, like the EFSF, to safeguard financial stability in the EU by providing financial assistance to EA member states. Its lending capacity initially was €500 billion, but in 2012 the lending ceiling of the ESM/EFSF was increased to €700 billion (Council of the EU n.d.). Just as with the EFSF, support from the ESM is offered only within the framework of a macroeconomic adjustment programme. The ESM is also permitted to recapitalize banks directly in connection with the banking union.

How is the ESM related to earlier EU institutions? As mentioned, the ESM is an institutional structure that is very similar to the EFSF. The earlier temporary body became a 'try-out' institution that, as mentioned above, can be seen as being somewhat similar to the EMI in a number of ways: it was temporary and directed only to EA countries. In terms of its management, the ESM follows the EFSF, but has taken over the management of the EFSF's loans and other financial instruments from the EIB. Again, the ESM was created as an intergovernmental treaty. As is the case with Schengen, it is anticipated that at some point in the future the ESM may well be incorporated into the EU treaty. Gocaj and Meunier (2013: 249) demonstrate that the ESM came about faster than many originally anticipated, mainly because of the need to have a timely response to the fact that the EFSF was seen as insufficiently capitalized and given the continuous difficulties in financial markets. They also stress that the ESM was easier to create than any other structure because the EFSF had already been ratified in all member states. Markets would be familiar with it; and the roles of other institutions (Commission and ECB) *vis-à-vis* the EFSF were already known and thus the relations with the ESM would be similar (Gocaj and Meunier, 2013: 249). Deeg and Posner (2015) also stress the great potential of an HI approach in analysing developments in European financial integration as do Salines *et al.* (2012).

In terms of the four ideal types, this second institution, the ESM, fits a little better, but not perfectly, the four ideal types. The ESM is clearly built to replace the EFSF, which still exists; however, since 2013 it no longer issues new loans. This relationship between the two can be seen to some extent as displacement: the ESM taking over as permanent institution after the EFSF's short-term oper-ations. But 'replacement' would have been a better ideal type. The ideal type 'layering' may perhaps fit better than the ideal type 'displacement'. The reason is that the ESM to some extent is layered on the EFSF, but not exactly the way Thelen and co-authors intend: there is no 'eating at the core' or 'siphoning off support'; it was fully intentional and planned (Streeck and Thelen 2005: 31). Again, 'copying' would perhaps also fit (also as per the above analysis of the legal structure chosen for the ESM).

The Six-Pack and the Two-Pack

As mentioned in the introduction to this collection (Ioannou *et al.* 2015), the Six-Pack aimed to amend and reinforce the earlier SGP (Heipertz and Verdun 2010). This was done in 2011 with the adoption of five regulations and one directive, which entered into force in December 2011 (European Com-mission 2011). The Six-Pack that applies to all EU member states covers fiscal and macroeconomic surveillance. It makes the debt criterion more important than before, when the SGP focused more on the deficit criterion. It has some specific rules for EA members, especially insofar as sanctions are concerned. For instance, it introduces reverse qualified majority vote (rQMV) when recom-mending sanctions (a rQMV is needed in the Council to oppose sanctions if recommended by the Commission), which makes it easier to impose sanctions on member states than previously, when such a recommendation had to be passed in the Council by qualified majority vote. Governance of EU budgetary and fiscal policy also now follows the European Semester, which has as its goal to co-ordinate economic policy. The European Semester is a procedure that starts at the beginning of a given year and proceeds in the following way: the European Commission adopts the Annual Growth Survey; EU heads of state and government provide policy orientations; member states submit their econ-omic plans. The next step is for the Commission to make detailed analyses of member states' economic programmes and to offer recommendations about the steps to take during the subsequent year to year-and-a-half. These rec-ommendations are first discussed by the Council and eventually endorsed by the European Council. The Council adopts the final formal country-specific recommendations. In the second half of the year member states implement their plans ('national semester'). This elaborate process seeks to be a more streamlined and disciplined way to ensure economic policy co-ordination than the arrangement under the previous SGP rules.

In 2013 a so-called 'Two-Pack' of regulations was introduced (European Commission 2013; Ioannou *et al.* 2015). It built on the Six-Pack by introducing additional surveillance and monitoring procedures; however, these are directed to EA member states only. The Two-Pack stipulates that the Commission will examine and give an opinion on the member state's draft budget by 30 November and will ask for revisions if these budgets do not comply with the SGP. This timing enables it to act in between two 'European Semesters'.

The reasons why the Six-Pack and later the Two-Pack were put together was that member states' leaders and EU level officials concluded from experience of the EA financial crisis that having solid national budgetary and fiscal policies should be seen as a matter of common concern. If one member state would be pursuing excessive deficits or continuously increasing its public debt, the thinking was, it might pose costs on the other member states through concerns displayed in financial markets. Not all were convinced that fiscal profligacy was the only reason for the EA financial crisis; it was nevertheless agreed that the earlier fiscal targets made sense and had to be reinforced. The institutional structure chosen for this new set of rules was based on the logic and general mode of the SGP's operation, but made it much stricter in terms of procedures.

In terms of the four ideal types, the Six-Pack (including the European Semester) and the two-pack fit nicely with one of the four ideal types. They are 'layered' on top of the provisions in the Treaty and additional secondary legislation that made up the earlier SGP.

Finally, contrary to the EFSF and the ESM, which were based on an intergovernmental treaty (outside the existing EU treaties), the Six-Pack and Two-Pack have been approved using the normal procedures in place to create/amend EU regulations and directives. It was possible to use these normal procedures because these rules revised and updated existing regulations and directives. It did not require a new treaty or treaty change because it concerned secondary legislation. The part that did require treaty change was put in the Fiscal Compact, to which we now turn.

Fiscal Compact

The Fiscal Compact or 'fiscal stability treaty' (formally the 'Treaty on Stability, Co-ordination and Governance in the Economic and Monetary Union') is an intergovernmental treaty[7] that flanks the Six-Pack and Two-Pack (for details, see Ioannou *et al.* [2015]; and Council of the EU [2012]). Given the lack of support of all member states, and the difficulty of changing the current EU treaty for some fiscal governance measures, it was decided to create an international treaty. But as is the case with the ESM, there are provisions that suggest that this treaty may in the future become integrated into the EU treaty (and in fact the Two-Pack has already integrated some of the elements of the Fiscal Compact, thereby adding to the EU *acquis communautaire*). An innovation of this treaty was that it would enter into force by 1 January 2013 provided that 12 member states had ratified the treaty. It would only be applicable to those who had ratified it (European Parliament 2013). Others would join as they completed their national ratification process. This innovation would ensure that no single member state could block this treaty from entering into force – something that has been hanging over the EU when founding treaties are revised and need the signature and ratification of all member states before they can enter into force. It meant that those member states willing to participate could create EU-like institutions, work with them for some time, and then eventually add them to the EU Treaty at some point in the future. Also this treaty would be open to other EU members. It was important, because it seems that the EU built new institutions on top of existing institutions as well as used information about how institutions could be amended to create intergovernmental treaties. The new institutions were created to circumvent the normal type amendment that is customary in the EU, because it was improbable that it would be approved by all member states (read: the UK would not agree) and without unanimity the treaty could not be amended. Yet, the institutions were carefully built on earlier experiences so that they could be operational first temporarily, then after a few years permanent institution could be inaugurated.

In terms of the four ideal types, this fourth institution, the Fiscal Compact, also fits the ideal types with difficulty. In a sense, it is an addition to the EU treaties because it is 'layered' onto existing provisions to some extent; however, legally it is totally separate. Just as with the EFSF/ESM, the intention is that this legal structure will eventually be inserted into a future revised EU Treaty text. The Fiscal Compact was created as a standalone treaty to ensure it could be created in a timely fashion and that no veto players could obstruct the new institutional design. Again, 'copying', offered above as a separate ideal type when a new institution is created, might be a better way to describe these new institutions.

CONCLUSION: LESSONS FROM HISTORICAL INSTITUTIONALISM

This contribution started off asking the question of how we can we understand the EU's responses to the EA financial crisis. By examining this question through the theoretical lens of historical institutionalism I sought to highlight the path that the EU took. I first examined the design of institutions and stressed that the asymmetric architecture of the design of EMU posed challenges on the EU when the crisis hit. On the one hand, there were insufficient checks and balances for member states to consider their national budgetary deficits and public debts as a matter of common concern. On the other hand, there did not exist an EU-level (supranational) tax and spending body with sufficient resources to assist a member state in need. The nature of the crisis meant that the responses to crisis in the first instance were national: member state leaders took unilateral decisions to solve the immediate problems of the day. It took some time for solutions to be offered by institutions at the EU level, as the EU structures are less suitable for speedy decisions. Furthermore, national institutions have 'deeper pockets' than does the EU. Finally, when EU solutions were created it meant having to co-ordinate many EU member states, which is more difficult because there is not an executive power that can decide on behalf of the EU as a whole. Hence the need to convince all member states.

As mentioned above, with the support for the EU on the decline, this crisis put the EU to the test: would the EU be willing to step up to the plate and create institutions and rules that would deepen integration, or would it decide to allow, for instance, Greece to leave the EA and risk contagion of that decision which could ultimately mean that the EA as we know it would come to an end (or become much smaller in size)? In the end the EU member states chose to find solutions that were supportive of trying to rescue the EA, and for that they needed to enhance existing, as well as develop new, institutional structures.

In many instances historical institutionalist approaches focus on critical junctures (Capoccia and Kelemen 2007; Collier and Collier 1991). One could argue that the decision to create EMU was such a critical juncture. This decision constrained member states when making the next decisions about macroeconomic and monetary policy-making in the EA and the EU at large. In a way, a next critical juncture was the sovereign debt crisis: the EU member states were sufficiently willing to continue to support EMU that it shaped what they thought were acceptable solutions to deal with the crisis. It reconfirmed they were unwilling to let EMU unravel. The height of the EA financial crisis presented a critical juncture: decision-makers had a fairly narrow window (a few years) in which they could make decisions that were different from the day-to-day decisions owing to the circumstances of the crisis. Usually when the critical juncture closes the institutional structure then in place will likely continue for a longer time afterwards.

This contribution examined a selection of institutions that were created in the wake of the onset of the euro debt crisis: the EFSF; the ESM; the Six-Pack and Two-Pack; and the Fiscal Compact. The analysis shows how these institutions were built on previous institutions or were inspired by structures that had been created before. Where possible, EU legislation was used to create new rules. Where that was not possible, and seeing that it was not likely that all member states would support EU treaty change, new intergovernmental treaties were created to ensure that a legal basis was found for these institutions, even if not immediately within the context of the EU treaty. Those that were chosen were those that were fairly easy to agree. Thus, they built on the provisions that came before and have been created in such a way that in the future they may well become incorporated within the EU treaties (much like the Schengen provisions). An HI approach offers us a lens to see how this process took place and why institutions took on the form they did. We saw how temporary arrangements were made that were subsequently firmed up in permanent institutional structures (EFSF and ESM). We also saw how the Six-Pack, Two-Pack and the Fiscal Compact were ways to strengthen the earlier deficient SGP. We sought to borrow the terminology of Streeck and Thelen (2005), Thelen (2009) and Mahoney and Thelen (2010) to see if those ideal types could describe fully the institutional change observed. We noticed that in those cases where fully new institutions were created (EFSF and Fiscal Compact) they were inspired by the institutional structures of the past. However, the four ideal types did not fit well. Perhaps an amendment could be made by offering the ideal type 'copying' in those cases where new institutions are created by borrowing in some way from earlier institutions. In the other cases we did find that institutions were 'layered' on top of existing institutions.

Although no complex problem can be truly understood by looking at it through one single theoretical lens, this contribution has argued that a large of part of the problems that emerged, and the solutions adopted, in the context of the EA financial crisis can be understood by examining it through a historical institutionalist lens.

Biographical note: Amy Verdun is professor of political science and Jean Monnet Chair Ad Personam at the University of Victoria.

ACKNOWLEDGEMENTS

This contribution forms part of a larger project entitled 'Europe's Sovereign Debt Crisis: Lessons for European Integration', which has received generous support from the Social Science and Humanities Research Council of Canada (SSHRC), grant number: 410-2011-0405. Earlier versions of this contribution were presented at a workshop held at the Johannes Gutenberg University of Mainz, 8–9 November 2013, and at the 55th Annual Convention of the International Studies Association in Toronto, 26–9 March 2014. The author thanks participants of those conferences, two anonymous referees, and in particular Patrick Leblond for comments. This contribution was finalized whilst the author was a fellow at the Netherlands Institute for Advanced Studies (NIAS) in Wassenaar.

SUPPLEMENTAL DATA AND RESEARCH MATERIALS

Supplemental data for this article can be accessed on the Taylor & Francis website (http://dx.doi.org/10.1080/13501763.2014.994023).

NOTES

1 For a literature review, see Sadeh and Verdun (2009). For an account of the creation of EMU, see Dyson and Featherstone (1999).

2 'Displacement: the removal of existing rules and introduction of new ones; Layering: the introduction of new rules on top of or alongside existing ones; Drift: the changed impact of existing rules due to shifts in the environment; Conversion: the changed enactment of existing rules due to their strategic redeployment' (Mahoney and Thelen 2010: 15–16). 'Displacement' is the type of institutional change when existing rules are replaced with new ones, either rapidly or more incrementally (the latter occurs when two systems may be in competition with one another). In 'layering', new rules are added to existing ones and, contrary to displacement, does not replace entire institutions or sets of rules. In the case of 'drift', the formal rules might stay in place but they have a different impact owing to changes in the external environment. Similarly, in the case of 'conversion', the rules also stay intact but are interpreted differently; this may be done actively by actors who are consciously using discretion and the ambiguity in the language of the institutional rules for instance, and in this way redeploy the institutions (Mahoney and Thelen 2010: 16–18). Streeck and Thelen (2005: 29) had a fifth category for institutions in decline: 'exhaustion'.

3 Posner (2007) argued that quite some progress had already been made on European financial integration, which in his words had the potential of being more far-reaching than the creation of Europe's single currency (Deeg and Posner [2015] further underline this general point). Grossman and Leblond (2011) have argued that a full European financial structure to respond to the financial crisis would take considerable time to create.

4 As mentioned above, at the same time the European Financial Stability Mechanism was also created to channel funds from the EU, but with a much smaller budget (€60 billion as opposed to €440 billion for the EFSF) and backed up implicitly by the EU budget (http://ec.europa.eu/economy_finance/eu_borrower/efsm/index_en.htm).

5 The 80 billion euros from member states was earmarked to be provided to member states in need in the period May 2010 through June 2013. Eventually the amount was reduced by 2.7 billion euros, because Slovakia withdrew support. Ireland and Portugal withdrew from the facility when the latter two needed to obtain financial assistance themselves from the Greek Loan Facility (http://ec.europa.eu/economy_finance/assistance_eu_ms/greek_loan_facility/index_en.htm).

6 The EIB (also in Luxembourg) only had a limited role, namely to assist the EFSF with technical matters to do with being in Luxembourg and an entity under that law (European Investment Bank 2010).

7 Although all EU treaties are strictly speaking 'intergovernmental treaties', this particular one was a standalone treaty: it is not officially an addition to the *acquis communautaire* of the EU body of laws and regulations. In this way, this treaty is similar to other intergovernmental treaties outside the EU domain similar to the Bologna Declaration (1999) to create a European Higher Education Area or the 1985 Schengen Agreement. The latter eventually entered the European Union Treaty. The Fiscal Compact is also created in a way that its contents may eventually be folded into future revised EU treaties.

REFERENCES

Ardagna, S. and Caselli, F. (2012) 'The political economy of the Greek debt crisis: a tale of two bailouts', LSE mimeo, available at http://personal.lse.ac.uk/casellif/papers/greece.pdf (accessed 19 January 2015).

Armingeon, K. and Ceka, B. (2014) 'The loss of trust in the European Union during the great recession since 2007: the role of heuristics from the national political system', *European Union Politics* 15(1): 82–107.

Buiter, W. (1999) 'Alice in Euroland', *JCMS: Journal of Common Market Studies* 37(2): 181–209.

Buti, M. and Carnot, N. (2012) 'The EMU debt crisis: early lessons and reforms'. *JCMS: Journal of Common Market Studies* 50(6): 899–911.

Capoccia, G. and Kelemen, R.D. (2007) 'The study of critical junctures: theory, narrative, and counterfactuals in historical institutionalism', *World Politics* 59: 341–69.

Collier, R.B. and Collier, D. (1991) *Shaping the Political Arena: Critical Junctures, the Labor Movement, and Regime Dynamics in Latin America*, Princeton, NJ: Princeton University Press.

Council of the EU (2012) 'Fiscal compact enters into force' 18019/12 PRESSE 551, Brussels, 21 December.

Council of the EU (n.d.) 'FACTSHEET: European Stability Mechanism', available at http://www.consilium.europa.eu/uedocs/cms_data/docs/pressdata/en/ecofin/132734.pdf (accessed 19 January 2015).

De Grauwe, P. (2006a) 'What have we learnt about monetary integration since the Maastricht Treaty?', *JCMS: Journal of Common Market Studies* 44(4): 711–30.

De Grauwe, P. (2006b) 'Flaws in the design of the Eurosystem?' *International Finance* 9: 137–44.

De Grauwe, P. (2011) 'The governance of a fragile eurozone', Discussion paper, Katholieke Universiteit Leuven, available at http://www.econ.kuleuven.be/ew/academic/intecon/Degrauwe/PDG-papers/Discussion_papers/Governance-fragile-eurozone_s.pdf (accessed 19 January 2015).

De Grauwe, P. (2012) 'The eurozone's design failures: can they be corrected?', Paper presented at the LSE Public Lecture, London, 28 November.

De Grauwe, P. and Ji, Y. (2012) 'Mispricing of sovereign risk and macroeconomic stability in the eurozone', *JCMS: Journal of Common Market Studies* 50(6): 866–80.

De Larosière Report (2009) 'The High-level Group on Financial Supervision in the EU', Rreport chaired by Jacque de Larosière, Brussels, 25 February 2009.

Deeg, R. and Posner, E. (2015) 'European politics: finance,' in O. Fioretos, T.G. Falleti and A. Sheingate (eds), *The Oxford Handbook of Historical Institutionalism*, Oxford: Oxford University Press, forthcoming.

Der Spiegel (2011a) 'Dutch finance minister on the debt crisis: "we are all threatened by contagion"', by Christian Reiermann, 22 August, available at http://www.spiegel.de/international/spiegel/dutch-finance-minister-on-the-debt-crisis-we-are-all-threatened-by-contagion-a-781622.html (accessed 19 January 2015).

Der Spiegel (2011b) 'Uncommon currency: a possible scenario for the end of the euro', A Commentary by Henrik Müller, 6 October, available at http://www.spiegel.de/international/europe/uncommon-currency-a-possible-scenario-for-the-end-of-the-euro-a-790352.html (accessed 19 January 2015).

Drudi, F., Durré, A. and Mongelli, F.P. (2012) 'The interplay of economic reforms and monetary policy: the case of the eurozone', *JCMS: Journal of Common Market Studies* 50(6): 881–98.

Dyson, K. and Featherstone, K. (1999) *The Road to Maastricht: Negotiating Economic and Monetary Union*, Oxford: Oxford University Press.

Economist, The (2008) 'Nightmare on Wall Street: a weekend of high drama reshapes American finance', 15 September, available at http://www.economist.com/node/12231236 (accessed 19 January 2015).

Economist, The (2011) 'The euro area's flagging economy: the shadow of recession', 24 September, available at http://www.economist.com/node/21530115 (accessed 19 January 2015).

Eichengreen, B. (2012a) 'European monetary integration with benefit of hindsight', *JCMS: Journal of Common Market Studies* 50(S1): 123–36.

Eichengreen, B. (2012b) 'When currencies collapse', *Foreign Affairs* 91(1): 117–34.

Eijffinger, S.C.W. (2012) 'Rating agencies: role and influence of their sovereign credit risk assessment in the eurozone', *JCMS: Journal of Common Market Studies* 50(6): 912–21.

Engineer, M.H., Schure, P. and Gillis, M. (2013) 'A positive analysis of deposit insurance provision: regulatory competition among European Union countries', *Journal of Financial Stability* 9(4): 530–44.

Eurobarometer (2011) 'Public opinion in the European Union' Standard Eurobarometer 75, spring.

Eurobarometer (2012) 'Public opinion in the European Union' Standard Eurobarometer 78, autumn.

European Commission (2009a) 'Commission adopts legislative proposals to strengthen financial supervision in Europe', Press release IP/09/1347, Brussels, 23 September, available at http://europa.eu/rapid/press-release_IP-09-1347_en.htm (accessed 19 January 2015).

European Commission (2009b) 'Greece: Commission assessment in relation to the Commission recommendation for a Council decision under Article 104(8) of the Treaty', 16243, Brussels, 11 November, available at http://ec.europa.eu/economy_finance/publications/publication16243_en.pdf (accessed 19 January 2015).

European Commission (2011) 'EU economic governance "six pack" enters into force' Memo/11/898, 12 December.

European Commission (2013) '"Two-pack" completes budgetary surveillance cycle for euro area and further improves economic governance', Memo/13/196, 12 March.

European Commission (2014) 'A comprehensive EU response to the financial crisis: substantial progress towards a strong financial framework for Europe and a banking union for the eurozone', Memo 14/244, 28 March, available at http://europa.eu/rapid/press-release_MEMO-14-244_en.htm?locale=en (accessed 19 January 2015).

European Investment Bank (2010) 'Limited services provision role for EIB in European Financial Stability Facility', 21 May, available at http://www.eib.org/infocentre/press/news/all/limited-services-provision-role-for-eib-in-european-financial-stability-facility.htm?lang=en (accessed 19 January 2015).

European Parliament (2013) 'Table on the ratification process of amendment of art. 136 TFEU, ESM Treaty and Fiscal Compact'. Directorate General for the Presidency Directorate for Relations with National Parliaments, Brussels, 27/09/2013 Legislative Dialogue Unit.

Feldstein, M. (2012) 'The failure of the euro: the little currency that couldn't', *Foreign Affairs*, 91(1): 105–16.

Gocaj, L. and Meunier, S. (2013) 'time will tell: the EFSF, the ESM, and the euro crisis', *Journal of European Integration* 35(3): 239–53.

Gros, D. and Mayer, T. (2010) 'How to deal with sovereign default in Europe: create the European monetary fund now!', *CEPS Policy Brief No. 202*, 17 May, available at http://ssrn.com/abstract=1610303 (accessed 19 January 2015).

Grossman, E. and Leblond, P. (2011) 'European financial integration: finally the great leap forward?', *JCMS: Journal of Common Market Studies* 49(2): 413–35.

Hall, P.A. and Taylor, R.C.R. (1998) 'The potential of historical institutionalism: a response to Hay and Wincott', *Political Studies* 46(5): 958–62.

Hay, C. and Wincott, D. (1998) 'Structure, agency and historical institutionalism', *Political Studies* 46(5): 951–57.

Heipertz, M. and Verdun, A. (2010) *Ruling Europe: The Politics of the Stability and Growth Pact*, Cambridge: Cambridge University Press.

Hobolt, S.B. and Wratil, C. (2015) 'Public opinion and the crisis: the dynamics of support for the euro', *Journal of European Public Policy*, doi:10.1080/13501763. 2014.994022.

Ioannou, D., Leblond, P. and Niemann, A. (2015) 'European integration and the crisis: practice and theory,' *Journal of European Public Policy*, doi:10.1080/13501763. 2014.994979.

Krugman, P. (2011) 'This is the way the euro ends' *New York Times Blogs*, 11 November, available at http://krugman.blogs.nytimes.com/2011/11/09/this-is-the-way-the-euro-ends-2/?_r=0 (accessed 19 January 2015).

Krugman, P. (2012) 'Greece and the euro: is the end near?' *Truthout*, 24 May, available at http://truth-out.org/opinion/item/9358-greece-and-the-euro-is-the-end-near (accessed 19 January 2015).

Lipset, S.M. and Rokkan, S. (1967) *Party Systems and Voter Alignements: Cross-National Perspectives*, New York: The Free Press.

Mahoney, J. and Thelen, K. (2010) 'A theory of gradual institutional change', in J. Mahoney and K. Thelen (eds), *Explaining Institutional Change: Ambiguity, Agency and Power*, New York: Cambridge University Press, pp. 1–27.

Meunier, S. and McNamara, K.R. (2007) 'Making history: European integration and institutional change at fifty', in S. Meunier, and K.R. McNamara (eds), *Making History: European Integration and Institutional Change at Fifty*, Oxford: Oxford University Press, pp. 1–20.

Peters, B.G., Pierre, J. and King, D.S. (2005) 'The politics of path dependency: political conflict in historical institutionalism', *Journal of Politics* 67: 1275–300.

Pierson, P. (1996) 'The path to European integration: a historical institutionalist analysis', *Comparative Political Studies* 29(2): 123–63.

Pierson, P. (2000) 'Increasing returns, path dependence, and the study of politics', *American Political Science Review* 94(2): 251–67.

Posner, E. (2007) 'Financial transformation in the European Union', in S. Meunier and K.R. McNamara (eds), *Making History: European Integration and Institutional Change at Fifty*, Oxford: Oxford University Press, pp. 139–55.

Roth, F., Nowak-Lehmann, F. and Otter, T. (2011) 'Has the financial crisis shattered citizens' trust in national and European governmental institutions?' *CEPS Working Document, No. 343* (June). Brussels: CEPS.

Sadeh, T. and Verdun, A. (2009) 'Explaining Europe's monetary union: a survey of the literature' *International Studies Review* 11: 277–301.

Salines, M., Glöckler, G. and Truchlewski, Z. (2012) 'Existential crisis, incremental response: the Eurozone's dual institutional evolution 2007–2011' *Journal of European Public Policy*, 19(5): 665–81.

Sanders, E. (2009) 'Historical institutionalism' *The Oxford Handbook of Political Institutions (Oxford Handbooks Online)*, Oxford: Oxford University Press, doi:10.1093/oxfordhb/9780199548460.003.0003.

Sargent, T. (2011) 'United States then, Europe now'. Nobel Prize speech, Stockholm, 8 December.

Schure, P. (2013) 'European financial market integration', in A. Verdun and A. Tovias (eds), *Mapping European Economic Integration*, Basingstoke: Palgrave Macmillan, pp. 105–24.

Sorkin, A.R. (2009) *Too Big To Fail: Inside the Battle to Save Wall Street*, London/New York/Toronto: Allen Lane (Penguin Group).

Steinmo, S. (2008) 'Historical institutionalism', in D. della Porta and M. Keating (eds), *Approaches and Methodologies in the Social Sciences*, Cambridge: Cambridge University Press, pp. 118–38.

Steinmo, S., Thelen, K. and Longstreth, F. (1992) *Structuring Politics: Historical Institutionalism in Comparative Analysis*, Cambridge: Cambridge University Press.

Streeck, W. and Thelen, K. (2005) 'Introduction: institutional change in advanced political economies', in W. Streeck and K. Thelen (eds), *Beyond Continuity: Change in Advanced Political Economies*, Oxford: Oxford University Press, pp. 1–39.

Thelen, K. (1999) 'Historical institutionalism and comparative politics', *Annual Review of Political Science* 2: 369–404.

Thelen, K. (2009) 'Institutional change in advanced political economies' *British Journal of Industrial Relations* 47(3): 471–98.

Thelen, K. and Steinmo, S. (1992) 'Historical institutionalism in comparative politics', in S. Steinmo, K. Thelen and F. Longstreth (eds), *Structuring Politics: Historical Institutionalism in Comparative Politics*, Cambridge: Cambridge University Press, pp. 1–33.

Verdun, A. (1996) 'An "asymmetrical" Economic and Monetary Union in the EU: perceptions of monetary authorities and social partners', *Journal of European Integration* 20(1): 59–81.

Verdun, A. (2000) *European Responses to Globalization and Financial Market Integration, Perceptions of EMU in Britain, France and Germany*, Basingstoke and New York: St Martin's Press and Macmillan.

Verdun, A. (2007) 'A historical institutionalist analysis of the road to Economic and Monetary Union: a journey with many crossroads', in S. Meunier and K.R. McNamara (eds), *Making History: European Integration and Institutional Change at Fifty*, Oxford: Oxford University Press, pp. 195–209.

Verdun, A. (2013a) 'The European currency in turbulent times – austerity policy made in Brussels as the only way out?', in D. Schiek (ed.), *The EU Social and Economic Model After the Global Crisis: Interdisciplinary Perspectives*, Farnham: Ashgate, pp. 45–69.

Verdun, A. (2013b) 'Small states and the global economic crisis: an assessment', *European Political Science* 12(1): 276–93.

Verdun, A. (2013c) 'The building of economic governance in the European Union', *Transfer: European Review of Labour and Research* 19(1): 23–35.

Public opinion and the crisis: the dynamics of support for the euro

Sara B. Hobolt and Christopher Wratil

ABSTRACT Further integration in the European Union (EU) increasingly depends on public legitimacy. The global financial crisis and the subsequent euro area crisis have amplified both the salience and the redistributive consequences of decisions taken in Brussels, raising the question of how this has influenced public support for European integration. In this contribution, we examine how public opinion has responded to the crisis, focusing on support for monetary integration. Interestingly, our results show that support for the euro has remained high within the euro area; however, attitudes are increasingly driven by utilitarian considerations, whereas identity concerns have become less important. While the crisis has been seen to deepen divisions within Europe, our findings suggest that it has also encouraged citizens in the euro area to form opinions on the euro on the basis of a cost–benefit analysis of European economic governance, rather than relying primarily on national attachments.

INTRODUCTION

The global economic crisis and the ensuing euro area crisis have highlighted the salience and the redistributive consequences of monetary integration. As a consequence, citizens have become increasingly aware of the interdependence of European economies and the importance of European Union (EU) institutions in determining the future of individual national economies. Institutional responses to the crisis have also brought about reforms to deepen integration in the EU and resulted in calls for greater democracy and enhanced legitimacy. The euro area crisis thus represents the clearest example to date of Europe-wide politicization of the integration issue, understood in Schmitter's sense as a 'widening of the audience or clientele interested and active in integration' (1969: 166). This can thus be seen as a critical step in the ongoing process leading away from the 'permissive consensus' of the early period of integration, where insulated leaders could make decisions without public consultation, towards a 'constraining dissensus' where public opinion is both more critical and more decisive (Hooghe and Marks 2009). With a proliferation of referendums on EU matters, politicization of EU issues in national elections and increased powers of the European Parliament, future reforms to deepen European integration hinge more than ever upon public support.

This raises the question of how greater public awareness of European integration and its economic consequences changes the nature and role of public opinion in the integration process. In this contribution, we address a key aspect of this question by examining how the dynamics of support for the EU have been shaped by the euro crisis. Specifically, we analyse how attitudes towards monetary integration have been influenced by the global financial crisis and the euro area crisis since 2008. Our findings demonstrate that, contrary to what one might expect, public support for economic integration has remained stable within the euro area, while it has declined in EU member states outside the euro area (see also Hobolt and Leblond [2014]; Roth *et al.* [2011]). However, the factors that shape euro support in the euro area have shifted from identity-based concerns before the crisis to more utilitarian considerations during the crisis. These results suggest that as citizens receive more information about the economic consequences of monetary integration, people's attitudes towards the euro are more likely to be based on a systematic evaluation of the costs and benefits of the integration process. Such a utility-based approach to integration implies that citizens assign greater weight to individual and societal economic benefits from integration when forming opinions about monetary integration and are less likely to oppose the euro because of their attachment to the nation. Hence, while support for the euro may appear stable, the continued legitimacy of EU economic governance could depend on whether the EU is seen to deliver effective solutions to economic problems.

PUBLIC OPINION AND EUROPEAN INTEGRATION

Grand theories of integration have largely neglected the role of public opinion, not least because the general public was considered to be of minimal importance for the process of integration. However, both major integration theories, liberal intergovernmentalism and neofunctionalism, allow for ways in which public opinion could potentially become relevant. Liberal intergovernmentalism theorizes the importance of domestic interests in shaping governments' preferences as a first 'level' of the two-level game of European integration. This could potentially provide a role for public opinion, assuming that EU matters are sufficiently salient to influence the electoral incentives of national politicians (Börzel and Risse 2009; Moravcsik 1998). Yet, the primary focus of liberal intergovernmentalism is domestically organized economic interests shaping national governments' positions, rather than the role of national electorates (Moravcsik 1998). Similarly, according to neofunctionalism, politicization of EU issues could render public opinion important; yet other drivers of integration, notably economic interests organized in transnational associations and the preferences of member states, are considered far more significant (Haas 1958; Hooghe and Marks 2006; Schmitter 1969). Hence, while grand theories have acknowledged that public opinion can potentially play a role if the integration process became more salient, they have only paid limited attention to the mechanisms through which it should become important, and they have not engaged with the question of how public opinion is shaped by the process of integration itself.

The increasing politicization of the EU since the 1990s, however, has led scholars to pay more attention to the impact of public opinion on integration. Notably, Liesbet Hooghe and Gary Marks (2009) have formulated an ambitious 'postfunctionalist theory', which incorporates the role of public opinion into a framework for understanding regional integration. They argue that more democratic control over EU decision-making and increased politicization of the EU issue in domestic party politics have brought the public into EU decision-making. Their focus is on the conditions under which an EU issue becomes politicized in the domestic context and the move from the 'distributional logic' to the 'identity logic' of integration. They argue that as the scope and depth of European integration has intensified and the tension over threats to national identity have become more salient, not least due to political entrepreneurs mobilizing the issue, identity also becomes the key factor shaping attitudes towards integration (Hooghe and Marks 2009).

This argument relates to the ongoing debate between two alternative perspectives on public support for European integration: a utilitarian and an identity-based approach. From a utilitarian perspective, generic support for European integration is determined by a rational cost–benefit analysis: those who benefit economically from European integration (particularly trade liberalization) are supportive, whereas those who stand to lose are more hostile (Gabel 1998; Gabel and Palmer 1995; McLaren 2006). Support for monetary integration has also been explained in utilitarian terms, arguing that individuals with high involvement in international trade should favour the euro more than individuals employed in the non-tradable sector (Banducci et al. 2009; Gabel 2001; Gabel and Hix 2005). Studies of support for the euro have also found that sociotropic economic concerns play a role: citizens in countries that benefit economically, or are perceived to benefit economically, from membership of the EU are more supportive of the euro (Banducci et al. 2003, 2009; Hobolt and Leblond 2014; Kaltenthaler and Anderson 2001). An alternative explanation for the variation in support for European integration, and the euro more specifically, focuses less on economic self-interest and more on the threat that European integration can pose to national identity and a country's symbols and values (Carey 2002; Hooghe and Marks 2004; McLaren 2006). Several studies have shown that attachment to the nation, and particularly exclusive national identity, is a powerful predictor of negative attitudes towards European integration (Hooghe and Marks 2004; McLaren 2006). In the context of the referendums on joining the euro in Denmark and Sweden, Jupille and Leblang (2007) found that 'identity concerns' played a greater role than 'pocketbook calculations'. Generally, citizens who thought that the EU undermined national sovereignty and democracy were more likely to vote against the euro's adoption (see also Hobolt and Leblond [2009]). In their recent study of support for European economic integration during the crisis, Kuhn and Stoeckel (2014) also show that both utilitarian considerations and national identity matter.

Hence, existing work has clearly demonstrated that economic calculations *and* identity concerns play an important role in explaining variation in support for the EU, and monetary integration more specifically. However, less work has examined how the balance between these concerns evolves once the integration process and its economic consequences become more salient.[1] The visibility of European economic integration undeniably increased during the euro crisis, as Kriesi and Grande (2014) have shown in their content analysis of the public debate in six Western European countries. They conclude that 'the debate [on the euro crisis] has been exceptionally salient and has contributed to the increased visibility of Europe in the politics of the European nation-states' (Kriesi and Grande 2014: 24). While previous bursts of interest in the EU have tended to concern constitutional matters (e.g., treaty changes) and be concentrated in specific countries (e.g., where referendums were held), the euro crisis is unique in that it has made the issue of European integration salient across Europe and that it has highlighted decisions at the European level that have very obvious redistributive consequences between and within countries (Cramme and Hobolt 2014). Since the crisis has highlighted the tangible economic consequences, we expect that it is unlikely to evoke an 'identity logic', but that it is rather likely to prompt citizens to employ a 'utility logic'. Below, we elaborate on this idea and develop our expectations concerning the public response to the crisis.

THE PUBLIC RESPONSE TO THE CRISIS

Citizens' response to the 'Great Recession' needs to be understood in the context of the increasing salience and public awareness of the consequences of monetary integration. The heightened public salience of integration can be attributed to a mixture of factors: the visibility of the euro crisis and the EU's attempt to deal with it; changes in individual circumstances linked to the crisis (e.g., unemployment); as well as deliberate attempts by certain political élites to mobilize the issue and thus expand issue-specific conflict beyond the narrow circle of political actors (Cramme and Hobolt 2014; De Vries and Hobolt 2012; Hooghe and Marks 2009). Moreover, in response to the crisis the EU made a number of interventions that can be seen to increase integration in the EU, including measures that were targeted at individual debtor states and more formal institutional reforms to deepen economic integration in the EU (see Ioannou *et al.* [2015]).

There is evidence that the crisis raised the public awareness through all of these mechanisms: initial awareness for the interdependencies monetary integration had created was already present at the outset of the crisis and this awareness became more acute after the reforms of European economic governance, when the issue was also politicized by political entrepreneurs. The question of the desirability and future of economic integration in the Union became commonplace in the national public spheres of euro area countries and a key feature of national party competition and domestic election campaigns (Cramme and Hobolt 2014; Kriesi and Grande 2014). As the crisis evolved from a financial crisis into a sovereign debt crisis and a euro area crisis, citizens also started to assign responsibility to the EU for its actions and inactions. These shifts in public awareness of the EU's impact on the national economies were particularly pronounced inside the euro area (Hobolt and Tilley 2014).

Our expectation is that as monetary integration became an issue of general public awareness and information on the issue was disseminated, the nature of opinion formation also shifted. We know from the literature in political psychology and behavioural economics that greater salience allows people to engage in more systematic and analytical evaluations, and causes them to rely less on predispositions and heuristics. Negative information in particular has been shown to encourage individuals to engage in systematic evidence-based opinion formation (Kahneman and Tversky 1979). Systematic processing means that individuals take heed of the decision-relevant information that is currently available, and based on this information they carefully piece together a decision. This can be contrasted with heuristic processing which requires much less effort by individuals, as new information is processed in accordance with these standing decisions, including affective attachments, such as identities or partisanship, and not taking into account new information (Chaiken 1980).

In the context of the EU, it has been shown that issue-based proximity voting, rather than protest voting, is more common in European elections and referendums when the EU issue receives more media coverage and is more salient in the political debate (de Vries 2007; Hobolt 2009; Tillman 2004). Equally, since the Great Recession made European integration, and particularly monetary integration, a more salient issue in the national public debates, we expect citizens to become more concerned with economic pros and cons of integration. Consequently, our expectation is that utilitarian considerations concerning the economic benefits from economic integration and the capacity of institutions to deliver these benefits have come to matter more and identity to matter less as the issue of economic governance has become more salient. We expect this to be the case primarily *inside* the euro area, where there was a fear not only that individual economies might default, but that the entire system would collapse, thus creating great uncertainty and risk for euro area members regardless of whether they were debtor or creditor states. In contrast, we do not expect change outside the euro area, where the economic implications of a potential euro area meltdown were more diffuse and received less public attention. We focus on support for the type of integration most clearly linked to the crisis, namely support for monetary integration and the euro. This leads us to the following hypotheses:

H1: Economic benefits of integration have become more important to citizen support for the euro inside the euro area after the onset of the economic crisis. Outside the euro area the importance of economic benefits has remained stable.

H2: Institutional capacity to deliver benefits from economic integration has become more important to citizen support for the euro inside the euro area after the EU commenced its institutional reform agenda in response to the crisis. Outside the euro area the importance of institutional capacity has remained stable.

H3: National identity has become less important to citizen support for the euro inside the euro area during the crisis compared to before the crisis. Outside the euro area the importance of national identity has remained stable.

To test these propositions we start by looking at aggregate-level trends in support for the euro, and thereafter we present the results from multilevel models of pre-crisis and crisis surveys of individual support for the euro.

MEASURING THE PUBLIC RESPONSE TO THE CRISIS

It is not straightforward to put a date on the beginning of the European economic and financial crisis. While the onset of the financial crisis is often dated back to the collapse of Lehman Brothers in September 2008, survey data show that Europeans were aware of the looming economic crisis as early as the beginning of 2008: the proportion of citizens of Europe thinking that the 'economy will get worse' increased by a remarkable 20 percentage points between the autumn 2007 and the spring 2008 Eurobarometer survey waves (see Eurobarometer surveys).[2] The so-called 'euro area crisis' only emerged a little later. At the heart of this evolution was the sovereign debt crisis that surfaced in 2009 with downgrading of government debt in many European states, particularly in the so-called 'GIIPS' countries (Greece, Ireland, Italy, Portugal and Spain). Concerns intensified in early 2010 and thereafter, leading the EU to implement a series of financial support measures such as the European Financial Stability Facility (EFSF) and specifically 'bailout funds' to countries facing a severe sovereign debt crisis. These euro rescue measures targeted at helping countries in a severe sovereign debt crisis were accompanied by more formal institutional reforms of the governance of the Economic and Monetary Union (EMU), including the decision by the ECB to undertake outright monetary transactions and the establishment of the European Stability Mechanism to safeguard and provide instant access to financial assistance programmes (see Ioannou et al. [2015]). Second, a series of new legal instruments (the so-called 'six-pack', the 'two-pack', the Macroeconomic Imbalances Procedure), new decision-making procedures (the European Semester) and a new intergovernmental treaty, the Fiscal Compact, were aimed at more tightly constraining national fiscal policy-making (see Ioannou et al. [2015]). These ongoing attempts to rescue countries on the brink of bankruptcy, and avoid the collapse of the euro area, as well as the more formal institutional changes, were extensively covered in the national media across Europe.

To examine the public response to the crisis and the reforms, we rely on data from the Eurobarometer (EB), which are conducted twice a year on behalf of the European Commission, surveying citizens in each of the member states with respect to their opinions on European matters. According to our theoretical argument, citizens would have responded to the increasing salience of European economic governance by adjusting their opinions, but this response would not have been identical inside and outside the euro area, since the cost–benefit calculus for insiders and outsiders differs significantly. To explore these claims at the aggregate level, we measure public attitudes over time, both before and during the sovereign debt crisis in Europe, distinguishing between insiders and outsiders. We look specifically at support for the common currency, and we expect different responses inside and outside the euro area, since the utility calculus differs significantly depending on membership status: for countries that are already members, an exit or potential collapse of the euro area could have potentially disastrous and highly uncertain economic consequences; whereas for countries not yet members, the risk-adverse response may be to stay out of a currency area in turmoil. Public euro support is captured by way of the most commonly used to measure support for monetary integration, namely the proportion of citizens who favour the EMU with a single currency.

Figure 1 shows, in line with our general argument, that support for the euro is lower outside the euro area than inside. We can also see that, whereas there has been a decline in support among euro outsiders since 2010, support inside the

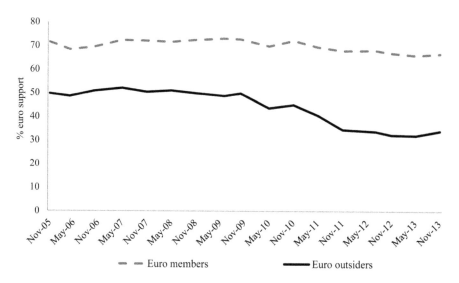

Figure 1 Support for the euro, inside and outside the euro area
Source: Eurobarometer surveys 2005–2013. (Eurobarometer Surveys data and documentation made available by GESIS. Reports available at http://ec.europa.eu/public_opinion).

euro area has remained fairly stable (see also Clements *et al.* [2014]; Roth *et al.* [2011]). This suggests that the choice facing insiders and outsiders is very different, and whereas insiders have remained supportive, outsiders have become less certain about the benefits of joining a monetary union in crisis (Hobolt and Leblond 2014).

Moreover, despite the severity of the crisis, citizens across Europe continued to regard the EU as relatively more effective at dealing with the crisis than other institutions, such as national governments. We can demonstrate this empirically by using the Eurobarometer question: 'Which of the following is best able to take effective actions against the effects of the financial and economic crisis?' The options include the national government, the European Union, the United States, the G20, the International Monetary Fund (IMF), other, and none. Figure 2 shows the proportion of citizens who selected the EU as the institution best able to take effective action. It is worth noting that, on average, EU citizens perceived the EU to be most effective at taking action against the crisis compared to all other options, even national governments.

Figure 2 shows that Europeans became more likely to name the EU as the most effective institution as the financial crisis evolved into a sovereign debt crisis in late 2009 and early 2010, especially inside the euro area, where the proportion of people mentioning the EU increased by 10 percentage points between May 2009 and May 2010. This increase also coincides with high-profile EU interventions, such as the first Greek bailout and the establishment of the EFSF to safeguard financial stability in Europe in May 2010. In other

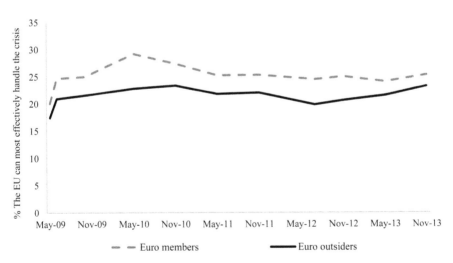

Figure 2 Citizens who think the EU takes most effective action against the crisis, inside and outside the euro area
Source: Eurobarometer surveys 2009–2013. (Eurobarometer Surveys data and documentation made available by GESIS. Reports available at http://ec.europa.eu/public_opinion).

words, as the crisis worsened in Europe and the EU started to intervene, more people thought that the EU is best placed to deal effectively with the consequences of the crisis. This remained stable throughout the crisis, however, despite the increased measures adopted by the EU in response to the crisis.

Overall, these descriptive data in Figures 1 and 2 suggest that the crisis has not led to reduced support for the euro inside the euro area, whereas this crisis has led to a sharp decline in support for the single currency outside the euro area. These results suggest that the utility calculus differed inside and outside the EA after the onset of the crisis, and that for citizens in the EMU a euro area collapse or exit was seen as the potentially most costly option, not least due to the widespread perception that the EU can deliver the most effective solution to the crisis. To examine more rigorously whether such a 'utility logic' was applied by citizens inside the euro area, we use individual-level data from before and during the crisis.

MODELLING INDIVIDUAL-LEVEL EURO SUPPORT

To assess the changing determinants of euro support, we estimate identical models of euro support using several waves of pre-crisis and crisis data. This allows us to closely track changes in effects over time. To do this, we use several Standard Eurobarometer waves for the years 2005 to 2013.[3] For all these waves we estimate the effects of all determinants of euro support that were asked in the respective wave. Unfortunately, we cannot estimate all predictors in one model, as they are rarely included in the same wave, and we thus estimate slightly different models (see Web Appendix for details [online supplemental material]).[4] Our dependent variable in all models is the respondent's (dichotomous) answer to the question whether he or she is for or against 'A European economic and monetary union with one single currency, the euro' (see Figure 1). This question has the convenient property that it captures support for the euro meaningfully both for citizens inside and outside the euro area, which any question on adopting or reforming the euro could not achieve. Turning to the operationalization of utilitarian concerns, we are interested in finding variables that capture the economic benefits of integration (H1) and the capacity of institutions to deliver those benefits (H2). To capture perceived country-level benefits from integration, we measure the respondent's perception of whether his country has benefited from integration: 'Taking everything into account, would you say that (OUR COUNTRY) has on balance benefited or not from being a member of the EU?' Using this operationalization of country-level benefits raises a question about the causal direction, since the respondent's view on the euro may influence his evaluations of how much benefit the EU provides, as well as vice versa. However, since our core argument is not about the direction of causality but about a stronger cognitive link between cost–benefit analysis and euro attitudes due to the crisis, this is less of a concern. Even if perceived benefits are partly endogenous to euro attitudes, a stronger association during the crisis can be interpreted as evidence of a change in the nature of support for the euro. Secondly, to operationalize the capacity of institutions to deliver benefits, we use the Eurobarometer question on the respondent's perception of which actor is most able to tackle the effects of the financial and economic crisis, constructing a dummy variable for those who consider the EU to be the most effective of all actors (see also Figure 2).

Our third expectation is that national identity will matter less during the crisis (H3). To capture identity, we use the following question: 'In the near future, do you see yourself as (1) [nationality] only, (2) [nationality] and European, (3) European and [nationality], or (4) European only?' This question on personal self-image has been viewed as the gold standard for measuring national identity by many scholars (e.g., Hooghe and Marks [2004, 2005]). In a comparison of different identity measures, Sinnott (2006) has found that 'identification ratings', such as this question, have the highest levels of predictive validity for attitudes on the EU. We use a simple four-level scale indicating different 'degrees of national identity' with 1 for 'European only' and 4 for '[nationality] only'. To test the importance of the specific national context, we also include a dummy for EMU membership.[5] In each model we include interactions between EMU membership and the independent variables. We also include standard controls for education, age and gender that have been shown to influence EU support.

Our estimates are based on multilevel logistic regression with random intercepts at the country level. By using logistic regression we essentially conceive of support for monetary integration as an unbounded, latent variable Y^* that is linearly related to our independent variables and linked to the probability of supporting the euro through the logit link function ($Pr(Y) = \Lambda(Y^*)$). All estimated models then take the following general form:

$$Y^* = \alpha + \beta_1 X + \beta_2 EMU + \beta_3(X*EMU) + \beta_4 CONTROL \dots$$
$$+ \beta_n CONTROL + u_j + \varepsilon_i \tag{1}$$

where X is the independent variable of interest, EMU is a dummy for euro area countries, u_j is the random intercept at the country level, and ε_i the individual-level error term.

Our primary interest lies in the changing effect of the independent variables Xs on latent support for monetary integration (Y^*) inside versus outside the euro area and before versus during the crisis. Therefore, we calculate the conditional marginal effects $\left(\dfrac{dY^*}{dX}\right)$ of each of the explanatory variables X and their 95 per cent confidence intervals depending on EMU membership. Figures 3A to 3C show how latent support for the euro (in terms of log odds) changes in response to a unit change in X inside versus outside the euro area and for each available wave. These plots are based on the full regression models (available in the Web Appendix [online supplemental material]) and the conditional marginal effects (EMU versus not EMU country) are calculated

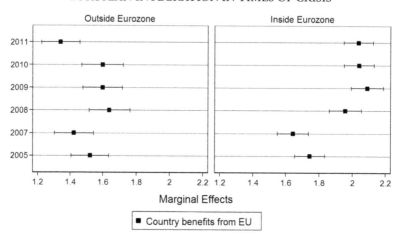

Figure 3A Determinants of euro support before and during the crisis: marginal effects of perceived benefits from EU membership

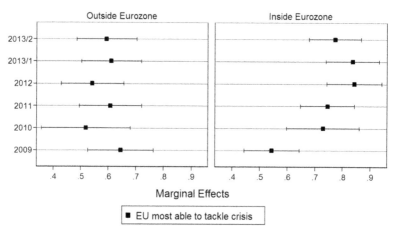

Figure 3B Determinants of euro support before and during the crisis: marginal effects of EU as most capable actor

from the interaction between the *EMU* dummy and the independent variable of interest (see Brambor et al. 2006). To further illustrate the changing effects of utility and identity concerns inside the euro area, we also plot the predicted probabilities of supporting the euro for a hypothetical individual with different values on the key independent variables before and over the course of the crisis (Figure 4).

Starting with our first hypothesis (H1), recall that we posited an increase in the association between benefits from EU membership and support for the euro inside the euro area. Figure 3A shows strong support for this hypothesis. While the effect of the variable fluctuates considerably outside the euro area

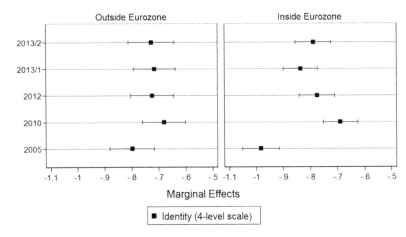

Figure 3C Determinants of euro support before and during the crisis: marginal effects of different degrees of national identity

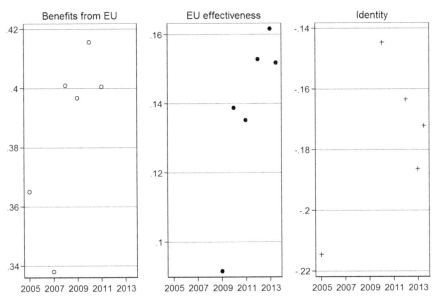

Figure 4 Difference in predicted probabilities of supporting the euro for individuals with different values on the independent variable (euro area)

Note: These figures show differences in predicted probabilities of supporting the euro for two hypothetical individuals (female, 47 years old, modal occupation and education level in a euro area country) who differ in terms of the variables of interest: perceived benefits from membership (benefits or no benefits); perceived EU effectiveness (EU as the most capable/EU not as the most capable); and identity ('national only' or 'national and European').

without a clear trend, the association has become much stronger within EMU over time. In particular, we witness a large shift in effects between the 2007 and the 2008 waves of the survey (pre- and post-crisis waves) that stabilizes and becomes even more pronounced in the subsequent years. This suggests the link between support for the euro and perceived national benefits from integration was changing from the very onset of the global financial crisis in 2008. This supports our conjecture that the crisis primed utilitarian concerns in citizens' reasoning about the euro. Indeed, the change is more immediate than one might have expected – it already occurred after the first signs of a crisis at the horizon. It coincides with a considerable worsening of citizens' economic expectations: whereas in autumn 2007 only about 26 per cent of EU citizens expected a worsening national economy in the next 12 months, this figure almost doubled to 46 per cent in just half a year. In accordance with our expectations, citizens in the euro area reoriented their stance on the euro in line with their assessment of whether integration provides benefits to their country. This is also reflected in predicted probabilities of supporting the euro: the difference between an individual who perceives benefits from integration and someone who does not was about 34–36 percentage points before the crisis but around 40 during the crisis (Figure 4). In other words, this factor clearly became more important in predicting support.

We find equally supportive evidence for our second hypothesis. Perceptions of the EU as the most effective actor to tackle the crisis became an increasingly important determinant of support for the euro as the crisis proceeded inside the euro area (Figure 3B). Regrettably, we can only observe the change from spring 2009 onwards, when the question was asked for the first time. However, the subsequent waves clearly demonstrate that concerns about the EU's institutional capacity to deliver effective solutions become more important for euro support, in particular between 2009 and 2012, when the EU adopted a number of reform measures in response to the crisis. This change is statistically significant and it is also substantial in terms of predicted probabilities. Figure 4 demonstrates that inside the euro area those who viewed the EU as most effective actor had a 9 percentage points higher probability of supporting the euro in 2009 compared to those who did not view the EU as the best able to take effective actions, and notably this difference increased to over 15 percentage points in 2012 and 2013. In contrast, we do not see any change in the importance of institutional effectiveness outside the euro area, in line with our theoretical expectation. Clearly, citizens outside EMU had less reason to respond to the euro area crisis by engaging in a cost–benefit analysis of economic integration as they were less directly affected by the fate of the euro area reforms.

Lastly, we turn to changes in the effect of national identity. Figure 3C plots the effect of degrees of national identity on a four-point scale between 2005 and 2013. The findings strongly support our third hypothesis. The effect of the variable has significantly diminished within the euro area over time. Notably, identity plays a much less important role for supporting the euro in 2010 compared to 2005, and the effect of identity remains at this lower level in the following years. As with benefits from integration, this again corroborates the finding that the cognitive shift we observe already took place during the early phase of the crisis. However, as we have fewer data points for identity, we cannot ascertain when exactly the shift occurred. We can, however, conclude that citizens clearly relied less on identity heuristics when forming their views on the euro as the crisis unfolded. Figure 4 shows that, before the crisis, individuals in the euro area conceiving of themselves as 'national only' had about 21 percentage points lower probability of supporting the euro than those with 'national and European' identity. In contrast, this difference due to identity diminished to 14–17 percentage points during the crisis. Hence, the role of identity in predicting support for the euro diminished during the crisis. Outside the euro area, however, the effect of identity remained largely stable.

Overall, we find that while both identity and utility concerns are important drivers of euro support both before and during the crisis, there is a significant shift in the balance of these determinants. This amounts to an increase in the differences in the predicted probabilities of euro support produced by perceived membership benefits and institutional benefits of about 4–7 percentage points over the course of the crisis, and a similar decrease in the differences in euro support due to identity. This is quite a substantial shift over a relatively short time period of four to eight years, and it is comparable in magnitude to those reported in existing studies on changing determinants of public support for European integration (see Hakhverdian *et al.* [2013]). Therefore, this analysis has demonstrated that while a simple glance at aggregate-level support for the euro inside the euro area reveals little change over the past eight years, a closer look at individual-level data demonstrates a significant shift in the factors shaping support. Inside the euro area the balance between rational cost–benefit considerations and identity factors has changed: economic benefits and institutional capacity now matter more, whereas identity matters less. In contrast, the determinants of support for the euro have remained stable outside the euro area.

CONCLUSION

Public opinion and voters play only a marginal role in classic theories of European integration. According to the dominant theories, the process of integration has been considered the remit of political and economic élites and of little interest to ordinary citizens. However, the euro area crisis has presented the EU with its most acute challenge to date, as it has pitted creditor states against debtor states, brought the negative consequences of monetary integration into focus and threatened the very survival of the new currency. As a result, Europe has become a more salient and divisive issue than ever before and European leaders can no longer rely on a 'permissive consensus'. In this contribution, we have addressed the important question of how the crisis has affected the nature of attitudes towards the euro.

Our findings show that despite the severity of the crisis, support for the euro inside the euro area has remained high, whereas it has declined significantly outside the euro area. Moreover, citizens have become more aware of these costs due the heightened salience of the economic consequences of the integration process during the crisis. We argue that utility calculations have become more important to euro insiders during the crisis, at the expense of identity heuristics that have come to play a less important role in shaping attitudes. Indeed we find strong support for these propositions in our analysis of cross-national individual-level survey data between 2005 and 2013, which demonstrates that the balance between rational cost–benefit considerations and identity factors has changed inside the euro area, whereas we find virtually no change outside the euro area. Hence, the analysis reveals a growing divide between insiders and outsiders: not only have citizens inside the euro area remained more supportive of the euro than those outside, but they also appear more readily persuaded by utilitarian considerations and arguments than citizens in other EU countries.

These findings contribute to the wider literature on the dynamics of support for European integration. Recent work on European integration, notably the theory of postfunctionalism (Hooghe and Marks 2009), has highlighted that national identity should become increasingly important for attitudes on European integration as the EU becomes politicized in domestic arenas. This is based on the observation that political entrepreneurs, often located on the fringes of the political spectrum, use identity frames to mobilize the integration issue in public discourses. This study suggests that the shifting determinants of EU support may depend on the type of politicization that takes place. Our findings show that as the issue of monetary integration became more salient and citizens more aware of it, identity concerns became *less* important to citizens, and utilitarian concerns about the EU's institutional effectiveness and benefits of integration became *more* important. This is not necessarily irreconcilable with the postfunctionalist propositions. Hooghe and Mark's expectation is that identity-based public opinion will be particularly pronounced if the integration issue that is contested has 'opaque economic implications' and 'transparent communal implications' (2009: 13). However, in contrast to previous periods of high politicization of the EU issue (notably referendums on treaty changes), the euro crisis has emphasized the economic and redistributive implications of integration (Hobolt and Tilley 2014; Kriesi and Grande 2014). Hence, this suggests that when the debate on European integration is focused on economic integration and its consequences, this may instead encourage citizens to think of integration more in terms of economic self-interest and less in terms of their national identity. It is also noteworthy that the increased salience of European integration has been driven not primarily by the issue entrepreneurship of political élites and challenger parties, but rather by an exogenous 'shock' to the EU's economic system in ways that have not only shaped the nature of the public debate, but also had tangible effects on the personal circumstances and future prospects of millions of citizens in the EU. Interestingly, our findings show that the shift in the dynamics of euro support took place before the worst effects of the crisis were felt by ordinary Europeans, and hence can be interpreted as a reaction to the heightened salience of integration and the fear of future repercussions, rather than actual changes in economic circumstances.

The increasing importance of the 'utility logic' over the 'identity logic' may also explain why support for the euro has remained high and stable inside the euro area, despite the severity of the economic crisis. Our results suggest that Europeans generally considered the EU to be more effective than any other institution, including their own national governments, in taking action against the crisis, and inside the euro area the perceived effectiveness of EU institutions played an increasingly important role in keeping support for the euro high. It is worth noting, however, that the shift away from identity-based opinions may be particularly pronounced because we are looking specifically at attitudes towards monetary integration, which arguably has clearer economic implications than other forms of integration, and it is not certain that these findings can be generalized to all types of integration support.

This study nonetheless has several implications for our understanding of European integration. First, it suggests that we should not necessarily expect greater politicization of the integration issue to equal more identity-based attitudes towards integration. Indeed, greater contestation that highlights the distributional consequences of the integration process may instead lead to opinions that are increasingly based on a cost–benefit analysis of the European project. A second and related contribution is that it challenges the prediction that national identities will continue to pose a significant constraint on the integration process in the long term. While our results show that identities matter, they also indicate that major shocks to the system can render them less important, certainly when it comes to attitudes towards economic integration. So far, the integration issue has been mobilized primarily by domestic political entrepreneurs emphasizing identity-based Eurosceptic concerns. Yet, our findings suggest that the public may also be receptive to the mobilization of the integration issue on the basis of utility-based arguments. Hence, while we are unlikely to return to the days where the European political élites could safely ignore public opinion, this study has illustrated that greater public contestation does not necessarily equal a public veto. Instead, the crisis demonstrates that public opinion on integration might be more dynamic and responsive to the changing nature of the integration process than stylized theories predict. This should be reflected in future studies as we continue to advance our models of public opinion formation on European integration by taking seriously the impact of the political and economic context.

Biographical notes: Sara Hobolt is the Sutherland Chair in European Institutions at the European Institute, London School of Economics and Political Science. Christopher Wratil is a PhD candidate at the London School of Economics and Political Science.

ACKNOWLEDGEMENTS

This work was supported by the UK Economic and Social Research Council [W88918G] and the Leverhulme Trust [RF-2013-245]. We would also like to thank Demosthenes Ioannou, Patrick Leblond, Arne Niemann and the anonymous reviewers for insightful comments and suggestions.

SUPPLEMENTAL DATA AND RESEARCH MATERIALS

Supplemental data for this article can be accessed on the Taylor & Francis website, http://dx.doi.org/10.1080/13501763.2014.994022.

NOTES

1 Only very few studies have examined how the economic and political context conditions the effect of identity and utility concerns on attitudes towards the EU. One exception is Garry and Tilley (2009), who find that the impact of identity in EU attitudes is conditional on economic context, as identity matters less in net beneficiary member states.

2 Eurobarometer Surveys. Data and documentation made available by GESIS. Reports available at http://ec.europa.eu/public_opinion.

3 We use all spring waves of the survey to create a coherent time series. Since the question item on national identity was unfortunately included less frequently in the surveys, we also use two autumn waves in which the identity item occurred: EB 64.2 (2005) and EB 80.1 (2013). (For source details of Eurobarometer Surveys please see note 2 above).

4 This reliance on different models and datasets may bias our estimates upwards or downwards, as we are not able to control for all independent variables while assessing the change in one of them. However, since we are more interested in the change of effects over time and less in the absolute magnitude of effects, such bias is less problematic, as it will apply to the estimates at both points in time.

5 One complication we have to address is that some countries joined the euro just before and even during the crisis (Cyprus, Estonia, Malta, Slovakia, and Slovenia). Excluding these countries is not a sensible option, as we would lose too many observations. Hence, we code all 17 countries that had joined the EA by January 2013 as part of EMU in all waves. Thereby, we make sure that we are drawing inferences about the same target population in the pre-crisis and crisis estimations of the models. However, the results are substantially the same if we, for instance, exclude Estonia and Slovakia from the analysis (both joined during the crisis).

REFERENCES

Banducci, S., Karp, J.A. and Loedel, P.H. (2003) 'The euro, economic interests and multi-level governance: examining support for the common currency', *European Journal of Political Research* 42: 685–703.

Banducci, S., Karp, J.A. and Loedel, P.H. (2009) 'Economic interests and public support for the euro', *Journal of European Public Policy* 16(4): 564–81.

Börzel, T.A. and Risse, T. (2009) 'Revisiting the nature of the beast – politicization, European identity, and postfunctionalism: a comment on Hooghe and Marks', *British Journal of Political Science* 39(1): 217–20.

Brambor, T., Clark, W.R. and Golder, M. (2006) 'Understanding interaction models: improving empirical analyses', *Political Analysis* 14: 63–82.

Carey, S. (2002). 'Undivided loyalties: is national identity an obstacle to European integration?', *European Union Politics* 3(4): 387–413.

Chaiken, S. (1980). 'Heuristic versus systematic information processing and the use of source versus message cues in persuasion', *Journal of Personality and Social Psychology* 39: 752–66.

Clements, B., Nanou, K. and Verney, S. (2014) 'We no longer love you, but we don't want to leave you: the eurozone crisis and popular Euroscepticism in Greece', *Journal of European Integration* 36: 247–65.

Cramme, O. and Hobolt, S.B. (eds) (2014) *Democratic Politics in a European Union under Stress*, Oxford: Oxford University Press.

De Vries, C.E. (2007) 'Sleeping giant: fact or fairytale? How European integration affects national elections', *European Union Politics* 8(3): 363–85.

De Vries, C.E., and Hobolt, S.B. (2012) 'When dimensions collide: the electoral success of issue entrepreneurs', *European Union Politics* 13(2): 246–68.

Gabel, M. J. (1998) *Interest and Integration: Market Liberalization, Public Opinion and European Union*, Ann Arbor, MI: University of Michigan Press.

Gabel, M.J. (2001) 'Divided opinion, common currency: the political economy of public support for EMU', in B. Eichengreen and J.A. Frieden (eds), *The Political Economy of European Monetary Unification*, 2nd edn, Boulder, CO: Westview Press, pp. 49–76.

Gabel, M.J. and Hix, S. (2005) 'Understanding public support for British membership of the single currency', *Political Studies* 53(1): 65–81.

Gabel, M.J. and Palmer, H.D. (1995) 'Understanding variation in public support for European integration', *European Journal of Political Research* 27: 3–19.

Garry, J. and Tilley, J. (2009) 'The macro economic factors conditioning the impact of identity on attitudes towards the EU', *European Union Politics* 10(3): 361–79.

Haas , E.B. (1958) *The Uniting of Europe*, Stanford, CA: Stanford University Press.

Hakhverdian, A., Van Elsas, E., van Der Brug, W. and Kuhn, T. (2013) 'Euroscepticism and education: a longitudinal study of 12 EU member states', *European Union Politics* 14(4): 522–41.

Hobolt, S.B. (2009) *Europe in Question. Referendums on European Integration*, Oxford: Oxford University Press.

Hobolt, S.B. and Leblond, P. (2009) 'Is my crown better than your euro? Exchange rates and public opinion on the European single currency', *European Union Politics* 10(2): 209–32.

Hobolt, S.B. and Leblond, P. (2014) 'Economic insecurity and public support for the euro before and during the financial crisis', in N. Bermeo and L.M. Bartels (eds), *Mass Politics in Tough Times: Opinion, Votes and Protest in the Great Recession*, Oxford: Oxford University Press, pp. 128–47.

Hobolt, S. and Tilley, J. (2014) *Blaming Europe? Responsibility without Accountability in the European Union*, Oxford: Oxford University Press.

Hooghe, L. and Marks, G. (2004) 'Does identity or economic rationality drive public opinion on European integration?', *PS: Political Science & Politics* 37(3): 415–20.

Hooghe, L. and Marks, G. (2005) 'Calculation, community and cues: public opinion on European integration', *European Union Politics* 6(4): 419–43.

Hooghe, L. and Marks, G. (2006) 'The neofunctionalists were (almost) right: politicization and European integration', in C. Crouch and W. Streeck (eds), *The*

Diversity of Democracy: Corporatism, Social Order and Political Conflict, Cheltenham: Edward Elgar, pp. 205–22.

Hooghe, L. and Marks, G. (2009) 'Postfunctionalism a postfunctionalist theory of European Integration: from permissive consensus to constraining dissensus', *British Journal of Political Science* 39(1): 1–23.

Ioannou, D., Leblond, P. and Niemann, A. (2015) 'European integration and the crisis: practice and theory', *Journal of European Public Policy*, doi: 10.1080/13501763.2014.994979.

Jupille, J. and Leblang, D. (2007) 'Voting for change: calculation, community, and euro referendums.' *International Organization* 61(4): 763–82.

Kaltenthaler, K.C. and Anderson, C.J. (2001) 'Europeans and their money: explaining public support for the common European currency', *European Journal of Political Research* 40(2): 139–70.

Kahneman, D. and Tversky, A. (1979) 'Prospect theory: an analysis of decision under risk', *Econometrica* 47(2): 263–92.

Kriesi, H. and Grande, E. (2014) 'Political debate in a polarizing Union', in O. Cramme and S.B Hobolt (eds), *Democratic Politics in a European Union under Stress*, Oxford: Oxford University Press.

Kuhn, T. and Stoeckel, F. (2014) 'When European integration becomes costly: the euro crisis and public support for European economic governance', *Journal of European Public Policy* 21(4): 624–41.

McLaren, L. (2006) *Identity, Interests and Attitudes to European Integration*, Basingstoke: Palgrave Macmillan.

Moravcsik, A. (1998) *The Choice for Europe: Social Purpose and State Power from Messina to Maastricht*, Ithaca, NY: Cornell University Press.

Roth, F., Jonung, L. and Nowak-Lehmann, F. (2011) 'The enduring popularity of the euro throughout the crisis', *CEPS Working Document 358*, Brussels: Centre for European Policy Studies.

Schmitter, P.C. (1969) 'Three neo-functional hypotheses about international integration', *International Organization* 23(1): 161–6.

Sinnott, R. (2006) 'An evaluation of the measurement of national, subnational and supranational identity in crossnational surveys', *International Journal of Public Opinion Research* 18(2): 211–23.

Tillman, E.R. (2004) 'The European Union at the ballot box? European integration and voting behavior in the new member states', *Comparative Political Studies* 37(5): 590–610.

Political legitimacy and European monetary union: contracts, constitutionalism and the normative logic of two-level games

Richard Bellamy and Albert Weale

ABSTRACT   The crisis of the euro area has severely tested the political authority of the European Union (EU). The crisis raises questions of normative legitimacy both because the EU is a normative order and because the construction of economic and monetary union (EMU) rested upon a theory that stressed the normative value of the depoliticization of money. However, this theory neglected the normative logic of the two-level game implicit in EMU. It also neglected the need for an impartial and publically acceptable constitutional order to acknowledge reasonable disagreements. By contrast, we contend that any reconstruction of the EU's economic constitution has to pay attention to reconciling a European monetary order with the legitimacy of member state governance. The EU requires a two-level contract to meet this standard. Member states must treat each other as equals and be representative of and accountable to their citizens on an equitable basis. These criteria entail that the EU's political legitimacy requires a form of *demoi*cracy that we call 'republican intergovernmentalism'. Only rules that could be acceptable as the product of a political constitution among the peoples of Europe can ultimately meet the required standards of political legitimacy. Such a political constitution could be brought about through empowering national parliaments in EU decision-making.

THE MAKING OF THE LEGITIMACY CRISIS

The crisis of the euro area (EA) has severely tested the political authority of the EU. Since 2010 the EU and its members states have been forced to improvise policies and processes to deal with the crisis, including the European Semester, a strengthened Stability and Growth Pact, the Treaty on Stability, Co-ordination and Governance, the European Financial Stability Facility (EFSF) and its successor in the European Stability Mechanism (ESM) (Begg 2013; Ioannou *et al.* 2015). The European Central Bank (ECB) has embarked upon two rounds of long-term refinancing operations to improve bank liquidity, in effect buying sovereign debt, as well as announcing its willingness to engage in outright monetary transactions (OMT), a policy allegedly leading Jens Weidmann, President of the Bundesbank, to say that this is tantamount 'to financing governments by printing banknotes' (Steen 2012). And still the prospect of deflation looms over European economies (House of Lords 2014c: 13 and *passim*).

The same conditions that gave rise to these policy imperatives have required the EU to find ways of supporting the governments of Greece, Ireland, Portugal, Spain and Cyprus in defiance of the no bail-out clause of the original monetary union (now Article 125 of the TFEU). They have resulted in the Troika imposing restrictions on the national budgets of debtor governments, policies that have been resisted by national parliaments and opposition movements. They have strengthened anti-EU parties, with a record number of Eurosceptic Members of the European Parliament (MEPs) elected in the European elections of May 2014. They have provoked legal actions in national constitutional courts in both creditor countries like Germany (Federal Constitutional Court 2014a, 2014b) and debtor countries like Portugal[1] resulting in judgements that question the legitimacy of the programmes. They have stimulated continued, and sometimes violent, demonstrations against public expenditure austerity packages. They have entailed the installation of technocratic governments in Greece and Italy in 2012 as a way of dealing with the inadequacies of their respective political institutions, as well as the electoral defeat of incumbent governments in Spain and France. In short, they have brought about a crisis of political legitimacy for the EU.

The Lisbon Treaty was widely regarded as having settled the institutional architecture of the EU after nearly two decades of constitutional debate. The EA crisis has reignited those issues. The new policies and processes that have been inaugurated have changed the balance of power within the EU and opened up questions about what 'deep and genuine' economic and monetary union (EMU) requires by way of institutional change (European Commission 2012; House of Lords 2014a). In these debates, issues of normative political legitimacy inevitably arise, because the EU is a normative order. That is to say, the agreements that it embodies contain principles and values defining norms of behaviour for member states and EU institutions. The Treaty on European Union (TEU) and the Stability and Growth Pact (SGP), strengthened through Title VIII of the Treaty on the Functioning of the European Union (TFEU), together with the Six-Pack and the Two-Pack, have required member states to make progressively stronger commitments to one another in respect of economic and fiscal policy (Ioannou *et al.* 2015). Those commitments have been reinforced by the Fiscal Compact contained in the Treaty on Stability, Co-ordination and Governance in the Economic and Monetary Union (TSCG), by which member states have undertaken to ensure that national budgets are in balance or in surplus 'through provisions of binding force and permanent character, preferably constitutional, or otherwise guaranteed to be fully respected and adhered to throughout the national budgetary processes' (TSCG, Article 3.2). Such measures provide a set of rules and principles by reference to which policies and institutional change are justified. Resting on agreed norms and principles, they form a political contract among member states.

However, questions of normative legitimacy are raised by the crisis not simply as a result of the EU's being a normative order, but also because the construction of EMU rested upon a set of constitutional principles that contained strong – and contestable – normative assumptions. In particular, economic and monetary union was constructed according to the principles of legal constitutionalism (Issing 2008; James 2012). Legal constitutionalism is a political doctrine to the effect that a legitimate political regime must rest on a set of legal rules that constrain the actions of politically responsive decision-makers. In some versions (e.g., Dworkin [1996]) such restrictions take a 'left liberal' form; in others (e.g., Hayek [1979]), they take a neoliberal form (see Bellamy [2007]). Our contention in this contribution is that the developing political contract underlying EMU has produced restrictions on member states with respect to their public budgets that amount to more than simply a treaty agreement; they have given rise to a treaty agreement underwritten by the principles of legal constitutionalism of a neoliberal kind, indeed of a specific kind within neo-liberalism.

The tradition of political analysis that fed into the construction of the single currency and its management is to be found in the work of thinkers associated with the Hayekian version of constitutional liberalism (see James [2012: 6–7]). According to this tradition, democratic governments have a tendency to fiscal irresponsibility owing to politicians having incentives to buy votes through excessive public expenditure. In seeking re-election, political representatives are motivated to respond to the wishes of special interest groups in the short term rather than framing legislation for the public interest in the long term. Particular manifestations of these tendencies might include the provision of price support schemes for agriculture, the protection of domestic industry from foreign competition, interference in controlling the terms of employment contracts that can be agreed, and expenditure on public works that benefit only localized constituencies. Hayek (1979) held that, to avoid these pitfalls, states need to be constrained by constitutional rules and mechanisms from engaging in excessive expenditure and unduly interfering in the operations of the free market. Behind the construction of the specific set of rules for EMU, therefore, lay a more general set of premises concerning the character of a democratic political order.

The problem with this construction, we argue, is that, when applied to EMU, it neglects the normative logic of two-level games. According to this logic, when governments make commitments to one another about their future behaviour, they *simultaneously* need to be responsible and accountable to their domestic populations in order to retain their political legitimacy. The logic of two-level games was originally developed by Putnam (1988) to account for the outcome of the Bonn economic summit of 1978, and has been subsequently applied to empirical cases ranging from security issues to economic diplomacy and North–South relations (Evans *et al.* 1993). As Pollack (2001: 225) has pointed out, it also lies behind liberal intergovern-mentalist accounts of EU integration such as that of Moravcsik (1998) and Schimmelfennig (2015). However, this framework of analysis neither implies fixed preferences (Crespy and Schmidt 2014), nor does it have only an empirical use. Beyond its empirical applications, the logic of two-level games also has a normative interpretation (Savage and Weale 2009) pro-viding a model by which we can evaluate the justifiability of constitutional arrangements.

The neglect of the normative logic of two-level games in the construction of EMU is compounded by a second problem within legal constitutionalism: namely, its disregard of the existence of reasonable differences in political judge-ment over the principles that should govern a monetary union made up of different sovereign states, each with their own traditions of economic and mon-etary policy. Indeed, even within the broadly neoliberal tradition of thinking about economic constitutions, there are important differences of substance as well as emphasis. When the conditions for continuing contestation over policy measures and organization exists, the putative political legitimacy of EU legal constitutionalist arrangements, such as those underlying EMU, the SGP and the TSCG, reinforce the practical contradiction of the two-level game implicit in the economic constitution. By contrast with this attempt to entrench legal constitutionalism, we suggest that the design of an economic con-stitution ought to respect the principles of political constitutionalism, with its requirement that governments be responsive to the public reasoning of their citi-zens within the continuing democratic conversation that makes up a political society (Bellamy 2007).

In pursuing this argument, the contribution proceeds as follows. In the next section we lay out the normative logic of the two-level game embodied in the construction of EMU. According to this logic, those participating in inter-national agreements have a dual duty: to deal fairly with one another, on the one hand; and to be responsive and accountable to the democratic reasoning of the people whom they represent, on the other. In acknowledging this dual duty, they should also acknowledge that their fellow negotiators have a similar duty in respect of their own peoples. The penultimate section indicates why, given reasonable disagreement about the principles that should govern an economic constitution, the legitimacy of EMU cannot be simply secured by framing the related fiscal rules in legal constitutionalist terms. The long-term legitimacy of EMU is compatible only with political constitutionalism. We con-clude that so long as the EU remains subject to the logic of delegation implicit in the normative logic of two-level games, EMU must remain subject to the equal control and influence of the different member state *demoi* – a position we characterize as 'republican intergovernmentalism'. We suggest this result can be achieved through the empowerment of national parliaments in EU policy-making.

THE NORMATIVE LEGITIMACY OF TWO-LEVEL CONTRACTS

At the centre of the issue of political legitimacy is the question of the credibility, and consequently the justifiability, of the reasoning underlying the norms and principles on which the construction of EMU is based. Yet, how might one evaluate such credibility? We approach this question through contractarian political theory. According to contractarian theory, political authority is to be understood as arising from a contract to mutual advantage implicitly or explicitly agreed among the members of a political association. The need for political organization can be modelled as the solution to dilemmas of collective action (Buchanan and Tullock 1962; Gauthier 1986; Ostrom 1990; Weale 2013). These dilemmas occur when unco-ordinated action by separate agents gives rise to potential gains from co-operation, as in an agreement on weights and measures or the rules of the road, or where unco-ordinated individual action leads to harmful side-effects from otherwise legitimate human activity, of which pollution and resource depletion are the obvious examples. If we think of political associations as having a contractarian logic in this sense, then we can address the issue of credibility by asking what conditions have to be satisfied for actors to find a contract that they can rationally support (Gauthier 1986).

The general logic of contractarian analysis can be applied not only to the study of natural persons but also to relations between states. States can impose harmful externalities on other states and their populations through cross-boundary pollution, trade restrictions or population movements. They can also fail to secure common advantages through a lack of political co-ordination. The EU has often been portrayed as a mechanism for overcoming these problems in the international arena (Moravcsik 1993). The assumption is that the policies that fall within the competence of the EU are in the long-term common interest of the member states, offering Pareto improvements over a prevailing *status quo* for all concerned. However, many such issues are subject to the logic of the prisoner's dilemma. Each member state may be better off with an agreed policy with which all other member states comply but with which it does not, than it would be when it complied as well, even if all would be worse off without any agreement. Yet, if this logic is clear to all, none would rationally comply and so the policy will either never be agreed or will unravel over time. Thus, the fundamental problem to be solved in any political contract between states is that of inducing credibility in others of one's commitment to the policy to be agreed to avoid defection from a mutually beneficial agreement. To overcome this free rider problem requires states to be able to make credible commitments to one another about their willingness to fulfil their obligations, even on those occasions when fulfilling those obligations proves onerous.

The logic of the N-person prisoner's dilemma was reflected in the construction of EMU. As Issing (2008: 234–6) has clearly explained, it was thought that, because democratic competition works to create deficit financing, thereby undermining the long-term stability of the currency and public finances, the euro was designed to represent depoliticized and hence stable money. On this analysis, the political benefits of deficit spending in the form of votes gained by governing parties are enjoyed by national players, while the potential negative effects, notably higher interest rates, are felt by all states. So, it is rational for prudent states to seek to ensure that they do not incur the spillover effects of others' deficit spending, and they can attempt to do this by institutionalizing a no bail-out rule. The alternative to such a rule is to leave discipline to the markets. However, within a currency union there is no exchange rate risk to a national government from deficit financing, and so borrowing premiums remain low over a period of time and credit risk builds up (Issing 2008: 193–4). Aware of this possibility, no rational state would prudently enter into a currency union without a no bail-out rule. Hence, in order for any such agreement to take place, states must commit to funding their own borrowing. Each state has to be able to make a credible commitment to other states about the maximum deficits that they are willing to tolerate in their public spending plans. This, in short, was the rationale of the no bail-out clause of the Maastricht Treaty. The SGP arose from the recognition that the Maastricht rules of no bail-out and no exit were insufficient to prevent member states continuing to run excessive deficits. The idea was that the scope for fiscal adjustments among participating states had to be defined once and for all. Political representatives at the member state level could still co-ordinate fiscal and monetary policy, but only on condition that the monetary component was fixed exogenously by an independent European Central Bank, the ECB, that had been deliberately isolated from political interference (see Issing [2008: 193–5]).

When Germany in 2002 and then France and Germany in 2003 breached the provisions of the SGP, member states within the contract of monetary union had an incentive to strengthen monitoring and compliance even more. With the coming of the financial crisis, the next stage of the contractarian logic was to embed the SGP in the European Semester, together with the Six-Pack and the Two-Pack, the effects of which were not only to increase the intensity of the monitoring of budgetary plans, but also to ensure co-ordination among member states *before* those plans were put to national parliaments. The Fiscal Compact, the aim of which is to alter the institutional structure of domestic political arrangements to prevent excessive deficits from arising or rectify them as quickly as possible if they do exist, reinforces these provisions. As contractarian theory predicts, these devices emerge where previous commitment has been shown wanting and there is no alternative to continuing collective association. In other words, when commitments turned out not to be credible, the contractarian logic leads actors to a search for greater compliance by increased monitoring, penalties and institutional restructuring (Weale forthcoming).

Does this contractarian rationale provide a justification of the political legitimacy of EMU as it has been constructed? It could only do so provided that the states in question could be regarded as unitary actors. Yet, treating states as unitary actors is merely a simplifying assumption, useful for the purposes of some types of analysis but distorting if taken as an accurate representation of an empirical situation. States are collective entities made up of constellations of many actors. In political associations modelled according to the norms of two-level games, the political representatives of each state simultaneously owe obligations to the political representatives of other states and to their own populations (Savage and Weale 2009), with implications for their ability to comply with their contractual commitments.

The credible commitment that each state has to be able to make to every other concerns such matters as the maximum budget deficits that they will allow in their public spending plans, the rate at which deficits will be rectified and the balance between the growth of GDP and the growth of public expenditure. However, the commitment of states with regard to these policy strategies can only be made credible provided that each state enjoys the confidence of its citizens. Only with the confidence of their citizens will these states possess the capacity to implement the policies implied by the international agreement. In the modern world, this confidence and the resulting capacity to implement policy rest upon democratic political legitimation. Monetary union implies, then, that each state can have the confidence that all other states can secure sufficient ongoing domestic support to meet their consequent obligations. Hence, only if states enjoy democratic legitimacy will other states have reason to believe that their commitments are credible.

A similar interlocking logic arises in the relationship of states to their citizens. For international agreements to be credible, the governments responsible for implementing them must be able to give domestic populations good reasons for compliance, showing how an agreement will serve the collective interest. At the same time, each state must recognize that all other states that are parties to the agreement are similarly acting as representatives of their citizens. The state parties are thus engaged in a two-level game, in which the terms of the agreement have to be simultaneously acceptable to other negotiating parties *and* to their domestic constituents. Simultaneity in this context does not mean 'occurring at the same time', but indicates that any international agreement must fulfil two sets of conditions. First, an international agreement requires 'fair dealing' among states in their relations with one another as the representatives of their peoples. Second, states must ensure the general acceptability of the agreement to their respective peoples and be able to justify their international commitments, including any provisions for side payments, as being a reasonable way of advancing their joint and several common interests. Unless this second condition is met, so that a state can guarantee the backing of the people it represents, no other state party to the putative contract can be confident that a commitment made to it is credible.

In short, the logic of collective commitment in a monetary union presupposes the logic of political democracy at the national level. Unless all the state parties to an agreement possess a credible democracy at the national level, it is a practical contradiction at the international level for them to enter into commitments with each other, since, in those circumstances, no state could rationally trust the commitments of the other states or be trustworthy itself. Consequently, *pace* certain analysts of the EU (Majone 2001; Scharpf 1999) input legitimacy at the domestic level cannot be substituted by output legitimacy at the international level – particularly if the beneficial effects of those outputs vary over time and between the different parties to the agreement in ways that might be regarded as unfair (Bellamy [2010]; a point acknowledged by the post-crisis analyses of Majone [2012] and Scharpf [2011]). Therefore, the search for 'an ever closer union of the peoples of Europe' is in effect a search for credible commitment devices among the contracting member states in respect of the peoples whom they represent (Bellamy 2013).

The need for domestic political legitimacy is not simply a political fact; it is also a reason within a normative order. An international agreement involves each state recognizing that all other states are embedded within a normative order that governs their internal and external relations. Consequently, each state requires democratic legitimation for its commitments. The most elaborately worked out example of the logic of such a normative order is that provided by the German Federal Constitutional Court in its jurisprudence on EMU starting with *Brunner* (Federal Constitutional Court 1993). That jurisprudence recognizes that the German state needs to be able to enter into long-term international commitments in order to be able to secure benefits that are only available through internationally co-ordinated action. At the same time, the jurisprudence of the Court insists that any international commitment must be consistent with those principles of the Basic Law that bind the German state in perpetuity to the principle of democratic authority stemming from the people. In particular, the voting rights of German citizens should not be compromised by the German parliament losing meaningful control over the direction of economic policy. Therefore, the Court has seen its task as being to make it legally and constitutionally possible for the German state to enter into and honour international agreements that are in its interests and in the interests of other states who are party to the agreement, whilst at the same time retaining the principle of the democratic self-determination of the German people that is a fundamental element of the Basic Law. In a series of judgements, the Court has reasoned that these different demands can be reconciled through the doctrine of delegation. So long as the international agreement could be said to rest on the delegated authority of the member state and the *Bundestag* retained the power of revoking Germany's participation in the international agreement, then the principle of democratic self-determination was respected.

As Gustavsson (1998) noted, the Court's reasoning in *Brunner* rested upon three assumptions about EMU: its revocability by the *Bundestag*; its marginality in terms of the scope of obligations it implied; and its predictability. The subsequent jurisprudence of the Court has had to deal with the failure of one or more of these assumptions to obtain in practice. Thus, in a recent judgement on the constitutionality of the policy of OMT by the ECB (Federal Constitutional Court 2014a), a majority of the judges ruled that OMT were unconstitutional, because they involved an open-ended commitment by the German government. In other words, the scope of the obligations implied by OMT was neither limited nor predictable. Although the Court referred the matter to the Court of Justice of the European Union, it offered its own (sceptical) interpretation of the compatibility of the ECB's planned action with treaty and constitutional requirements. However, the kernel of its judgment turned on the force of Article 38 (1) of the German Basic Law. In line with its previous jurisprudence, the Court interpreted this Article as requiring that state authority could not be transferred to the extent that democratic control becomes nugatory. The right to vote is in effect defined as the right to vote in an election where the result will lead to meaningful parliamentary control over the conditions of collective life, thereby expressing the self-determination of the people. Democratic self-determination means that the scope of the *Bundestag's* authority cannot be rendered nugatory, and, if the German government failed to contest the policy of OMT, then its actions can be revoked (for this logic, see also Lindseth [2010: 24]).

On many matters of international agreement, domestic acceptability can be presumed by national decision-makers because the issues involved are technical, have low political salience or can be negotiated with the agreement of specific interest groups who share a consensus on which polices best serve their mutual advantage. In other words, they satisfy something like a marginality requirement. Prior to EMU, the EU's competences largely concerned such low salient issues and hence aroused comparatively little democratic contestation (Moravcsik 2002). However, the logic of monetary union does not fall into any of these categories. Although it is technical, its ramifications are wide. Few items are as politically salient as the reliability of a nation's currency. And interest groups typically take different and incompatible positions on the desirability of different monetary policies. In these circumstances, the assumption that states are acting as authorized representatives of their populations will break down, unless there are good reasons for thinking that the authorization is open-ended (hence the shift in the post-crisis analyses of Scharpf [2011] and Majone [2012], which, unlike Moravcsik [2012], have moved close to the argument made here). However, as the jurisprudence of the German Federal Constitutional Court shows, after 1993 no other state had reason to think that the authorization was open-ended in the case of Germany. It was predictable that at some stage the limits of monetary integration would be met. This line of argument can be generalized. For just as other states had no reason for thinking that Germany would have an irrevocable commitment to all the implications of EMU, so no one in Germany could reasonably think that all other states could retain a democratic mandate for abiding by the rules of EMU when those terms became unpredictably onerous.

The practical contradiction at the heart of EMU is that member states could only find the terms of the contract credible on condition that they could assume that the commitments entered into by all other member states went beyond the scope of democratic legitimation within those states. That the contradiction revealed itself in the instability of the political contract on which EMU rested arose in part from the predictable unpredictability of monetary union. That feature in turn stemmed from the fallibility of political judgement within the circumstances of politics, an element of the normative logic that we discuss in the next section.

LIBERALISM VERSUS LEGAL CONSTITUTIONALISM

Legal constitutionalism of the sort that underlies the constitution of EMU represents one tradition within the liberal inheritance, one that is notably counter-majoritarian in its implications. According to that tradition, if modern democracies have the characteristics attributed to them by neoliberal legal constitutionalists, these commitments could not be credible, since the governments of the same states that entered into the contract would be prone to myopic and short-term sectional pressures such that they would take any opportunities that might arise to free ride on the co-operation of others. If the temptation to free ride is built into democratic governments in this way, then there is no credible basis for commitment on the part of any potential party to the contract. The only basis for a credible agreement on monetary union would be through the general establishment of legal economic constitutions at the national level, underpinned by powerful counter-majoritarian institutions, so as to break the link between public expenditure and responsiveness to the preferences of the population. Of course, this proposal is an implication of the neoliberal legal constitutionalist analysis, and the first steps along such a path are embodied in the requirements of the TSCG.

However, counter-majoritarian legal constitutionalism in the economic realm is only one way of reading the liberal inheritance. Indeed, that tradition is at odds with another liberal idea: namely, the claim that any constitutional political contract should recognize the 'burdens of judgement' in its construction (Rawls 1996: 54–8). The burdens of judgement arise from such general features of human judgement as the complexity of empirical evidence, the different weight that different persons will put on different types of evidence, the vagueness of relevant concepts and the problems of assessing evidence. Given the burdens of judgement, a constitution should refrain from imposing requirements on those subject to it that will be matters of reasonable disagreement, matters, in other words, in which no knockdown arguments are possible. Rawls used this argument to exclude the constitutional entrenchment of religious doctrines because they rested on controversial philosophical premises, an issue that also arose in the convention on the putative EU constitution (Olsen 2004). However, Rawls (1996: 225) also gives the example of disputed 'elaborate economic theories of general equilibrium' as involving inherently controversial views that should not be given constitutional status. If one takes this view of disputed economic theories, the fair value of political liberties cannot be maintained if some views are given a privileged constitutional position *vis-à-vis* other views.

Does the entrenchment of a particular form of Hayekian theory in the constitution of EMU fall foul of this condition? There are a number of reasons to suppose that it does. Firstly, Hayek himself opposed EMU in part because he recognized economic policy, even of a libertarian kind, was not a matter that could be legally entrenched. Instead, he advocated free competition between rival currencies provided by private rather than public banks (Hayek 1978).

Although this is a position that Issing (2000) attempted to contest on neo-Hayekian grounds, Hayek's scepticism about EMU was a logical consequence of his belief that viable economic orders were the evolutionary product of human action but not of human design (Hayek 1979). In other words, the attempt to construct an international monetary order by political fiat would replicate the fallacies of central planning on which the road to serfdom was based.

Secondly, even within neoliberalism, there are other traditions of theory that take a non-evolutionary view of the economic order. Although sometimes identified with a Hayekian perspective, even by Hayek (1967: 252–3) himself on some occasions, German ordoliberal economists like Eucken and Röpke, took the view that a functioning economy presupposes a moment of constitutional founding in which the rules of its operation are determined (Eucken [1951a, 1951b]; compare Goldschmidt [2000]; Nicholls [1994]; Peukert [2000]). As various commentators (for example, Sally [1998]; Streit and Wohlgemuth [2000]) have noted, this ordoliberal tradition contrasts with the Hayekian position in being rationalist and constructivist. It presupposes that the institutional form of the economy is determined within an already established legal order and political community. Economic integration is not an instrument to create a political community, but an expression of the political choices of that community.

Thirdly, this ordoliberal view is consistent with the worries many economists and policy-makers had expressed about the sequencing of European political union and monetary union and the design flaws built into EMU before the euro crisis had revealed these problems. For example, in a paper summarizing a wide range of work, Bordo and Jonung (2003: 43–4) pointed out that EMU lacked both a lender of last resort, by contrast with other modern monetary systems where central banks were able to ensure liquidity, and a central authority to supervize financial systems, including the commercial banks. They went on to point out that the absence of any central co-ordination of fiscal policies within EMU combined with 'unduly strict criteria for debt and deficits ... implies that EMU will not be able to respond to asymmetric shocks and disturbances in a satisfactory way'. Finally, and as many other economists also noted, they pointed out that Europe is too large and diverse an area to form a well-functioning currency union, with the efficiency gains from increased trade not large enough to outweigh the costs of surrendering control over national monetary policies.

Fourthly, it is well established that different national traditions of economic policy-making fed into the creation of EMU. For reasons of history and intellectual tradition, German policy-making gave pride of place to the goal of price stability underpinned by the independence of the central bank. By contrast, French thinking gave priority to *gouvernement économique*, a view of the relationship between government and the economy in which executive action played a large role in securing the day-to-day steering and co-ordination of the economy, as well as providing capital for investment in major projects (Dyson and Featherstone 1999; Jabko 2006: 168–72). Historically and institutionally rooted traditions do not disappear in a new policy framework, but manifest themselves in different ways. In particular, when it comes to questions of how countries recover from large economic shocks, there will be differences in what is seen as justifiable requirements; for example, how quickly and by what methods to re-establish internationally credible debt levels within the framework of the Excessive Deficit Procedure. Similar differences of judgement will affect how countries think about the institutionalization of debt brakes and other constitutional devices under the TSCG.

The implication of these points is that legal constitutionalism presupposes that there can be agreement on the basis of the constitutional essentials of a European monetary order, although the epistemic conditions do not exist to establish that agreement. Indeed, even the German *Bundesbank*, so often presented as a model apolitical central bank, had its independence from the German government tested both by Adenauer and Schmidt (Kennedy 1991: 37–42). If within a single country, with powerful political and intellectual traditions justifying a strong independent central bank, the issue can be contested, it is not surprising that a rigid pan-European economic constitution based on the idea of automatic rules will be contested even more.

POLITICAL CONSTITUTIONALISM AND EUROPEAN ECONOMIC GOVERNANCE

The argument so far may be summarized as follows: credible commitment by governments at the international level presupposes political legitimacy at the domestic level; but the domestic legitimacy of democratic governments in turn presupposes that commitments may be modified or altered through political processes. Moreover, the epistemic conditions arising from the burdens of judgement reinforce the need for open discussion and democratic deliberation. Legal constitutionalism at the international level, therefore, risks undermining rather than reinforcing the credibility of state commitments if the measures legally entrenched are matters that should be subject to ongoing political debate by domestic electorates.

Political constitutionalism offers an alternative to legal constitutionalism (Bellamy 2007). By contrast to legal constitutionalism, political constitutionalism contends the terms of the political contract must be subject to ongoing debate among citizens with regard to both the procedures of decision-making and the substance of decisions. Judgments about either cannot be legitimately entrenched or handled by judicial or technical bodies that are isolated from democratic processes because such isolation fails to recognize the equal legal and political status of citizens. Political constitutionalists argue that the functional complexity, ethical diversity and openness of liberal societies make individual judgements about the public good inevitably partial and fallible. Because we are inescapably limited in our knowledge and experience, even the most conscientious persons will tend to reason from their own values and interests and be prone to error with regard to the present and future interests of others. If the collective decisions needed to regulate social life are to be not only impartial but also well informed with regard to the views and circumstances of those to whom they apply, so that they treat citizens with equal respect and concern, then citizens must have equal influence and control over the direction of public policy. *Pace* neoliberal thinkers, such as Hayek, such equal influence and control cannot be provided by markets but only by a democratic process, albeit indirectly through the election of decision-makers (Bellamy 1994).

Legal constitutionalism in its purest form tries to place the legal and political system itself and even many public policies beyond political contestation, defining in substantive and concrete terms how both might be best configured so as to realize equal concern and respect. By contrast, political constitutionalism in its purest form regards legitimacy as dependent upon the ability to employ existing political procedures to contest the procedural and substantive adequacy of the democratic system and its policies through the constant struggle of citizens to exercise equal influence and control over both. Most liberal democracies combine different degrees of each of them, some nearer to the political constitutionalist end of the spectrum and others more at the legal constitutionalist end. The various member states manifest considerable diversity in this respect, making all but the most abstract and procedural forms of legal constitutionalism difficult to agree. Hence the need for political constitutionalism between even those member states that have legal constitutionalist regimes (compare Glencross [2013]).

From the perspective of the normative logic of two-level games, the legitimacy of the integration process depends on its taking the form of what might be termed 'republican inter-governmentalism' (Bellamy 2013); that is, the governments and their agents can only enter into credible commitments with each other to the extent that they possess ongoing democratic authorization to represent their respective peoples, and acknowledge the equal right and obligation of all the other governments to represent their peoples (Pettit 2010). This logic stands behind the largely consensual character of much EU decision-making, not least the unanimity rule for any treaty change and the need for such changes to obtain domestic ratification within all 28 member states. Such features have led a number of commentators to remark on how the EU is best characterized not as a democracy, with EU citizens forming a pan-European demos, but as a *demoi*cracy between the different peoples of the member states (Chevenal and Schimmelfennig 2013; Nicolaidis 2013).

We have argued that the legal constitutionalist mechanisms embodied in the TSCG cannot provide EMU with political legitimacy of a normative kind. It is not possible to model the choices of the actors according to the normative logic of the two-level contract in such a way that their practical reasoning is credible. If such reasoning cannot be modelled in a contractarian way in theory, it will not be credible in practice. Instead, EMU must remain part of the political constitution provided by the ongoing democratic influence and control of those subject to it. Within the EU as presently constituted, this political constitution must reflect the normative logic of two-level games. As such, political legitimacy comes not from a single EU *demos* but from an agreement among the different *demoi* of the eurozone, as negotiated by their elected representatives. For EMU to be legitimate, therefore, it must be under the *demoi*cratic control of European states. The logic here is that of the delegation of authority, with the problem of democratic legitimacy in the EU, not that of the democratic deficit but that of the democratic disconnect – the failure to ensure policy-making remains under the equal influence and control of the constituted peoples of the Union via their domestic democratic processes (Lindseth 2010: 234).

Can such *demoi*cratic control be achieved in the case of a currency union? A detailed response lies outside the scope of this contribution. Here, we wish merely to indicate the institutional structures needed to place EMU under a political rather than a legal constitution, and to note how these structures exist within the EU to a sufficient degree for this proposal to be plausible. The main lines of such an approach can be found in the German Constitutional Court's judgements from 1993 onwards referred to earlier. According to the Court, the national parliament, the *Bundestag*, as the representative body of the German people, plays an integral role in realizing the 'right to democracy' guaranteed by the German Constitution. Moreover, its budgetary responsibilities form an intrinsic aspect of that role, given that decisions on revenue and expenditure constrain the choice of public policies that shape the collective life of citizens. Adopting reasoning that encapsulates both political constitutionalism and the *demoi*cratic approach, the Court has argued that 'sufficient space' has to exist for the citizens of the member state to be able to interpret the fundamental rights that underlie their 'economic, cultural and social living conditions'. Given reasonable disagreements about the relative importance and nature of these rights and how they might be best interpreted and realized – disagreements that have been resolved in different ways over time within each of the member states, as their different political and constitutional traditions attest – European unification could not be conducted in such a way as to leave no space for the *demoi* of the contracting parties to determine their collective life according to their differing 'cultural, historical and linguistic perceptions' through 'public discourse in the party, political and parliamentary spheres of public politics' (Federal Constitutional Court 2009). As a result, the Court has insisted on the *Bundestag's* right of participation in ESM, particularly in authorizing extensions of the guarantees for the fund (Federal Constitutional Court 2014b).

Drawing on this reasoning, two roles for national parliaments emerge within EMU. The first, domestic, role is to ensure that in negotiating budgetary rules at the EU level, the elected executives of each of the contracting member states act on the authority of their national parliament, and that the subsequent undertakings remain subject to their control and scrutiny. There are signs that other national parliaments are following the German lead. For example, Spain has set up a parliamentary budget office – the *Oficina Presupuestaria de las Cortes Generales* – that checks and assesses the execution of the budget and provides information to the legislature. The French and Italian Parliaments have likewise requested higher standards of information and transparency on issues of European economic governance. The second, inter-parliamentary, role involves national parliaments working together to ensure that EU measures treat each of the member states with equal concern and respect as self-governing polities. That role was developed formally with Lisbon and the measures relating to their mutual guardianship of subsidiarity, such as the Early Warning Mechanism. Such measures have increased the Commission's obligation to inform and give reasons to parliaments for their policies, while encouraging parliaments to develop the requisite scrutiny and control procedures. Most importantly, the role of national parliaments was explicitly acknowledged in Article 13 of the TSCG, which provided the basis for the creation of the Interparliamentary Conference on Economic and Financial Governance of the European Union. Although both these roles remain as yet rudimentary and untested, they are the subject of considerable policy interest at present (see, for example House of Lords [2014b]) and provide the beginnings of the sort of *demoi*cratic political constitution we have advocated for EMU.

CONCLUSION

We have argued that the normative order of the EU requires that contracts between member states be seen as a two-level game, in which executives can only sign credible agreements as the duly authorized agents of their domestic peoples. We termed this *demoi*cratic structure 'republican intergovernmentalism'. We argued that the attempt to view the neoliberal budgetary constraints of the Fiscal Compact as a supranational legal constitution not only conflicted with this normative order, but also was unjustifiable in denying the reasonable disagreements among both citizens and member states about economic policy. Instead, such measures have to be subject to a political constitution of a *demoi*cratic kind. The continuing role for national parliaments insisted on by the German Constitutional Court in its Lisbon Judgment and elsewhere (Federal Constitutional Court 2009) provide the basis for such a political constitutional framework for EMU.

Biographical notes: Richard Bellamy is director of the Max Weber Programme, European University Institute, Florence and professor of political science, UCL, University of London; Albert Weale is professor of political theory and public policy, UCL, University of London.

ACKNOWLEDGEMENTS

We are grateful to the special issue editors, two anonymous referees, Peter Lindseth and Christine Reh for their comments. Richard Bellamy acknowledges the support of a Leverhulme Trust Research Fellowship RF-2012-368 and a Fellowship at the Hanse Wissenschaft Kolleg; and the comments of Sandra Kröger and other members of the Colloquium on 'Democracy and multi-level governance in the EU' at the University of Bremen.

NOTE

1 Portuguese Constitutional Court Decisions 187/2013, 474/2013, 602/2013.

REFERENCES

Begg, I. (2013) 'Are better defined rules enough? An assessment of the post-crisis reforms of the governance of EMU', *Transfer: European Review of Labour and Research* 19(1): 49–62.

Bellamy, R. (1994) '"Dethroning politics": constitutionalism, liberalism and democracy in the political thought of F. A. Hayek', *British Journal of Political Science* 24: 419–41.

Bellamy, R. (2007) *Political Constitutionalism: A Republican Defence of the Constitutionality of Democracy*, Cambridge: Cambridge University Press.

Bellamy, R. (2010) 'Democracy without democracy? Can the EU's democratic "outputs" be separated from the democratic "inputs" provided by competitive parties and majority rule?', *Journal of European Public Policy* 17: 2–19.

Bellamy, R. (2013) 'An ever closer union of peoples: republican intergovernmentalism, *demoi*-cracy and representation in the EU', *Journal of European Integration* 35(5): 499–516.

Bordo, M.D. and Jonung, L. (2003) 'The future of EMU: what does the history of monetary unions tell us?', in F.H. Capie and G.E. Wood (eds), *Monetary Unions: Theory, History, Public Choice*, London and New York: Routledge: pp. 42–69.

Buchanan, J. and Tullock, G. (1962) *The Calculus of Consent*, Ann Arbor, MI: University of Michigan Press.

Chevenal, F. and Schimmelfennig, F. (2013) 'The case for *demoi*cracy in the European Union', *Journal of Common Market Studies* 51(2): 334–50.

Crespy, A. and Schmidt, V. (2014) 'The clash of titans: France, Germany and the discursive double game of EMU reform', *Journal of European Public Policy* 21(8): 1085–101.

Dworkin, R. (1996) *Freedom's Law: The Moral Reading of the American Constitution*, Oxford: Oxford University Press.

Dyson, K. and Featherstone, K. (1999) *The Road to Maastricht: Negotiating Economic and Monetary Union*, Oxford: Oxford University Press.

Eucken, W. (1951a) *The Foundations of Economics: History and Theory in the Analysis of Economic Reality*, trans. by T.W. Hutchinson, London: William Hodge.

Eucken, W. (1951b) *The Unsuccessful Age or The Pains of Economic Progress*, Edinburgh: William Hodge.

European Commission (2012) 'A blueprint for deep and genuine monetary union: launching a European debate', Brussels, *COM (2012) 777 final.*

Evans, P.B., Jacobson, H.K. and Putnam, R.D. (eds) (1993) *Double-Edged Diplomacy: International Bargaining and Domestic Politics*, Berkely, CA: University of California Press.

Federal Constitutional Court (1993) *Brunner*, available as BVerfG (1994) C.M.L.R. 57.

Federal Constitutional Court (2009) *Lisbon Judgement*, available as BVerfG, 2 BvE 2/08.

Federal Constitutional Court (2014a), *Outright Monetary Transactions*, available as 2 BvR 2728/13 vom 14.01.2014, Absatz-Nr (1-105), available at https://www.

bundesverfassungsgericht.de/entscheidungen/rs20140114_2bvr272813.html. (accessed 15 August 2014.)

Federal Constitutional Court (2014b), *European Stability Mechanism*, available as 2 BvR 1390/12 vom 18.3.2014, Absatz-Nr. (1-245), available at https://www.bundes verfassungsgericht.de/entscheidungen/rs20140318_2bvr139012.html. (accessed 15 August 2014.)

Gauthier, D. (1986) *Morals by Agreement*, Oxford: Clarendon Press.

Glencross, A. (2013) 'The absence of political constitutionalism in the EU: three models for enhancing constitutional agency', *Journal of European Public Policy* 21(8): 1163–80.

Goldschmidt, N. (2000) 'Theorie auf Normativer Basis: Anmerkungen zum ordoliberalen Konzept von Walter Eucken', in P. Commun (ed.), *L'ordoliberalisme allemand: aux sources de l'économie sociale de marché*, Cergy-Pontoise: CIRAC, pp. 119–31.

Gustavsson, S. (1998) 'Defending the democratic deficit', in A. Weale and M. Nentwich (eds), *Political Theory and the European Union: Legitimacy, Constitutional Choice and Citizenship*, London: Routledge/ECPR, pp. 63–79.

Hayek, F.A. (1967) *Studies in Philosophy, Politics and Economics*, London: Routledge & Kegan Paul.

Hayek, F.A. (1978) *Denationalization of Money - The Argument Refined*. 2nd edn London: The Institute of Economic Affairs.

Hayek, F.A. (1979) *Law, Legislation and Liberty*, 3 vols, London: Routledge.

House of Lords (2014a) '"Genuine economic and monetary Union" and the implications for the UK', *European Union Committee, 8th Report of Session 2013–14, HL Paper 314*, London: The Stationery Office Limited, available at http://www. publications.parliament.uk/pa/ld201314/ldselect/ldeucom/134/134.pdf

House of Lords (2014b) 'The Role of National parliament in the European Union', *European Union Committee, 9th Report of Session 2013–14, HL Paper 151*, London: the Stationery Office Limited, available at http://www.parliament.uk/ documents/Role-of-National-Parliaments.pdf

House of Lords (2014c) 'Euro area crisis: an update', *European Union Committee, 11th Report of Session 2013–14, HL Paper 163*, London: The Stationery Office Limited, available at http://www.publications.parliament.uk/pa/ld201314/ldselect/ldeucom/ 163/163.pdf

Ioannou, D., Leblond, P. and Niemann, A. (2015) 'European integration and the crisis: practice and theory,' *Journal of European Public Policy*, doi: 10.1080/13501763. 2014.994979.

Issing, O. (2000) 'Hayek, currency competition and European monetary union', *Occasional Papers 111*, London: The Institute of Economic Affairs.

Issing, O. (2008) *The Birth of the Euro*, Cambridge: Cambridge University Press.

Jabko, N. (2006) *Playing the Market: A Political Strategy for Uniting Europe, 1985–2005*, Ithaca, NY: Cornell University Press.

James, H. (2012) *Making the European Monetary Union: The Role of the Committee of Central Bank Governors and the Origins of the European Central Bank*, Cambridge, MA: The Belknap Press.

Kennedy, E. (1991) *The Bundesbank: Germany's Central Bank in the International Monetary System*, London: Pinter, The Royal Institute of International Affairs.

Lindseth, P. (2010) *Power and Legitimacy: Reconciling Europe and the Nation State*, Oxford: Oxford University Press.

Majone, G. (2001) 'Nonmajoritarian institutions and the limits of democratic governance: a political transaction cost approach', *Journal of Institutional and Theoretical Economics* 157(1): 57–78

Majone, G. (2012) 'Rethinking European integration after the debt crisis', *UCL European Institute Working Paper 3/2012*, London: University College London.

Moravcsik, A. (1993) 'Preferences and power in the European Community: a liberal intergovernmentalist approach', *Journal of Common Market Studies* 31(4): 473–524.

Moravcsik, A. (1998) *The Choice for Europe: Social Purpose and State Power from Messina to Maastricht*, London and New York: Routledge.

Moravscik, A. (2002) 'In defence of the "democratic deficit": reassessing legitimacy in the EU', *Journal of Common Market Studies* 40(4): 603–24.

Moravscik, A. (2012) 'Europe after the crisis: how to sustain a common currency', *Foreign Affairs* 91(3): 54–68.

Nicholls, A.J. (1994) *Freedom with Responsibility: The Social Market Economy in Germany, 1918–1963*, Oxford: Clarendon Press.

Nicolaïdis, K. (2013) 'European *demoi*cracy and its crisis', *Journal of Common Market Studies* 51(2): 351–69.

Olsen, T.V. (2004) 'Europea: united under God? Or not?', in L. Dobson and A. Follesdal (eds), *Political Theory and the European Constitution*, London and New York: Routledge, pp. 75–90.

Ostrom, E. (1990) *Governing the Commons: The Evolution of Institutions for Collective Action*, Cambridge: Cambridge University Press.

Pettit, P. (2010) 'Legitimate international institutions: a neo-republican perspective' in S. Besson and J. Tasioulis (eds), *The Philosophy of International Law*, Oxford: Oxford University Press, pp. 139–60.

Peukert, H. (2000) 'Walter Eucken (1891–1950) and the Historical School', in P. Koslowski (ed.), *The Theory of Capitalism in the German Economic Tradition: Historism, Ordo-Liberalism, Critical Theory, Solidarism*, Hamburg: Springer-Verlag, pp. 93–145.

Pollack, M.A. (2001) 'International Relations theory and European integration', *Journal of Common Market Studies* 39(2): 221–44.

Putnam, R.D. (1988) 'Diplomacy and domestic politics: the logic of two-level games', *International Organization* 42(3): 427–60.

Rawls, J. (1996) *Political Liberalism: With a New Introduction and "Reply to Habermas"*, New York: Columbia University Press.

Sally, R. (1998) *Classical Liberalism and International Economic Order: Studies in Theory and Intellectual History*, London and New York: Routledge.

Savage, D. and Weale, A. (2009) 'Political representation and the normative logic of two-level games', *European Political Science Review* 1(1): 63–81.

Scharpf, F. (1999) *Governing in Europe: Effective and Democratic?* Oxford: Oxford University Press.

Scharpf, F. (2011) 'Monetary union, fiscal crisis and the preemption of democracy', *MPIfG Discussion Paper 11/11*, Munich: Max Planck Instituten für Gesellschaft.

Schimmelfennig, F. (2015) 'Liberal intergovernmentalism and the euro area crisis', *Journal of European Public Policy*, doi: 10.1080/13501763.2014.994020.

Steen, M. (2012) 'Weidmann isolated as ECB plan approved', *The Financial Times*, 6 September.

Streit, M.E. and Wohlgemuth, H. (2000) 'The market economy and the state. Hayekian and ordoliberal conceptions', in P. Koslowski (ed.), *The Theory of Capitalism in the German Economic Tradition: Historism, Ordo-Liberalism, Critical Theory, Solidarism*, Hamburg: Springer-Verlag, pp. 224–69.

Weale, A. (2013) *Democratic Justice and the Social Contract*, Oxford: Oxford University Press.

Weale, A. (forthcoming) 'Political legitimacy, credible commitment and euro governance', in Hertie School of Governance (ed.), *The Governance Report 2015*, Oxford: Oxford University Press.

Europe's ordoliberal iron cage: critical political economy, the euro area crisis and its management

Magnus Ryner

ABSTRACT Orthodox integration scholarship failed to identify the factors leading to the euro area (EA) economic and financial crisis because of weaknesses that Horkheimer identified in 'traditional' theory: disciplinary splits and a tendency to idealize from particular instrumental perspectives. By contrast, critical political economy offered a plausible and coherent elucidation of the emergent properties and limits of finance-led capitalism and their concrete manifestation in the EA. This contribution both reviews state-of-the-art critical political economy research on the EA crisis and makes a distinct contribution to it. In addressing the puzzle of why not only the Economic and Monetary Union persists despite morbid symptoms but why crisis management is extending and deepening a discredited finance-led capitalism, the contribution synthesizes theories of transnational class formation and inter-state relations, and proposes that Europe is caught in an ordoliberal iron cage.

INTRODUCTION

The financial crisis reaped its academic casualties. Asking why economists had not seen it coming, Queen Elizabeth surprisingly became emblematic for those finding their assumptions wanting (e.g., Boyer [2012: 292–6]). As the financial crisis morphed into the euro area (EA) crisis, reasons also arose to question European integration scholarship. A survey of the *Journal of Common Market Studies* found that of the 732 articles published between the inception of the Single European Market (SEM) and mid-2009, only five had anything relevant to say about the factors that had generated the crisis (Ryner 2012: 649).

Yet, the dominant response to the anomalies that the EA crisis poses for European integration scholarship has been minimalist and complacent. First, the supposed prudence induced by Economic and Monetary Union (EMU) was compared favourably with American profligacy, leading to off-the-mark musings about a European 'decoupling' from the American economy (International Monetary Find [IMF] 2007). The collapse of Lehman Brothers, revealing exposure of European finance to toxic assets with crucial counterpart liabilities within the European Union (EU) itself, dispelled any illusions on that score. Then the effect of the financial crisis on the EU was acknowledged, but the institutions agreed at Maastricht were held to be fit for purpose (e.g., Pisani-Ferry and Posen [2009: v]). This became untenable when the price of credit default swaps and bond-yield spreads rapidly increased first in Greece in late 2009, and then in Portugal, Ireland, Italy and Spain. The symptom of rapidly increasing public deficits was henceforth treated as cause, facilitating macroeconomic *ex post* rationalization and justification for fiscal and structural conditionality to the European Stability Mechanism (ESM), and the European Central Bank's (ECB's) Long Term Refinancing Operations (LTRO) and, above all, the Outright Monetary Transactions (OMT), which were necessary for saving the euro and which then could be construed as indicating successful European governance and even spillover.

This contribution argues that accommodating the anomalies in question ought to motivate a more radical theoretical recasting. Drawing on Horkheimer's (1937[2002]) famous distinction, the analysis of critical political economy of the emergent properties of the EA crisis and its management is compared favourably to that of traditional integration scholarship. But also critical political economy must be judged as a progressive research programme. Dispelling charges of tendentiousness, much excellent critical, yet highly formal and quantitative analysis has been done in recent years on European capital accumulation. As argued in the first section, some such works can even claim to have predicted the coming crisis. However, there is a tendency in such works to view the crisis and its management with reference to policy mistakes. Compelling findings about macroeconomic proportions, tensions and risks entailed in crisis management, and policy alternatives are offered. But resilience of current crisis-management is underestimated, the endurance of the euro remains unexplained, and difficult questions about agency required to advance alternatives are elided. By contrast, in the second section, this article contributes to works that see crisis management as a form of rule that may endure for some time.

The particular contribution here is to steer clear of two oversimplifying tendencies in critical political economy to either reduce rule to that of a transnational capitalist class or German dominance. An account is offered that integrates an inter-state understanding of how German EA leadership works as a common but variegated European response to predatory post-Bretton Woods American hegemony over finance-led transnational capitalism. This configuration, though far from optimal for Europe, is not easily changed. Invoking Parsons's translation of Weber's *Stahlhartes Gehäuse* to denote a deeply troubled situation from which it is impossible to escape, despite the disenchanted realization that the Celestial City will never be reached (Baehr 2001), I suggest that the paradox of a monetary union that endures despite its contradictions, social costs and conflicts can be seen as an ordoliberal iron cage.

ANALYSING THE EA CRISIS: TRADITIONAL SCHOLARSHIP AND CRITICAL POLITICAL ECONOMY

European integration scholarship was successful primarily because instrumental purposes served in addressing questions about rendering the transatlantic alliance organic on a pluralist template (Milward and Sørensen 1993). But this 'structure of thinking' was not appropriate for addressing the financial and EA crisis because of idealizations eliding the mechanisms that generated the crisis (Ryner 2012: 655).

Most European integration scholarship rests on two common paradigmatic assumptions inherited from foundational works that shape terms of debate *a priori* (Ryner 2012: 653–5). The *disciplinary split* results in an obstinately conventional division of labour between 'economics', 'sociology' and 'politics' of integration. Concerned with the allocation of scarce resources, economics of integration abstracts its sphere of analysis from social power relations. Analysing social relations becomes the remit of the sociology of integration, but conceiving these in terms of the 'density' of social interaction and postulating a positive functional relation between such density and rational order, also here power is ignored. Delegated to the concern of political scientists, power is seen as residing in the 'political system' without concern sources in the social and economic 'environment'. With the *integration telos*, all of the aforementioned assume that integration expresses rational potentials inherent in human nature. Debates between 'optimists', 'pessimists' and 'middle positions', originating with Hoffman's (1966) critique of Haas (1968), concern the prospects of realizing these potentials in the face of power-laden and arbitrary constraints that the weight of Europe's statist history poses. Horkheimer (1937[2002]: 198) sees such assumptions as symptomatic of traditional social science when it itself becomes an input in the politico-economic system but nevertheless attempts to shroud itself in a general-scientific aura. It does so by universalizing its particular instrumentality through idealization. By doing so, however, it creates blind-spots.

By contrast, critical theory seeks holistic analysis of the co-constitution of economic, political and cultural forms in the stratified, complex, contradictory and historically specific capitalist mode of production. This is a complex enterprise with emancipatory intent, seeking to reveal 'coercive illusions' that appear objective whilst being socially constructed and preventing humans from becoming what they could become (Connerton 1976: 18). It is impossible to do full justice to this enterprise here, where not the least the Frankfurt School is divided over the very possibility of emancipatory reason in modern society. The focus is on a subset of this enterprise, concerning how we can understand the EA in terms of 'regulatory effects' (Horkheimer 1937[2002]: 225), which provisionally secure capitalist order in certain epochs *but within definite limits*.

Economic analysis of the EA has followed Balassa's (1962) foundational work resting on Ricardian trade theory, which has ruled out considerations of mechanisms generating the crisis *a priori*. High-level export reports from the Cecchini to the Sapir Reports are cases in point (European Commission 1988; Sapir *et al.* 2003). Money and finance are here seen as commodities like any other, and no reasons are entertained to regard them as exceptions to the Pareto-optimal effects supposedly engendered by the fundamental freedoms. Most economic analyses of the EA are specialized refinements that follow the assumptions and agendas of these reports. Hence, suggesting an end of the Feldstein–Horioka Puzzle, Blanchard and Giavazzi (2002) argued that current account deficits in southern EA member states were not a concern. Being the consequence of capital inflows motivated by higher returns, investments would generate the requisites for their servicing and repayment. It is hard to imagine a more hubristic belief in the rational market-creating properties of the monetary union.

Work close to the ECB qualifies the record slightly, and a case has been made that it issued the relevant warnings. It is not based on the obvious source of optimum currency area theory, because the predominance of the 'endogenous' variant of that theory that held the very formation of the EMU and SEM as solutions to the problem (e.g., Frankel and Rose [2002]). Rather, it rests on macroeconomics of the neoclassical synthesis, where short-run assumptions about the market compulsion towards equilibrium are relaxed because of information imperfections and 'sticky' oligopolistic pricing. Attention focuses on inflows that followed when the monetary union eliminated exchange rate risks in the European periphery, where stability culture was not entrenched. In this analysis, the attendant reduction of domestic savings, widening indebtedness and current account deficits should have been countered with even more stringent and precautionary fiscal policy than the Stability and Growth Pact (SGP) required (e.g., Fagan and Gaspar [2008]).

But the case is not compelling. Indebtedness and deficits are seen as adjustment problems caused by the transition to monetary union. Misallocation of finance to residential rather than high-tech business investments is not explained. That the financial crisis started in the highly developed role-model system of the United States (US) is not addressed. Of course, it could be argued that the problem ultimately resided in overly expansionary macroeconomic policies in the US and the GIIPS (Greece, Ireland, Italy, Portugal and Spain). But then one must entertain the possibility that it was such expansionary policy that explains the output and productivity gap between the US and the EU in the first place, and not the supply-side institutional differences that the Sapir report sought to eliminate. Furthermore, EA economic growth would have been even more anaemic without US expansionary policies and with tighter fiscal policies in the GIIPS prior to the financial crisis. In short, the analysis does not consider that debt expansion was not an abnormality but an integral and necessary part of the sort of capitalism that the SEM had promoted (Crouch 2009).

This motivates a more radical, critical–theoretical, departure from conventional analysis of the EA, offered most systematically by regulation theory in a broad sense (Jessop [1990]; for early analyses see Boyer [1990]; Leborgne and Lipietz [1990]). Just as for Horkheimer (1937[2002]), the emergent properties of the EA are historically specific crisis-prone regularities associated with capitalism as a mode of production. These are seen as inherently unstable and contradictory, because of constitutive properties in the power relation between capital and labour. Marx (1973 [1857]: 410) famously maintained that capitalism tends towards over-accumulation. On the one hand capitalists act on the profit motive, requiring market expansion; but on the other surplus augmentation depends on containing wages, which holds back expansion of final demand relative to accumulated capital. When the total mass of capital cannot be profitably deployed, this generates crisis tendencies. The key contributions of regulation theory has been to elucidate how bourgeois society draws on technological and institutional innovation (modes of regulation) to counter such crisis tendencies and temporarily stabilize particular regimes of accumulation in particular epochs. This facilitates a synthesis with radical (so-called post-) Keynesians that agree that capitalist dynamics cannot be separated from power relations between capital and labour and market dynamics are prone to under-consumption. From this perspective, the EA crisis is understood as a particularly European manifestation of the crisis of *finance-led accumulation.*

In contrast to Fordism, which predominated from the 1950s to the 1970s and was based on the integration of mass production and mass consumption underwritten by productivity growth, wage increases have been delinked from productivity and output growth with the neoliberal flexibility agenda and the wage-share as a proportion of value added has fallen dramatically (Onaran and Galanis 2013; Stockhammer 2013). Over-accumulation tendencies have rather been counteracted through the extension of debt underwritten by asset values. The crisis should be understood as financial markets driven to ever riskier investments in pursuit of profitable deployment of the expanding mass of accumulated capital (Boyer 2012: 285–6).

American capital accumulation was at the centre of this system, enabled by dollar seigniorage, the dominance of the US financial industry in financial intermediation, and institutional complementarity between global finance, American corporate governance, a residual welfare state and the role of private loans and savings in everyday political economy (especially in housing and pensions) (Konings 2011; Schwartz 2009). European capital accumulation was articulated to American capital accumulation in two subordinate ways. The first was through export-led manufacturing in the north, with wage increases set below productivity growth, depending on the locomotive effect of the American economy (Becker and Jäger 2012: 175–6; Bellofiore *et al.* 2011; Lapavitsas *et al.* 2010; Onaran and Galanis 2013; Stockhammer 2008). A leaner form of corporatism was promoted by financial liberalization, which included institutional investors among the stakeholders (Vitols 2004). Another articulation was through peripheral financialization, whereby debt-based consumption and growth were sustained for some time, despite the absence of relational density and intermediary capacity found in financial centres such as New York and London (Konings 2008: 256, 262, 265, 270). Surplus capital, above all from north-western Europe, was invested in undervalued assets in southern and eastern Europe, not primarily in productive enterprise, but in housing and mortgages in search of leverage opportunities (Becker and Jäger 2012: 176–7: Charnock *et al.* 2014). Temporarily, access to cheap loans sub-stituted as a lever of demand expansion also in southern Europe, despite lower wage-shares (Milios and Sotiropoulos 2010: 236). Financial market liber-alization and the elimination of exchange rate risks by the EMU facilitated this development. This highlights that, in the absence of high-productivity growth, finance-led accumulation has a decidedly extensive quality, and depends on the opening of new frontiers of commodification in space but also in socioeconomic life, driven by privatization of previously public or common assets (Harvey 2006: 41–50, 52–3). In this process, the US has been consumer and clearer of balances in the last resort of the European economy (Bellofiore *et al.* 2011: 121).

If anyone identified the EA crisis in the making it was Engelbert Stockham-mer (2008), working with formal macroeconomic modelling derived from the social structure of accumulation variant of regulation theory (Bhaduri and Marglin 1990). Stockhammer argued that although, unlike American finance-led accumulation, the European variant inherently suffered from mediocre growth, it was at least as fragile. As expected when securitization makes loans readily accessible, just like in America, household savings rates decreased. But in contrast to the US, European consumption propensity did not increase (except in Greece), because of two counteracting tendencies: rapidly falling wage-shares; and retrenchment of pay-as-you-go pensions. Wage moderation contracted output and did not stimulate employment as growth in the EA as a whole is wage-led (see also Onaran and Galanis [2013]). EMU motivates member states to contain growth to protect the balance of payments, resulting in a collective action problem, which contains the expansion of aggregate demand (Stockhammer *et al.* 2009: 15–56). Just as in the US, investment rates did not increase either, despite increased profitability. This is consistent with the expectation that increased mobility of financial capital increases the required return on capital through higher asset–yield ratios associated with 'shareholder value', prompting a change of management strategy from 'retain and reinvest' to 'downsize and redistribute'. Contrary to the American situation, and in accordance with Boyer's (1990) warnings a decade and a half earlier, the intended expansionary impulses of the SEM did not materialize and did not generate a dynamic accumulation regime based on virtuous relations between productivity growth and aggregate demand. Estimates of so-called Verdoorn elasticities suggest that a percentage of foregone output growth equals just under 0.5 per cent of foregone productivity growth (Storm and Naastepad 2013: 104–8).

Concerning the uneven effects of European 'competitive austerity', Stock-hammer *et al.* (2009) were pioneers in identifying the dangers of the cavernous internal imbalances between export-led and peripheral finance-led accumu-lation regimes. These were manifested in massively diverging relative unit labour costs. Since German core inflation is close to zero, the only route of adjustment on the current account that was available to deficit countries (save a productivity growth miracle) would be highly destabilizing deflationary policies. Internal payments balances were therefore dependent on highly volatile flows on the capital account. Whilst the common currency prevented the sort of turbulence associated with the ERM crisis, Stockhammer deemed the situation as unsustainable. The only issue that puzzled him was that this configuration had not displayed the instabilities that one would have expected (Stockhammer 2008: 197–8). The lag time between him writing those lines and publication would 'resolve' his puzzle, since it coincided with the outbreak of the financial crisis.

Painting catastrophic scenarios, such formal analysis of social structures of accumulation is now used to assess EA-crisis management. Warnings are issued against a strategy trying to transpose the export-oriented models of northern Europe to the rest of the EA. These can be summarized by two key questions: what will generate final effective aggregate demand? And, how is uneven development in the EA to be mediated? Fallacy of composition is stressed: it is not possible for all EA member states to run surpluses, unless there is a massive increase in the current account surplus to the rest of the world. Grahl's (2012) estimate of the first fiscal semester has been that in the unlikely event that all national plans were successful, it would generate an EA surplus of 6 per cent of gross domestic product (GDP). That is twice the surplus that China is running with an economy half the size of the EA. It is inconceivable that the rest of the world could or would absorb such surplus production. Furthermore, a one-sided 20 per cent adjustment of relative unit labour costs by the periphery to Germany would require a contraction equivalent to two 1930-style depressions (Stockhammer 2011).

This literature contributes to understanding macroeconomic proportions and tensions in crisis management. But to see crisis management simply in terms of policy mistakes compounds a danger that Jessop (1990: 315; 321–2) long ago identified in regulation theory: despite its emphasis on regulatory practices and historical contingency, methodological bracketing entailed in formal analysis of capital accumulation tends to neglect rigorous analysis of the power-laden processes, through which the constellation of accumulation regimes and regulation modes are forged and replaced through accumulation strategies and hegemonic projects. This problem becomes particularly acute problem when analysing crisis management, which as a form of rule might have more method to its madness than these analyses suppose.

EA CRISIS MANAGEMENT AS A FORM OF RULE

The extension of regulation theory as developed in this section argues that EA-crisis management seeks to preserve and extend an accumulation strategy and a hegemonic project based on ordoliberalism as a particular variant of neoliberalism. As such, ordoliberalism is an ideological point of reference for moral and intellectual leadership (Gramsci 1971: 181) that distances rule from the corporate-economic interests served by engendering an intersubjective framework for deliberation in the EU over the general economic good. The theory of ordoliberalism emerged out of the crisis of inter-war Weimar Germany. It postulates that market society does not emerge spontaneously but that its autopoiesis must be politically framed by constitution-like rules. Hence, it is a theory of how market society can be depoliticized through politics and attendant entrepreneurial socialization through what it calls *Vitalpolitik* (Bonefeld 2012). Whilst historical change in ordoliberalism can be debated, there are essential features that continue to give intellectual content to EA-crisis management. When translated into stylized tropes such as Merkel as the prudent 'Swabian Housewife', it also has popular appeal in northern European civil societies that have enjoyed export-oriented recoveries (Young 2011). Such tropes played a crucial role in recasting the narrative of the financial crisis from one of dysfunctional financial markets to one of public finances and competitiveness (Heinrich and Kutter 2014). Ordoliberalism has long informed EU governance, notably in competition and monetary policy (Dyson and Featherstone 1999; Gerber 1998). In the current crisis management it influences the disciplinary conditionalities as codified by the Treaty on Stability, Co-ordination and Governance (TSCG), the attendant EuroPlus Pact, and the 'Six-Pack' of Regulations on macroeconomic surveillance (see Ioannou *et al.* [2015]).

The TSCG (European Council 2012) resuscitates and firms up the 1996 SGP, which in turn attempted to lock in the fiscal Maastricht Convergence Criteria. It is worthwhile recalling that the SGP had been broken by France and Germany in November 2003, when overly anaemic growth rates undermined their capacity to meet the 3 per cent deficit target. Subsequently, when the Council refused to enact disciplinary measures, the SGP became a fudge. The TSCG most certainly removes any ambiguities. Compared to the 3 per cent norm of the SGP, Article 3.1.b of the TSCG specifies that structural deficits of member states may not exceed 0.5 per cent of GDP. This norm can only be infringed in 'deep recessions' and 'exceptional circumstances' (Article 3.3.b). When member states exceed the 0.5 per cent threshold, Excessive Deficit Procedures (EDP) are activated by default and can only be suspended by qualified-majority voting in the Council. This is in contrast to the SGP, when activation required a vote. Article 5 specifies that EDPs require states to enter into Economic Partnership Programmes (EPPs) with the EU. These are detailed agreements on macroeconomic *and structural* reforms. Progress reports are to be regularly submitted to the Commission and the Council for surveillance and endorsement. Notably, the EPPs are encoded in EU law, and infringement claims can be made by the Commission or any member state to the ECB (TSCG, Article 8). Already being pursued in the rescue packages of the GIIPS, the EPPs mobilize hard EU authority to transpose the export-oriented models of northern Europe to the rest of the EA.

Potentially catastrophic macroeconomic implications of such crisis management, as outlined in the previous section, raise questions about why the bumble bee is still flying. No doubt, the announcement that the ECB would embark on OMTs if required has calmed markets over the last two years. This lends some credence to traditional–theoretical approaches in the sociological mould that argue that social density, and credible commitments by France and Germany, are sufficient to maintain EMU (e.g., Enderlein and Verdun [2009]). This is not incorrect, and as a mid-range explanation even valuable. But in its deference to equilibrium-based economics, it remains suspect as an account of the fundamental emergent properties that have generated suboptimal economic developments and, of course, the crisis itself. After all, even the more cautious intergovernmentalist versions of such theory had concluded that credible commitments at Maastricht had made the EU 'institutionally stable' (Moravcsik 2006).

An alternative critical explanation starts from the formal analysis of capital accumulation of the previous section and agrees that one-sided adjustments by deficit countries would be catastrophic. But putting power and interests at the centre of analysis, it queries the chief objective of crisis management. It is unlikely to be primarily about eliminating payments imbalances, but more about mobilizing EU authority to deepen market reform. Crisis management serves the interests of the financial industry and is premised on a continuation of finance-led accumulation (Radice 2014). Credence to such analysis is given by the stalling of the agenda of financial regulation (Bieling 2014) and in Commission President Barroso's pronouncement of a market-oriented 'silent revolution' (Haar 2011). Ordoliberal crisis management is hence a manifestation of the 'shock doctrine' (Klein 2009) as the crisis serves as an occasion to move forward the boundaries of the possible. Privatization and making previously public assets available for financial leveraging, further enabled by legal authority through the structural provisions of the TSCG, is thus the chief policy priority. Whilst such a policy orientation is likely to remain tension ridden, and is likely to generate another bubble-crisis dynamic eventually, its prospects should not be underestimated. It may prove viable for some time. The Organization for Economic Co-operation and Development (OECD) world still has $2 trillion-worth of state-owned enterprises that could be privatized (Christiansen 2011). According to IMF estimates, public non-financialized assets in real estate and land, including subsoil resources, have a value equalling three-quarters of GDP of developed economies. Greek state-owned residential properties are currently estimated at €3.3 billion, but could reach €20 billion in 10 years. Creditor member states and consultants to the ESM are considering mechanisms through which such public assets could be brought to market from reluctant debtor states whose institutions sometimes cannot even account for them. Proposals include holding companies located in other member states and pledges of future cash flows from state assets (for instance rents or ticket sales) as security against new bonds (*The Economist* 2014: 18).

The 'silent revolution' resonates with the perspective of the Amsterdam School, which augments regulation theory by analysing how transnational class agency exercises leadership in the transition from one accumulation regime to another. Van Apeldoorn has shown that mobilization of capitalist élite unity at a European level was crucial in forging a coherent neoliberal accumulation strategy and hence the finance-led accumulation regime. He emphasizes the importance of Europe-level 'private planning bodies', notably the European Roundtable of Industrialists, which *inter alia* resolve differences and conflicts between different 'factions' of capital and exert strategic leadership over the direction of Single Market reform. Similar forces can be seen to be at play at present (van Apeldoorn 2014).

The Amsterdam School answers questions begged to those who, drawing on classical Marxist theories of imperialism, reduce the EA crisis management to German dominance (e.g., Lapavitsas [2012]). Though German origins of ordoliberalism are undeniable, this understates active élite internalization, consent and co-ordination of crisis management in other member states. It neglects the extent to which crisis management is the 'outcome of struggles between transnational social forces and shaped by the agency of a transnational capitalist class' (van Apeldoorn 2014: 197). Bearing in mind that classical theories of imperialism anticipated sharpened inter-imperialist rivalry that only socialist transformation would resolve, the fundamental question to the German neomercantilist thesis is: how was European integration possible at all? The most significant contribution of the Amsterdam School is a theoretical breakthrough by van der Pijl (1998: 9–24) that makes it possible to answer that question, which offers nothing less than a critical–theoretical counterpoint to Haas. Following the cue of a seminal piece by Poulantzas (1974), van der Pijl argues that whilst capitalist classes and societies, emerging out of late-feudal absolute states, originally see one another as part of external nature forming potential threats and objects of conquest, the molecular nature of capitalism creates strong tendencies toward 'interiorization'. Progressively, capitalist societies begin to interiorize each others' social relations and international relations are transformed to become part of the management of internal nature. Being Marxist, the Amsterdam School sees this development as uneven, imbricated by power relations, and 'network experts' representing big capital enjoy structurally privileged positions and exercise leadership over this process. But it explains why inter-imperialist anarchy can be overcome in capitalism, and it was taken to a higher level after World War II under American leadership and the diffusion of Fordism. After the 1970s, the social content of transnational capitalist relations has become increasingly neoliberal. It is in this context that the Amsterdam School understands developments in the EU.

When this is understood as producing international organization that shapes inter-state relations akin to Bull's (1977) 'international society', the Amsterdam School is at its most convincing. But it tends to 'bend the stick' too far and understate the importance of the state and interstate relations, which become seen as passive receivers of transnational ruling class hegemony. This is empirically problematic. National fault lines remain relevant, even in as 'transnational' a policy area as European financial services (Macartney 2011). Furthermore, Drainville's critique still stands that the Amsterdam School neglects that neoliberalism is not only a 'broad strategy of restructuring' but also 'a succession of negotiated settlements of concessions to the rigidities and dynamics of structures as well as the political possibilities of the moment' (Drainville 1994: 116). This has been borne out by research on the variegated nature of neoliberalism in different countries and sites (Birch and Mykhnenko 2009). This is illustrated by simple examples such as that of Italy becoming more determined to join the EMU after the crisis of the Exchange Rate Mechanism, whilst the United Kingdom (UK) definitely decided to opt out (Talani 2003). The theoretical implication is that states and inter-state relations remain crucial to capitalism, because, as the ultimate site of collectively binding decisions in a given territory, their roles in managing uneven development, reproduction and maintaining social legitimacy by mediating the potentially antagonistic relations between classes and social groups. Hence, when focus changes from accumulation strategies to mass legitimacy through hegemonic projects, states and inter-state relations remain essential.

It is in that context that the role of Germany, or rather Germany in relation to America, in ordoliberal EA-crisis management should be understood. Such understanding begins by paying closer attention to what Poulantzas (1974), arguably the greatest of Marxist state theorists, had to say about capitalist interiorization. Poulantzas also focused on the international developments after World War II, but stressed their organic roots in the particularities of American society. Hence, whilst European capitalist groupings had their autonomous base in market competition and formed no 'comprador bourgeoisie', a particular dependency on America developed (Poulantzas 1974: 161–4, 166–9). Influenced by the French industrialist intellectual Servan-Schreiber (1967), Poulantzas pointed towards the particular form of foreign direct investment (FDI), which the export of American capital had taken in Europe after 1945. This was not primarily about the volumes, which to Poulantzas underestimated European dependence. Far more significant was US investments in leading sectors that fed strategic inputs to other sectors and shaped socialization of production processes. To this, Poulantzas added the US-centred concentration of money-capital, which at that time was beginning to effect the terms of credit access. Poulantzas argued that this interpenetration of European capital with US capital determined a whole series of corporate 'practices, know-how, modes and rituals to do with the economic sphere'; 'ideology' in a broad and materialist sense (Poulantzas 1974: 164). European capital was increasingly articulated with American capital on terms shaped by American society and its power bloc (1974: 164–7). This increasingly alienated European capital from the specificities of the various European social formations, creating problems for European states in performing their mediating functions between capital accumulation and social legitimation.

Poulantzas clearly overestimated the importance of US FDI in Europe. But stressing the role of US-centred finance, and its qualitative effect on European corporate practice, outlook and strategy, was prescient. Recent research verifies that liberalized and global financial markets cultivated by US hegemony

(Panitch and Gindin 2012) are specifically organic to American corporate governance and liberal welfare residualism and enabling the finance-led, consumption-based economic growth dynamic in the US. It was underpinned by dollar seigniorage, which has given the US unique capacities in the post-Bretton Woods world to 'delay and deflect' adjustment costs (Cohen 2006) for pursuing deficit-financed expansionary policies, especially low tax rates and military expenditure, to other parts of the world. In the absence of any challenge to this financial system, anything equivalent to the US federal Treasury bills, and its 'anti-growth bias', the EMU does not as much pose a challenge to post-Bretton Woods US hegemony as it reflects a particular method of adjustment (Cohen 2003, 2009; Grahl 2011). The lack of complementarity between global financial markets and European welfare institutions resulted in pernicious effects on growth as outlined in the previous section, which in turn has compelled welfare state retrenchment in violation of deeply entrenched norms of legitimacy, resulting in a corrosion of sociopolitical representation and giving rise to especially right-wing populism (Cafruny and Ryner 2007: 73–104).

The pivotal role of German ordoliberalism in this method of adjustment can hence be specified, as can the reasons why, despite its pernicious effects, it is so hard to escape. European monetary integration, culminating in monetary union, developed as a response to no less than six major adjustments to such US-induced externalities (Henning 1998). To all intents and purposes, German foreign exchange reserves, the consequence of cumulative surpluses, offered buffers whereby a degree of protection from the externalities of US deflection could be secured (Jones 2003). Whilst benefits seem more equivocal today than during the first decade of the euro, the threat of turbulence and lack of pooled protection against the vagaries of a US dollar-denominated global finance seems sufficient to keep EA member states in line.

This method of adjustment originated with Franco–German agreement on the European Monetary System (EMS) in 1978. Turbulence on global money markets compelled West Germany to abandon coronation doctrine, and to treat European monetary co-operation as a lever rather than result of economic convergence. With the EMS, West Germany found a way to shield itself from US dollar inflation and to revalue on acceptable terms. Given its composition, revaluation strengthened the German export sector as price increases had less of an impact on sales than reduced costs on imports, provided that European competitors could be locked into fixed exchange rate arrangements (Lankowski 1982). This is a formula that still applies, and if anything to a more pronounced extent (Bellofiore et al. 2011: 141). The general need to shield against dollar-induced turbulence, not least illustrated during the first years of Mitterand's presidency in France, offered the inducement required for others to agree to an EMS on German terms.

Crucially, ordoliberal monetary arrangements anchored a more composite social compromise in West Germany itself. Organized labour and welfare state constituencies that were not 'hailed' by ordoliberal appeals but social democratic ones were served by welfare mechanisms that distributed economic rents generated by favourable terms of trade secured by EMS (Ryner 2003). These included co-ordinated wage bargaining, whereby for a time the German wage-share of value added actually increased, and where work-time reduction and early retirement provided a social safety net for those laid off by industrial rationalization (e.g., Esser 1982). Over time, reflecting the relative dislocation of German transnational corporations from the German social formation, the terms of this social compromise have changed and become less labour inclusive. After 'Agenda 2010', promotion of low-wage and increasingly casual employment replaced work-time reduction and early retirement. Such 'competitive corporatism' has been at work throughout northern Europe (e.g., Bieling and Schulten 2003). Despite the composite nature of German compromises, the external discipline of European monetary co-operation and competition policy is decisively ordoliberal (Bonefeld 2002; Clift 2003). At the same time, in other societies, when export-generated rents are scarce, it is increasingly difficult to render ordoliberal discipline compatible with entrenched legitimation norms to the extent that the situation became critical with the EA crisis.

CONCLUSIONS

Critical political economy contributes to understanding of the EA crisis and its management with plausible and coherent accounts of their emergent properties. Since traditional theory serves instrumental functions for management practices, and following Horkheimer's (1937[2002]), the critique of such theory served as a starting point for this article in analysing of 'real concrete' developments. Recent economic applications in the regulation–theoretical tradition were then reviewed to elucidate the EA crisis as the consequence of an unstable and anaemic version of finance-led accumulation. But such works were also critiqued for not appreciating the political rationality of EA-crisis management. Drawing on pioneering work by Poulantzas (1974), the contribution suggested that the ordoliberal iron cage metaphor captures this rationality, produced by a particular configuration of inter-state relations within transnational capitalism, where the relationship between America and Germany is central. German leadership in Europe should be seen in terms of a European method of adjustment to cope with the externalities resulting from a more predatory form of American hegemony post-Bretton Woods, but with differential effects. EA-crisis management is marked by continuity on that score.

The ordoliberal iron cage is deeply and structurally embedded. This does not alter the fact that it also has produced, and is likely to continue to produce, the highly unstable and anaemic socioeconomic dynamics that are likely to be extraordinarily harsh in Europe's periphery. Whilst another phase of finance-led accumulation seems possible, based on extension and deepening of what Harvey (2003) calls the 'political economy of dispossession' of public assets, a deeper social crisis is unfolding. The interaction of economic shock, fiscal austerity and stress on social protection systems generated by austerity is related to dramatic increases in suicide rates, infectious diseases and human immuno-deficiency virus (HIV) (Karanikolos *et al.* 2013). There are also good grounds to expect a crisis of reproduction in the European periphery. During the bubble, access to cheap credit and expansion of family welfare services provided a means to support reproduction, as extended family networks were attenuated by modernization (Milios and Sotiropoulos 2010; Rhodes 2002: 312–13). The credit crunch, austerity and unemployment forced populations to return to the reliance of these weakened networks, and their capacity to carry the strain is in question (e.g., Salido *et al.* [2012]). Given what research has told us about the importance of the welfare state for relieving such pressures and for rendering democracy compatible with capitalist markets (Flora and Alber 1981; Wilensky 1975), doubts are appropriately raised over the prospects of an ordoliberal European project retaining legitimacy. Eurosceptic, and even neo-Nazi parties, and reterritorialization of sociopolitical cleavages in some member states offer plenty of morbid symptoms. With the EPPs constraining what is possible in electoral politics, authoritarian tendencies are becoming increasingly apparent in governance (Bruff 2014). Finally, given the effect of the financial crisis in speeding up change in global geopolitics, a crisis strategy is risky that presupposes either that the US can maintain its role as consumer and clearer of balances of last resort or that China soon will fill that role. Indeed, whilst the euro is not fit to replace the hegemonic role of the dollar, it may serve, within a new geopolitical constellation where the investment strategies of the BRICs (Brazil, Russia, India, China) are important, to unhinge a dollar-based top currency system (Otero-Iglesias and Steinberg 2013). Is it really advisable for European political economy to be so dependent on the vagaries of developments in the US and China?

In this context, it is worth exploring what critical political economy in recent years has said about policy alternatives. One of the most striking things about it is how pro-EU it is (for an exception, see Lapavitsas [2012]). The problem is not that there is too much Europe, but too little (of a different) Europe. The Euro-Memorandum Group (e.g., EuroMemo 2012), where many of Europe's most eminent critical political economists are leading figures, is consistently arguing for federalist measures: mutualization of debt (e.g., Eurobonds); EU-wide industrial policy; fiscal transfer payments and a larger EU budget; EU-wide capital controls; EU-wide wage co-ordination norms; a common expansionary fiscal policy; and external policies that require collective European agency such as new approaches to Association Agreements and the World Trade Organization (WTO). Macroeconomic projections suggest that the outcomes of this sort would result in higher, more even and environmentally more sustainable development (Eatwell *et al.* 2014).

But even if this is recognized as an ambitious project, the radical implications of what is required to realize it are often underestimated. That a higher wage-share would generate higher output productivity growth through Kaldor–Verdoorn effects is certainly plausible; however, this is likely to result in increased capital intensity, leading exactly to jobless growth and attendant fiscal pressures on social insurance systems that motivated competitive–corporatist wage restraint in the first place (Storm and Nastepaad 2013: 104). In addition, using the shift to a more ecologically sustainable system as a lever for alternative growth strategies is more difficult than is supposed (Brand 2012). The implications of rendering these policy alternatives viable on taxation-levels and public as opposed to private consumption and investment are very radical (Bellofiore 2013) relative to prevailing norms in European societies.

If critical political economy aspires to unity in theory and practice, this raises some extremely thorny conundrums. In their analysis of the formidable normalizing capacities of capitalist society, the Frankfurt School that Horkheimer helped form would appreciate these conundrums and its members did not hesitate to be bearers of bad news. One does not have to agree with Adorno (2004 [1948]) that escape can only be found in highly esoteric aesthetic experiences as induced by Schoenbergian tonal scales. Nevertheless, the implication of my analysis about how current forms of rule are *both* deeply imbricated in transnational capitalism and in the state system is sobering. It means that it is not easy for any member state to exit a German-dominated regional system because the costs for doing so are real. Nor is it simply a matter of finding an alter-transnational agency to counter a transnational ruling class. The various transnational protest groups that have developed worldwide and in Europe face structural limitations (Scholl and Freyberg-Inan 2013). Arguments that ignore this seriously underestimate the degree to which states and the state-system still integrate, and at the same time divide, mass society, including trade unions, that would have to be hailed in the formation of political agency that could push developments in an alternative direction. And whilst marginalization certainly means that the integrative capacities have diminished, opposition movements that grow out of marginalization often generate paradoxical results. Indeed, movements such as the Indignados represents as much decomposition of the old socialist left and its power resources as it represents mobilization of new resources (e.g., Cotillo 2014). This may actually increase policy space for neoliberal reform in the foreseeable future. And that is the point with iron cages. They are not easily escaped.

Biographical note: Magnus Ryner is a reader in international political economy at King's College London.

REFERENCES

Adorno, T. (2004 [1948]) *Philosophy of Modern Music*, New York: Continuum.
Baehr, P. (2001) 'The "iron cage" and the "shell as hard as steel": Parsons, Weber and the *Staalhartes Gehäuse* metaphor in *The Protestant Ethic and the Spirit of Capitalism*', *History and Theory* 40: 153–69.

Balassa, B. (1962) *The Theory of Economic Integration*, London: Allen & Unwin.

Becker, J. and Jäger, J. (2012) 'integration in crisis: a regulationist perspective on the interaction of European varieties of capitalism', *Competition & Change* 16(3): 169–87.

Bellofiore, R. (2013) '"Two or three things i know about her": Europe in the global crisis and heterodox economics', *Cambridge Journal of Economics* 37(3): 497–512.

Bellofiore, R., Garibaldo, F. and Halevi, J. (2011) 'The global crisis and the crisis of European mercantilism', in L. Panitch, G. Albo and V. Chibber (eds), *The Socialist Register 2011: The Crisis this Time*, London: Merlin Press, pp. 120–46.

Bhaduri, A and Marglin, S. (1990) 'Unemployment and the real wage: the economic basis for contesting political ideologies', *Cambridge Journal of Economics* 14: 375–93.

Bieling, H.-J. (2014) 'Shattered expectations: the defeat of European ambitions of global financial reform', *Journal of European Public Policy* 21(3): 346–66.

Bieling, H.-J. and Schulten, T. (2003) '"Competitive restructuring" and industrial relations within the European Union: corporatist involvement and beyond', in A. Cafruny and M. Ryner (eds), *A Ruined Fortress? Neoliberal Hegmony and Transformation in Europe*, Lanham, MD: Rowman & Littlefield, pp. 231–60.

Birch, K. and Mykhnenko, V. (eds) (2009) *The Rise and Fall of Neo-Liberalism*, London: Zed Books.

Blanchard, O. and Giavazzi, F. (2002) 'Current account deficits in the euro area: the end of the Feldstein–Horioka puzzle?', *Brookings Papers on Economic Activity 2/2002*, Washington, DC: Brookings Institute, available at http://www.brookings.edu/~/media/Projects/BPEA/Fall%202002/2002b_bpea_blanchard.PDF.

Bonefeld, W. (2002) 'European integration: the market, the political and class', *Capital & Class* 77: 117–42.

Bonefeld, W. (2012) 'Freedom and the strong state: on German ordoliberalism', *New Political Economy* 17(5): 633–56.

Boyer, R. (1990) 'The impact of the single market on labour and employment: a discussion of macroeconomic approaches in light of research in labour economics', *Labour and Society* 15(2): 109–42.

Boyer, R. (2012) 'The four fallacies of contemporary austerity policies: the lost Keynesian legacy', *Cambridge Journal of Economics* 36(1): 283–312.

Brand, U. (2012) 'Green economy – the next oxymoron? No lessons learnt from implementing sustainable development', *GAIA* 21(1): 28–32.

Bruff, I. (2014) 'The rise of authoritarian neoliberalism', *Rethinking Marxism* 26(1): 113–29.

Bull, H. (1977) *The Anarchical Society*, New York: Columbia University Press.

Cafruny, A and Ryner, M. (2007) *Europe at Bay: In the Shadow of US Hegemony*, Boulder CO: Lynne Rienner.

Charnock, G, Purcell, T. and Ribera-Fumaz, R. (2014) *The Limits to Capital in Spain*, Basingstoke: Palgrave Macmillan.

Christiansen, H. (2011) 'The size and composition of the SOE sector in OECD countries', *OECD Corporate Governance Working Papers #5*, Paris: Organisation for Economic Cooperation and Development.

Clift, B. (2003) 'The changing political economy of France: *Dirigisme* under duress', A. Cafruny and M. Ryner (eds), *A Ruined Fortress? Neoliberal Hegmony and Transformation in Europe*, Lanham, MD: Rowman & Littlefield: 173–200.

Cohen, B. (2003) 'Global currency rivalry: can the euro ever challenge the dollar?', *Journal of Common Market Studies* 41(4): 575–95.

Cohen, B. (2006) 'The macrofoundations of monetary power', in D. Andrews (ed.), *International Monetary Power*, Ithaca NY: Cornell University Press, pp. 117–38.

Cohen, B. (2009) 'Dollar dominance, euro aspirations: recipe for discord?', *Journal of Common Market Studies* 47(4): 741–66.

Connerton, P. (1976) 'Introduction', in P. Connerton (ed.), *Critical Sociology*, Harmondsworth: Penguin, pp. 11–39.

Cotillo, A. (2014) 'Political disaffection or crisis of the ideological left? Political effects of the debt crisis in Spain', in N. Petropoulos (ed.), *The Debt Crisis in the Eurozone: Social Impacts*, Newcastle: Cambridge Scholars Publishers, pp. 305–41.

Crouch, C. (2009) 'Privatised Keynesianism: an unacknowledged policy regime', *British Journal of Politics and International Relations* 11(3): 382–99.

Drainville, A. (1994) 'International political economy in the age of open Marxism', *Review of International Political Economy* 1(1): 105–32.

Dyson, K. and Featherstone, K. (1999) *The Road to Maastricht: Negotiating Economic and Monetary Union*, Oxford: Oxford University Press.

Eatwell, J, McKinley, T. and Petit, P. (eds) (2014) *Challenges for Europe in the World 2030*, London: Ashgate.

The Economist (2014) 'Setting out the store: briefing state owned assets', *The Economist*, 11–17 January, 17–20.

Enderlein, H and Verdun, A. (2009) 'EMU's teenage challenge: what have we learned and what can we predict from political science', *Journal of European Public Policy* 16(4): 490–507.

Esser, J. (1982) *Gewerkschaften in der Krise*, Frankfurt: Suhrkamp.

EuroMemo Group (2012) 'European integration at the crossroads: democratic deepening for stability, solidarity and social justice', available at http://www2.euromemorandum.eu/uploads/euromemorandum_2012.pdf (accessed 29 March 2013).

European Commission (1988) 'Europe 1992: the overall challenge', *SEC 88 (524) Final*, 13 April, Brussels: European Commission.

European Council (2012) 'Treaty on stability, coordination and governance', *TSCG/en 16*, 2 March, Brussels: European Council.

Fagan, G. and Gaspar, V. (2008) 'Macroeconomic adjustment to monetary union', *ECB Working Paper #946*, Frankfurt: European Central Bank.

Flora, P. and Alber, J. (1981) 'Modernization, democratization and the development of welfare states in Western Europe', in P. Flora and A. Heidenheimer (eds), *The Development of Welfare States in Europe and America*, New Brunswick, NJ: Transaction Books, pp. 37–80.

Frankel, J. and Rose, A. (2002) 'An estimate of the effect of common currencies on trade and income', *The Quarterly Journal of Economics* 117(2): 437–66.

Gerber, D. (1998) *Law and Competition in Twentieth Century Europe: Protecting Prometheus*, Oxford: Oxford University Press.

Grahl, J. (2011) 'The subordination of European finance', *Competition & Change* 15(1): 31–47.

Grahl, J. (2012) 'The first European Semester: an incoherent strategy', Paper presented at the Political Economy Research Group Workshop 'Europe in Crisis', April, Department of Economics, Kingston University, London.

Gramsci, A. (1971) *Selections from the Prison Notebooks*, New York: International Publishers.

Haar, K. (2011) 'EU's silent revolution in economic governance undermines democratic control', Corporate Europe Observatory, available at http://corporateeurope.org/pressreleases/2011/eus-silent-revolution-economic-governance-undermines-democratic-control (accessed 12 May 2014).

Haas, E. (1968) *The Uniting of Europe: Political, Social and Economic Forces*, 2nd edn, Stanford, CA: Stanford University Press.

Harvey, D. (2003) *The New Imperialism*, Oxford: Oxford University Press.

Harvey, D. (2006) *Spaces of Global Capitalism*, London: Verso.

Heinrich, M. and Kutter, A. (2014) 'A critical juncture in EU integration? The euro-zone crisis and its management 2010–12', in F. Panizza and G. Phillip (eds), *Moments of Truth: The Politics of Financial Crisis in Comparative Perspective*, London: Routledge, pp. 120–39.

Henning, R. (1998) 'Systemic conflict and regional monetary intetgration: the case of Europe', *International Organization* 52(3): 537–74.

Hoffman, S. (1966) 'Obstinate or obsolete? The fate of the nation state and the case of Western Europe', *Daedalus* 95: 862–915.

Horkheimer, M. (1937 [2002]) 'Traditional and critical theory', in *Critical Theory: Selected Essays*, compiled by S. Aronowitz, New York: Continuum, pp. 188–243.

IMF (2007) 'De-coupling the train? Spillovers and cycles in the global economy', *World Economic Outlook*, Chapter 4, Washington, DC: IMF, available at http://www.imf.org/external/pubs/ft/weo/2007/01/pdf/text.pdf.

Ioannou, D., Leblond, P. and Niemann, A. (2015) 'European integration and the crisis: practice and theory,' *Journal of European Public Policy*, doi: 10.1080/13501763.2014.994979.

Jessop, B. (1990) 'Regulation theory in retrospect and prospect', *Economy and Society* 19(2): 153–216.

Jones, E. (2003) 'Liberalized capital markets, state autonomy and European monetary union', *European Journal of Political Research* 42(2): 197–222.

Karanikolos, M. *et al.* (2013) 'Financial crisis, austerity and health in Europe', *The Lancet* 381: 1323–31.

Klein, N. (2009) *The Shock Doctrine*, Toronto: Knopf Canada.

Konings, M. (2008) 'European finance in the American mirror: financial change and the reconfiguration of competitiveness', *Contemporary Politics* 14(3): 253–75.

Konings, M. (2011) *The Development of American Finance*, Cambridge: Cambridge University Press.

Lankowski, C. (1982) 'Modell Deutschland and the international regionalization of the West German state', in A. Markovits (ed.), *The Political Economy of the German Model: Modell Deutschland*, New York: Praeger, pp. 90–115.

Lapavitsas, C. (2012) 'Default and exit from the eurozone', in L. Panitch, G. Albo and V. Chibber (eds), *The Socialist Register 2012*, London: Merlin Press, pp. 288–97.

Lapavitsas, C. *et al.* (2010) 'Eurozone crisis: beggar thyself and beggar thy neighbour', *Journal of Balkan and Near Eastern Studies* 12(4): 321–73.

Leborgne, D. and Lipietz, A. (1990) 'How to avoid a two-tiered Europe', *Labour and Society* 15(2): 77–99.

Macartney, H. (2011) *Variegated Neoliberalism: EU Varieties of Capitalism and International Political Economy*, London: Routledge.

Marx, K. (1973 [1857]) *Grundrisse*, Harmondsworth: Penguin.

Milios, J. and Sotiropoulos, D. (2010) 'Crisis of Greece or crisis of the euro? A view from the European "periphery"', *Journal of Balkan and Near Eastern Studies* 12(3): 223–40.

Milward, A.S. and Sørensen, V. (1993) 'Interdependence or integration? A national choice', in A.S. Milward, F. Lynch, R. Ranieri, F. Romero and V. Sørensen (eds), *The Frontier of National Sovereignty: History and Theory*, London: Routledge, pp. 1–32.

Moravcsik, A. (2006) 'What can we learn from the collapse of the European constitutional project?', *Politische Vierterjarhesschrift* 47(2): 219–41.

Onaran, Ö. And Galanis, G. (2013) 'Is aggregate demand wage-led or profit-led?', in M. Lavoie and E. Stockhammer (eds), *Wage-Led Growth: An Equitable Strategy for Economic Recovery*, Basingstoke: Palgrave Macmillan/ILO, pp. 71–99.

Otero-Iglesias, M. and Steinberg, F. (2013) 'Reframing the dollar vs euro debate through the perceptions of financial elites in key dollar holding countries', *Review of International Political Economy* 20(1): 180–214.

Panitch, L. and Gindin, S. (2012) *The Making of Global Capitalism*, London: Verso.

Pisani-Ferry, J. and Posen, A. (2009) 'Introduction: the euro at ten – successful but regional', in J. Pisani-Ferry and A. Posen (eds), *The Euro at Ten: The Next Global Currency?* Washington, DC and Brussels: The Peterson Institute of International Economics and Bruegel, pp. 1–15.

Poulantzas, N. (1974) 'Internationalisation of capitalist relations and the nation state', *Economy and Society* 2(1): 145–79.

Radice, H. (2014) 'Enforcing austerity in Europe: the structural deficit as a policy target', *Journal of Contemporary European Studies* 22(3): 318–28.

Rhodes, M. (2002) 'Why the euro is – or may be – good for European welfare states', in K. Dyson (ed.), *European States and the Euro*, Oxford: Oxford University Press, pp. 305–33.

Ryner, M. (2003) 'Disciplinary neoliberalism, regionalization and the social market in German restructuring', in A. Cafruny and M. Ryner (eds), *A Ruined Fortress? Neoliberal Hegemony and Transformation in Europe*, Lanham, MD: Rowman & Littlefield, pp. 201–28.

Ryner, M. (2012) 'Financial crisis, orthodoxy, heterodoxy and the production of knowledge about the EU', *Millennium: Journal of International Studies* 40(3): 647–73.

Salido, O., Carabana, J. and Torrejon, S. (2012) 'Unemployment and poverty in Spain: a portrait of recent changes in the "welfare mix"', Paper presented at the Interim Conference of the Disaster, Conflict and Social Crisis Research Network of the European Sociological Association, University of the Aegean, Mytilene, Greece, 13–14 September.

Sapir, A. *et al.* (2003) *An Agenda for a Growing Europe: The Sapir Report*, Oxford: Oxford University Press.

Scholl, C. and Freyberg-Inan, A. (2012) 'Hegemony's dirty tricks: explaining counter-globalization's weakness in times of neoliberal crisis', *Globalizations* 10(4): 1–20.

Schwartz, H. (2009) *Subprime Nation: American Power, Global Capital and the Housing Bubble*, Ithaca, NY: Cornell University Press.

Servan-Shreiber, J.-J. (1969) *The American Challenge*, Harmondsworth: Pelican.

Stockhammer, E. (2008) 'Some stylized facts on the finance-dominated accumulation regime', *Competition & Change* 12(2): 184–202.

Stockhammer, E. (2011) 'Peripheral Europe's debt and German wages', *International Journal of Public Policy* 7: 83–96.

Stockhammer, E. (2013) 'Why have wage shares fallen? An analysis of the determinants of functional income distribution', in M. Lavoie and E. Stockhammer (eds), *Wage-Led Growth: An Equitable Strategy for Economic Recovery*, Basingstoke: Palgrave Macmillan/ILO, pp. 40–70.

Stockhammer, E., Onaran, Ö. and Ederer, S. (2009) 'Functional income distribution and aggregate demand in the euro area', *Cambridge Journal of Economics* 33(1): 139–59.

Storm, S. and Nastepaad, C.W.M. (2013) 'Wage-led or profit-led supply: wages, productivity and investments', in M. Lavoie and E. Stockhammer (eds), *Wage-Led Growth: An Equitable Strategy for Economic Recovery*, Basingstoke: Palgrave Macmillan/ILO, pp. 100–24.

Talani, L.S. (2003) 'The political economy of exchange rate commitments: Italy, the United Kingdom and the process of European monetary integration', in A. Cafruny and M. Ryner (eds), *A Ruined Fortress? Neoliberal Hegemony and Transformation in Europe*, Lanham, MD: Rowman & Littlefield, pp. 123–46.

Van Apeldoorn, B. (2014) 'The European capitalist class and the crisis of its hegemonic project', in L. Panitch, G. Albo and V. Chibber (eds), *The Socialist Register 2014*, London: Merlin Press, pp. 189–206.

Van der Pijl, K. (1998) *Transnational Classes and International Relations*, London: Routledge.

Vitols, S. (2004) 'Negotiated shareholder value: the German variant of an Anglo-American practice', *Competition & Change* 8(4): 357–74.

Wilensky, H. (1975) *The Welfare State and Equality: Structural and Political Roots to Public Expenditure*, Berkeley, CA: University of California Press.

Young, B. (2011) 'Germany's puzzling response to the eurozone crisis: the obstinate defence of ordnungspolitik', *EUSA Review* 24(3): 5–6.

Index